VCs of the First World War

1914

VCs OF THE FIRST WORLD WAR

1914

GERALD GLIDDON

SUTTON PUBLISHING LIMITED

First published in the United Kingdom in 1994
Alan Sutton Publishing Ltd, an imprint of Sutton Publishing Limited
Phoenix Mill · Thrupp · Stroud · Gloucestershire

Paperback edition first published 1997

British Library Cataloguing in Publication Data

Gliddon, Gerald
  VCs of the First World War: 1914
  I. Title
  940.460922

ISBN 0-7509-1444-0

Library of Congress Cataloguing in Publication Data applied for

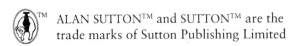
ALAN SUTTON™ and SUTTON™ are the
trade marks of Sutton Publishing Limited

Typeset in 10/13pt Sabon.
Typesetting and origination by
Sutton Publishing Limited.
Printed in Great Britain by
WBC Limited, Bridgend.

CONTENTS

PREFACE

After the publication of *VCs of the First World War: The Somme* it occurred to me that it would be a good idea to produce other books on some of the 634 men who won the Victoria Cross in the First World War. *1914* is therefore the second volume in the series to be published.

I began my *1914* research with the files of the late Canon Lummis (who was with the Cavalry in 1914 and who built up a filing system that dealt with all winners of the VC) that are cared for by the Military Historical Society and are housed at the National Army Museum in London. A similar set of files with supplementary material is kept at the Department of Printed Documents at the Imperial War Museum. Any would-be researcher should inspect both sets of files.

I wrote to all the Regimental archives kept by the various units, where they still existed, and to many local newspapers throughout the British Isles. Response to these requests was uneven but occasionally very fruitful indeed. I visited various museums including the Royal Artillery Institution who have individual files on the artillerymen who won the VC in the First World War. I also visited the Public Record Office at Kew but the majority of the researching there was carried out most efficiently by Maurice Johnson.

As for the illustrations I have once again used the famous Gallahers Cigarette Card set and also many artists' impressions, mostly from the book *Deeds that Thrilled the Empire*. These pictures are by no means always accurate but do give a feeling of the period and also depict attitudes that prevailed at the time. Most of the other photographs have been taken in recent years and I have been able to secure pictures of the graves of all the men where they exist. During this research I have once again been able to draw on the considerable kindness of Mr D.C. Jennings who lives in Florida, USA.

I have been unable to commission a brand new set of maps and have, therefore, reproduced some of the ones first used by David Ascoli in his book *The Mons Star* and also some of the maps used in the *Michelin Guide to Ypres*.

Lastly I have attempted to read as many published accounts of the 'Deeds' as possible. Readers will find some of these listed in the Bibliography.

ACKNOWLEDGEMENTS

I would like to thank the staff at the following institutions for their help and patience during the research for this book: The Commonwealth War Graves Commission, the Imperial War Museum, London, the National Army Museum, London, the Public Record Office, Kew, the Royal Artillery Institution, London, and the Royal Engineers Museum, Chatham, Kent.

Illustrations have been obtained from the following: D. Ascoli, *The Mons Star*, pp. 2, 35, 69, 81, 144, 156; *The Bugle*, p. 47; the Cheyne family, p. 83; Evelyn Clark, p. 188; Courage Ltd, p. 150; A. Fullaway, p. 204; Brenda Hands, p. 39; *The Illustrated London News*, pp. 58, 72, 147, 174; Illustrated Michelin Guide, *Ypres and the Battles of Ypres*, p. 120; Charlie McDonald, p. 117; David Rowlands, p. 9; M. Scott, p. 141; Ian Uys, p. 171; S. Wall, p. 33; L. Wiltshire, pp. 65, 105; The Collection of the Woolton Society, p. 37; Michelle Young, p. 60.

I have also received considerable assistance from the following individuals who have all helped in various ways: Peter Batchelor, John Bolton, Tom Brophy, John Cameron, Jack Cavanagh, Colonel Terry Cave CBE, Peter Harris, Donald C. Jennings, Maurice Johnson, Dennis Pillinger, Joan Purcell, David Rowlands, Steve Snelling, Tony Spagnoly and Andrew Vollans. My wife Wynne has, as always, been a great support.

ABBREVIATIONS

ASH	Argyll & Sutherland Highlanders	LDV	Local Defence Volunteers
BEF	British Expeditionary Force	MC	Military Cross
		NF	Northumberland Fusiliers
BWM	British War Medal	OTC	Officers Training Corps
BSM	Battery Sergeant Major	OCA	Old Comrades Association
CB	Commander of the Bath		
CG	Coldstream Guards	OP	Observation Post
CRA	Commander Royal Artillery	Ox & Bucks	Oxfordshire and Buckinghamshire Light Infantry
CRE	Commander Royal Engineers	PO	Petty Officer
		PRO	Public Record Office
CCS	Casualty Clearing Station	RAMC	Royal Army Medical Corps
DCLI	Duke of Cornwall's Light Infantry	RA	Royal Artillery
DG	Dragoon Guards	RE	Royal Engineers
DUKES	Duke of Wellingtons (West Riding)	RFA	Royal Field Artillery
		RFC	Royal Flying Corps
GOC	General Officer Commanding	RHA	Royal Horse Artillery
		RSF	Royal Scots Fusiliers
HLI	Highland Light Infantry	RWF	Royal Welch Fusiliers
KOSB	King's Own Scottish Borderers	SAA	Small Arms Ammunition
		SWB	South Wales Borderers
KOYLI	King's Own Yorkshire Light Infantry	TF	Territorial Force
		VC	Victoria Cross
KRRC	King's Royal Rifle Corps	VM	Victory Medal

INTRODUCTION

The Victoria Cross is the most coveted decoration that can be awarded to any member of the British and Commonwealth armed services. It can also be awarded posthumously. The medal was instituted in 1856 by Queen Victoria and is made from gun metal in the design of a Maltese Cross. It measures 1½ inches across. The ribbon used in 1914 was red for the Army and blue for the Royal Navy and below the crown were the words *For Valour*. The date of the deed is inscribed on the reverse side. A small pension is paid to holders of the Cross.

The British Army was considerably altered in the period between the end of the Boer War in 1902 and the beginning of the First World War in 1914. There were lessons to be learnt and in South Africa the numerically inferior army of Boers had for much of the time out-thought and out-gunned the much larger British Army. There were also lessons to be learnt from the Russo-Japanese war of 1904–05. Instrumental in these changes was Lord Haldane, the War Minister, who brought in the Haldane reforms and instigated the Territorial Army in 1908. Its role was at first to be a supplementary one, in that it was to be a back-up to the regular Army who in turn would call on its reservists in the event of hostilities.

The War Office had planned for the possibility of a European Campaign for some time and when it became clear that the German nation was set on invading and conquering France with the use of the Schlieffen Plan, the British Army was ready. Within less than two weeks the first troops of what were to be initially six infantry divisions and a cavalry division, together with a headquarters staff and back-up, were arriving in France and Belgium. Their role was one of support to their Belgian and French Allies.

At no time in 1914 and even after the arrival of the Indian Corps did the British Expeditionary Force number more than a quarter of a million men. It was this comparatively small size that led it to be known by the enemy as 'Contemptible' and thus the men who took part in the early fighting became known as the 'Old Contemptibles'. At the time of writing (1994) there are still a handful of British survivors alive from this early period of the war.

The medal known as the Mons Star was struck in 1917 and was the first campaign medal of the First World War. It was awarded to those men of the Army and Royal Flying Corps who served in France and Belgium between 5 August and 30 November 1914. In October 1919 a bar was awarded to those who were 'under fire' in France or Belgium between 5 August and 22 November

1914. By early December the British casualties came to nearly 90,000 and fewer than 230,000 bars were awarded.

There was a gap of nearly ten years when no VCs were awarded, between the action at Somaliland and the opening weeks of the First World War. The first two medals to be awarded in the early part of the fighting in the war were for gallantry on 23 August 1914. A further forty-four were won by the end of the year and not all in France and Belgium but also in Africa and the Dardanelles. Thirteen VCs out of forty-six were awarded posthumously and eleven of these were to officers. It is difficult to say with hindsight whether this figure was on the high side. However, the circumstances of the campaign were so unusual and the British and Indian Armies so outnumbered by the German Army that it was hardly surprising that many deeds of heroism and gallantry were committed in the opening months of the fighting.

In many people's minds mention of the First World War immediately summons up images of trench warfare, a muddy landscape and broken bodies. It is true that the latter battles to capture the siege town of Ypres did produce conditions of warfare which surely can never be repeated. However this did not apply to the early days of the fighting in August and September 1914. For then the war was one of continuous movement and change, beginning at Mons and continuing with the retreat to the Marne, only 20 miles from Paris. After the Allies 'stood on the Marne' the campaign changed dramatically when they pursued their German foe until they reached the valley of the River Aisne. Here the Germans made a stand, using the considerable advantage of the Aisne heights, on top of which stood the Chemin des Dames, or 'Ladies Road'. This was no casual stand as the Germans had surveyed the area very thoroughly before the war with the help of students studying the area. They knew exactly where to place their guns and troops to the best advantage against any army that endeavoured to cross the River Aisne and attempt to push them back.

Much of the August fighting had been carried out in very warm weather, and this combined with a considerable amount of marching led to both armies becoming exhausted, with men and horses dropping by the roadside. In September, however, conditions on the Aisne were often very cold and were accompanied by an abnormal amount of rain for the region. Contrary to popular belief, trench warfare began on the Aisne and not later in the Ypres Salient. At the end of September the early fighting on the Aisne came to an inconclusive end and the British handed over their positions to the French Army and marched north through France to Flanders. Their new role was to help save the Channel ports and the town of Ypres from falling into enemy hands. They were also to become heavily involved in fighting to the south of Ypres especially at Festubert, Messines and Neuve Chapelle. By the end of the year the Western Front stretched for about 350 miles from the Belgian coast to the Swiss border and the period of static trench warfare had begun. Both sides were to face each other across a shattered landscape for nearly four years until the Germans were finally overcome with exhaustion and pursued an Armistice in November 1918.

The men who won the VC in 1914 came from a varied social background; they were 'taken up' by the Press and became famous for a short period. The Press followed the lives of the thirty-three survivors with avid interest and this also included the reporting of any misdemeanours that they committed. Some of these men had tragic lives after the war as a result of the experience of the war itself and were often never to be fit again, along with the burden of unemployment. Britain did not look after its 'heroes' very well, yet the authorities had been keen to use the men in drumming up support for further recruits and volunteers for the war effort.

For one man, Francis Grenfell, the coming of war brought about the culmination of all of his soldierly ambitions. He came from a privileged background and after seeing many of his friends die, as well as his twin brother, he was to become disillusioned by the time he was shot through the heart in a gas-filled landscape in May 1915. The early 'big adventure' had turned into a nightmare. Lt. P. Neame, on the other hand, another career soldier, seemed to have been able to take the whole thing in his stride and within the pages of his autobiography, he does not 'let his guard fall' or show any form of weakness at all. Neame had considerable social advantages and was not short of money; he rose to a high rank in the Army and played an active role in the Second World War as well. He retired from the Army steeped in honours.

The holders of the Victoria Cross must feel that they belong to the most exclusive club of all. It is one for which membership is not one of payment but of gallantry and heroism in battle.

In my book on the men who won the Victoria Cross on the Somme in 1916, I wrote it in such a way as to allow each man's biography to stand up in its own right. This led to a small amount of repetition of introductory matter, but I assumed that readers might want to turn to individuals and not necessarily read the book in chronological order. However, I have decided to change this format for the present volume in order to cut down on repetition. Thus Mons, Le Cateau and Nery, for example, have a 'block' approach rather than an individual one. For the section on Le Cateau it looks as though Driver Luke has been rather 'short changed' but I would hope that he was read about in the context of the Le Cateau battle. I would be interested to hear which of these approaches readers prefer and would also be very grateful for any additional information that they may have to tell me.

Finally my admiration for the men from both sides, who took part in the First World War, remains undimmed and this book is dedicated to their memory.

M.J. DEASE

Mons, Belgium, 23 August

The first shots exchanged between the British and German Armies rang out at Soignies on 22 August 1914 on the northern outskirts of the Belgian city of Mons. Close by, the Condé Canal bends round in a wide loop, passing through the suburb of Nimy, thus making a salient. When the German and British Armies found themselves face to face across the canal on 23 August it was the British Expeditionary Force which was at the greater disadvantage. The drawbacks were simply that the British could be attacked from three sides.

Basically the Mons position followed the Condé Canal from Condé in the west to Binche in the east, where the 5th Cavalry Brigade was situated. The German threat came from almost all northerly directions and the BEF ran a considerable risk of becoming surrounded. The enemy intended to exploit the weakness of the Condé 'loop position' right from the start and if they captured it the British would have to evacuate the defence line along the straight road to Condé. At Nimy the way across the canal was by two bridges, one road and one rail bridge to its left.

Nimy turned out to be one of the earliest flashpoints of the First World War and no fewer than five Victoria Crosses were to be won in Mons and its environs on 23 August 1914.

The 4 Royal Fusiliers (9th Brig. 3rd Div.) had reached the outskirts of Mons on 22 August and were made very welcome by the inhabitants of the town who gave them eggs and fruit and other provisions. The battalion marched through the town and crossed the Condé Canal at Nimy and at first took up positions which were far from being ideal as there was a thick wood to the north-west. They were then ordered to retire to the canal itself and make that their line of defence along with the two bridges that crossed it. The Middlesex Regiment (8th Brig.) were to their right beyond the road bridge, and the 1st Royal Scottish Fusiliers (9th Brig. 3rd Div.) to their left, just north of Lock 6, about 800 yards to the left of the railway bridge.

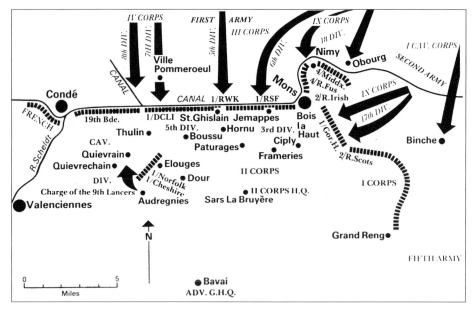

Mons, 23 August

In the early hours of 23 August, Gen. Sir H.L. Smith-Dorrien, the new Commander of the British 11 Corps gave divisional orders that the bridges over the Mons-Condé canal should be prepared for demolition. The timing, however, would depend on knowledge at local level and the bridges were not to be destroyed without permission.

The 4 Royal Fusiliers had B, C and D Companies in the firing line with A Company in reserve at Nimy railway station, B and C Companies were in and around Nimy itself and were responsible for the two bridges and the embankment. The road bridge (which was a swing bridge) was to be defended by Capt. Forster with two platoons of C Company. The rail bridge was to be defended by two platoons and Company Headquarters under Capt. Ashburner with the machine-gun section of two guns under Lt. M.J. Dease. Railway sleepers were set up to act as emplacements for the gunners. The left-hand gun was atop the embankment and the right-hand gun was below the bridge. In addition the infantrymen had support from 107th Battery Royal Field Artillery (RFA) who were in trenches behind them and who were to capture the enemy range with great accuracy.

During the night one man in every three had kept awake and the rest roused themselves at first light on the 23rd. They had continued to improve the defences; the day before, Dease had ordered that flour sacks of shingle be filled to give some protection for his two machine guns. Dease had taken off his coat and helped to shovel the shingle into the sacks.

The enemy strength consisted of six German battalions from 18th Division 111 Corps and they first showed themselves at around 07.00 hours and the battle for the railway bridge began in earnest an hour or so later, on what turned out to be a very hot day. The Germans took cover in small plantations which helped to hide their positions, and at 09.00 hours attacked the narrow position at the head of Nimy bridge in close formation which resulted in considerable casualties from the British machine guns and rapid firing riflemen. The survivors retreated in some haste and took cover behind the plantations where they hid for half an hour, before renewing the attack, but this time in extended order. The attack was not stopped in its tracks and Capt. Ashburner's company of Royal Fusiliers was under extremely heavy pressure. Very soon after the firing began Dease was hit for the first time. Lt. J.F. Mead was sent up with a platoon to help out but on arrival he was immediately wounded in the head. He had the wound dressed and on returning to the bridge was shot again in the head, this time fatally. Capt. Bowdon-Smith and Lt. Smith also went up to the bridge with another platoon but within a few minutes they too became casualties. Smith was killed and Bowden-Smith was wounded and died a few days later.

Capt. Ashburner received a head wound and Capt. Forster, in a trench to his right, was injured in the stomach and arm, and died two hours later. Dease was hit in the neck and was told by Lt. F.W.A. Steele 'to lie still and don't move. We are getting it all our own way.' Dease asked, 'How's the machine gun getting on?' and stood up but was hit again. He struggled up to handle one of the guns himself and was hit once more, this time seriously. Dease had spent some time before serving one of the two guns with ammunition but he became impatient and crawled his way to the right-hand gun and dragged the wounded gunner away. He then began to fire the gun himself and rolled the wounded man down the embankment which must have saved his life. Dease was exposed to murderous rifle, machine gun, and artillery fire, and kept calling for gunners to take the place of the men who were dead or wounded in the fighting. Dease's head was especially vulnerable, as were those of his colleagues, and it was only a matter of time before he was going to be killed and he must have known it. When he fell for the last time his body slumped across the railway lines and he probably died later at around 15.30 hours, after the infantry had withdrawn. During the action which lasted only a few hours this extremely brave officer 'fussed over' his guns and was only happy when both guns were firing in unison. He had rejected any attempts of sending him to hospital and on his death became an immediate hero to his battalion. Dease and his colleagues had fought as long as they were able and everyone involved was either killed or wounded. The position at Nimy bridge grew desperate and D Company to the left at Ghlin Bridge was going through a similar experience. Six burning barges on the canal added to the confusion.

When orders for the inevitable retirement came at 14.00 hours B and C Companies of the Royal Fusiliers were to leave first. They had to move from their dangerous position across 250 yards of exposed ground which was swept by shrapnel and machine-gun fire. Lt. Steele was said to have gathered up the mortally wounded Dease in his arms but this was not so, although Steele seems to have been the only man to have escaped without any injury. Pte. S.F. Godley who had been on the bridge since the start of the day had taken over one of the machine guns and kept it firing until long after his companions got away. He then proceeded to destroy the gun and fling the pieces into the canal. The retirement was carried out efficiently and the battalion was able to re-assemble in an open space in the centre of Mons. According to an eye-witness C Company looked in a bad state. The battalion, after forming up, marched through the town to an old château in front of which they bivouacked for the night.

For reasons that cannot easily be explained the casualties of 4 Royal Fusiliers on 23 August were not published for several weeks. This naturally caused considerable distress to their families. The blame must lie with the Royal Fusiliers themselves or with the War Office. The war being so young at this stage may have meant that systems had yet to be set up properly for the recording of casualties.

In mid-September, twenty-three days after Dease died of his wounds, his family learned of his injuries from a letter written to another officer by Capt. W. Hill, the Adjutant of the Royal Fusiliers. It said that Dease had been seriously wounded and might even be dead according to some witnesses. Eventually, Capt. Hill, now back at Aldershot, interviewed some of the survivors from the Nimy bridge fighting and listed the casualties which he admitted included Maurice Dease as killed. Still no names of casualties had been published concerning the Royal Fusiliers but on 16 September the Dease family finally received more firm evidence about Dease's death from a Sergeant who was on the bridge at Nimy during the fighting. He wrote, 'Dease, as far as we know, was killed in this action.' The next day the family heard from a Mrs Harter whose son James had been with the Battalion Staff that he had told her of Maurice's death on 2 September. However, as this was not official information the family still clung on to the slim hope that Maurice might have been taken prisoner.

They contacted the War Office but this brought forth no hard facts about Maurice's fate and they learned that 'nothing had been reported about Lt. Dease.' Finally, on 18 September the family had to accept the stark truth that they would never see Maurice alive again when they heard of his death in a letter written by Maj. Maltlock, second in command of the 4 Royal Fusiliers. Four days later the War Office sent a telegram saying that Dease had been dangerously wounded. This was followed four days later by an announcement of his death. However the confusion did not end there as the War Office, changing its mind again, sent a third telegram on the 28th stating that Dease was missing and not dead. By this time the family had accepted the inevitable and wisely ignored the third communication.

On 25 September the Dease family received a letter from Lt. K. Tower which told them that Maurice had 'died gallantly and certainly deserved the VC. I am trying to see that he is mentioned in Despatches. The whole regiment were really proud of him and the way he worked his machine gun on the bridge at Mons and everyone mourns the loss of one of the most popular and best officers in the Regiment.'

On the 27th Lt. Steele wrote to the family as well saying:

Poor Maurice got shot below the knee or thereabouts about 9am while he was attending to a machine gun on the left side of the bridge. Ashburner and I begged him to go off and get fixed up at the hospital, but he refused. He then crawled over to the right-hand side gun. Almost as soon as he got there he was again shot somewhere in the side. I made him lie down near me and with difficulty kept him quiet as he was worried about his guns. I promised to look after these for him and he settled down a bit quieter. I asked him if he was in any pain and he said, 'No' and smiled more or less cheerfully. As soon as I managed to get the guns going again he seemed much more happy. He seemed to have been hit again while I was busy on his left. For the next two hours there was a perfect hail of machine-gun fire as well as Artillery and Infantry fire. Maurice during this time became very quiet, and I fancy unconscious. When we retired Maurice had to be left behind . . .

A Pte. Marshall also wrote to Dease's sister:

. . . All went well (on the bridge) until we saw some German cavalry galloping across our front and C Coy. opened fire upon them and when they ceased firing, a German cavalry officer came and gave himself up as prisoner. Shortly afterwards we saw some Germans dodging about between some houses and your brother told a Private to lay the gun on the space between the houses and when he saw the Germans again to open fire. We fired and in about half an hour the Private got wounded in the head, and your brother told him to go and get it bandaged up and then I took over the gun and then I saw the Germans advancing towards us . . .

Another letter from Lt. K. Tower read as follows:

You really ought to hear the men back from the 4th Battalion talk of Maurice, it would do your heart good. They simply adore him and it's quite funny to see so many of them have brought photographs of him taken in the old groups of the Battalion and cut him out . . . Sir A. Conan Doyle is lecturing on the Great Battles of the war in several places, and he talks at some length about Maurice and his VC at Mons. I sent him my diary on the subject . . . You ought to have heard the cheers at the town hall at Folkestone – it would have made you feel proud . . .

A Patriotic Meeting took place at the Royal Albert Hall in London and a member of the audience wrote: 'Young Maurice Dease, VC and Captain Ranken, VC were both shown on the screen and the thousands present rose to their feet and cheered enthusiastically. It was a wonderful tribute from Great Britain and if the mothers of those boys who gave their lives for their country could have seen it, it might comfort their sad lonely hearts.'

Dease's Victoria Cross was gazetted on 16 November 1914 and although others were approved on that day, his was the first act of gallantry to warrant such an award. Dease was recommended for the award by Lt. Col. McMahon, probably on the evidence of Lt. Steele who had witnessed the fight to hold Nimy railway bridge. Dease was buried at St Symphorien Military Cemetery 3½ miles to the south-east of Mons. The cemetery, which is one of the most beautifully designed war cemeteries

on the Western Front, was laid out by the Germans who must have picked up Dease's body at Nimy bridge from the rail track. His grave is numbered V, B, 2 and the German and British graves are laid out in groups or clumps in a most attractive design.

Maurice James Dease was born in Gaulstown, Coole, County Westmeath, Ireland on 28 September 1889. He was the only son of Edmund Fitzlawrence Dease and Katherine, eldest daughter of Maurice Murray of Beech Hill, Cork. He was also the grandson of James Arthur Dease, JP, DL, the Vice-Lieutenant of Cavan. At the age of eight he went to the Frognal Park preparatory school in Hampstead, London. In 1903 he left and went to the Roman Catholic

Stonyhurst College. The college is able to claim seven holders of the Victoria Cross among its former students, and their portraits are on display there. Dease took his religion seriously and became a server in the college chapel. He was also interested in natural history and wrote articles on birds for the college magazine.

He left Stonyhurst for the Army College in Wimbledon about four years later before going on to the Royal Military College at Sandhurst.

He joined the 4 Royal Fusiliers in May 1910 as a Second Lieutenant and was promoted to full Lieutenant in April 1912. He later became machine-gun officer and was for a time Acting Adjutant. When war broke out in early August 1914 the battalion was stationed at Parkhurst and had mobilized within three days; by the 13th it was in France at Le Havre. The battalion journeyed to Belgium in a circuitous route via Amiens and ended up on the Belgian-French border, arriving at Mons on 22 August from the direction of Brussels.

After Dease's death at Nimy on 23 August his family received his Victoria Cross by post on 11 January 1915. He was later commemorated in Westminster Cathedral, on the Catholic Officers' Association Roll of Honour. There is also a plaque to his memory and that of Pte. Godley at Nimy. The plaque was unveiled in April 1939 on the original bridge and later hidden from the Germans.

In 1964 a service of remembrance was held at the Nimy memorial. This was attended by Brig. P.R. Ashburner, the son of Capt. Ashburner who commanded the company defending the two Nimy bridges, fifty years before. Others who attended included Dease's sister and his nephew, Maj. French.

There is a picture of Dease at the museum in Mons. Any visitor today will find the Nimy landscape very different from 1914, for a few years ago the canal was drained and turned into a motorway. The canal now exists as only little more than a drainage ditch. In the 1980s a painting of the action on the bridge at Nimy was commissioned for the Royal Fusiliers.

Although Dease's medals had been displayed at the Regimental Museum which is in the grounds of the Tower of London they belonged to his nephew Maj. French. In the mid-1980s the Major wrote to the Regimental Association informing it that he wished to sell them in order to raise some money for his grandchildren's education. However, he offered to give the regiment 'first refusal'. The sale transaction was carried out with the minimum of fuss and the medals were valued by an expert at about £18,000. It was felt by both parties that they would fetch more at auction but selling them privately would keep the costs down. Maj. French was paid in instalments.

The Victoria and Albert Museum in London was empowered to pay half of the cost providing that the regiment found the rest of the money. As the VC medal had the extra cachet of being the first awarded in the First World War there was no real means of estimating its value at auction. Dease's other medals included the 1914 Star with Mons Clasp, the British War Medal and the Victory Medal.

S.F. GODLEY

Mons, Belgium, 23 August

Pte. Sidney Frank Godley was a member of the 4 Royal Fusiliers and was part of Lt. Dease's machine-gun section at Nimy rail bridge on 23 August. Some accounts say that he was one of those men called upon to take over a gun and yet Godley himself said that he was on the bridge all the time, helping to provide ammunition. The main point of his story is that he was asked to man one of the machine guns by Lt. F.W.A. Steele when orders had been given to retire. Godley knew that this would result in him being captured by the Germans, dead or alive.

He took over a machine gun from Dease when the latter had been mortally wounded and although badly wounded himself, he managed to hold the bridge single-handed for two hours, while the Royal Fusiliers carried out their retirement. Eventually, after running out of ammunition, his final act was to destroy his gun and to toss the pieces into the Condé Canal. He had inflicted tremendous damage on the German infantry. The enemy had allowed many lives to be squandered in the Nimy fighting.

Godley crawled back from the bridge to the main road and was helped to a hospital by two Belgian civilians. When he was having his wounds dressed the hospital was taken over by the Germans and he was taken prisoner. He was asked many questions, such as which unit he belonged to and who was his Commanding Officer. He refused to answer. He was sent to Berlin for surgery and skin grafts; his back alone needed 150 stitches. When he was fit enough he was transferred to a POW camp at Doberitz. The senior German officer at the camp was the first man to tell Godley of his award of the Victoria Cross and Godley was congratulated by his jailer! This was after 25 November 1914 when his award was gazetted. Godley remained a prisoner of war for four years, and was able to walk out of the camp in 1918 when the camp guards deserted their posts during the revolution in Berlin. He returned to England having made his escape via Denmark. He was presented with his VC in the ballroom at Buckingham Palace on 15 February 1919.

Mons Canal railway bridge, 23 August. Lt. Maurice Dease and Pte. Sidney Frank Godley, 4 Royal Fusiliers, in the action that won them the first two Victoria Crosses to be awarded in the First World War

He was later welcomed home by the Mayor of Lewisham on 26 February and presented with 50 guineas and a copy of the Lewisham Roll of Honour.

Sidney Frank Godley was born on 14 August 1889 at East Grinstead, Sussex and went to school at the Sidcup National School. Later he moved to St John's Wood in London where he attended the Henry Street School. His mother had died when he was six years old and he moved to Willesden in North London to live with his uncle and aunt. Before enlisting with the Royal Fusiliers on 13 December 1909 he worked briefly at an ironmonger's shop in Kilburn High Road. In the Army he was a noted sportsman.

At the outbreak of war in August 1914 his battalion was one of the first to embark for France and Belgium and he arrived at Mons along with Lt. Dease and the rest of the 4 Royal Fusiliers on 22 August. In 1954 he recorded a programme for the BBC on the 40th anniversary of the Mons battle and said:

> . . . a little boy and girl came up on the bridge, and brought me some rolls and coffee. I was thoroughly enjoying the rolls and coffee, and talking to the children the best I could, when the Germans started shelling. So I said to this little boy and girl; 'You'd better sling your hooks now, otherwise you may get hurt.' Well, they packed their basket and left.

Godley became a school caretaker and retired in 1951 after thirty years' service. In 1919 he married a friend of his sister at St Mark's Church, Harlesden. Her name was Helen Eliza, daughter of George Norman. Between the wars Godley worked very hard on behalf of service charities. On occasions he dressed up as 'Old Bill' the character created by the artist Bruce Bairnsfather. It is true that he did bear some likeness to 'Old Bill'. This became his nickname and there are several photographs which bear this out. However the writer is one of those who considers that the character was not really based on one individual soldier but rather on an amalgam of characters and individuals. He was more of a symbol of the typical British Tommy of the First World War than a real person. Godley, however, used the likeness to good effect and wore a walrus moustache, and combined this with sporting a pipe and wearing his hat at a raffish angle. On occasions he wore a helmet with the design of a Union Jack covering it. He never ceased to attend ceremonies commemorating the war or special functions arranged for the 'Old Contemptibles' and in November 1931 he took part in the Armistice Service at the Cenotaph in London.

In April 1939, nearly twenty-five years after the Battle of Mons took place, a party of fifty men from the Royal Fusiliers attended the unveiling of a new bridge at Nimy. During the service a plaque commemorating the heroism of Lt. Dease and Pte. Godley was unveiled. Godley was also presented with a special medal in the previous year by the people of Mons. Altogether he made seven visits to Mons, his last being in 1939. The mayor of Mons gave a lunch at the Hotel de Ville and Godley was guest of honour. Another of the guests, who signed a menu of the luncheon, was one of the children who had fed Godley with rolls and coffee in 1914.

In 1940 the plaque was taken down from Nimy bridge and hidden for the duration of the war. In 1954 Godley gave an interview to the *Daily Express* on the occasion of the 40th anniversary of the Mons battle on 23 August and said, 'It was Sunday. People in their best suits were going to church . . . They didn't know the Germans were so near, of course. No one did . . . Then suddenly the Germans were everywhere.'

Godley was virtually a 'local boy' to the Regimental Museum at the Tower of London and was very fond of London's East End. He had connections with Tower Hamlets and Bethnal Green. The school where he worked was the Cranbrook School, and his home address was Digby Street off Globe Road, E1. However late in his life he moved to No. 164 Torrington Drive, Loughton in Essex, and died there on 29 June 1957. He was buried in grave number 3051 at Loughton Cemetery, St John's church. At his funeral the Revd B.W. Ottaway was assisted by the Revd Mellish VC who, although retired, travelled up from Somerset for the service. Mellish had also married the Godleys back in 1919.

A firing party from the Royal Fusiliers fired a volley over the grave and provided a bearer party. An 'Old Contemptible's' badge was placed on the grave.

In 1976 a new housing estate in Bexley, close to Sidcup, consisting of forty-one houses, was named after Godley.

On 23 August 1985 another ceremony was arranged at Mons which was organized by the Royal Fusiliers, and many of Godley's family attended.

In the 1980s a decision was taken to build a housing block in Tower Hamlets and to name it after a 'local hero'. At first the name of Blair Peach was suggested by the left wing council. Peach had been 'roughed up' in a racial disturbance some years before. There was a lot of discussion in the council and Godley's name was put forward as a more appropriate name for the housing block to be named after. Eventually the plaque was unveiled on 8 May 1992 and the block was called Sidney Godley VC House. Godley's son, members of the Royal Fusiliers and members of the local council attended the ceremony.

Godley's medals are not publicly held.

T. WRIGHT

Mons, Belgium, 23 August

Gen. Sir H.L. Smith-Dorrien in charge of 11 Corps gave orders early on 23 August that the various bridges over the Mons-Condé Canal should be prepared for demolition by the Royal Engineers. However the timing of the destruction of the bridges was to be a decision made by divisional commanders or at local level. Thus each bridge was prepared for blowing, even while some of them were being fought over. During this whole operation there were many examples of heroism. Unfortunately the end result did not do much to slow the advance of the German Army.

It was the 3rd Division that was mainly responsible for the Mons-Condé line and we already know that the 4 Royal Fusiliers (9th Brig.) were covering the two bridges at Nimy, with the 1st RSF to their left close to Lock 6, then came the 1st NF.

Two companies of the Royal Engineers were part of the 3rd Division, the 56th and 57th Field Companies. Capt. Theodore Wright was the Adjutant divisional Royal Engineer under the command of the divisional CRE, Lt. Col. C.S. Wilson.

Wright was detailed to supervise 57th Field Company's preparation of the destruction of eight of the bridges over the canal. 56 Field Company also had some bridges to supervise.

After Mariette Bridge had been prepared by Sgt. Smith and Sapper Dabell, Capt. Wright was seen, by some Engineers, to be coming from the direction of Lock 2 where he had been wounded by shrapnel. He had been hit when trying to cross a gap of 20 yards between the barricade, set up by the infantry, and Cpl. Jarvis's (57th Field Coy.) boat from which Jarvis was attempting to lay charges under heavy fire going on overhead. Occasionally Jarvis and Sapper Neary had to dash back to the barricade to fetch more explosives and to run out their leads. In the afternoon it was discovered from a despatch rider, who was on his way to the RSF, that orders for the retirement had been given. Wright's problem was then how to blow up five bridges, on a front of 3 miles with only one exploder. Sensibly he used a car to get him from bridge to bridge in the shortest period of time, taking the exploder with him. He first visited Dayos Bridge and Jemappes was blown at around 15.00 hours.

Capt. T. Wright setting the charges under Mariette Bridge

Lt. A.F. Day attempted to blow the bridges at Nimy but lacked an instantaneous fuse which slowed operations down. He worked on the rail bridge judging it to be the more important one but before he could finish fixing his charges, he was wounded and taken prisoner. The bridge at Lock 2 was omitted from the list owing to a lack of time to detonate it and the one next to it. The next bridge on Wright's list was the important bridge at Mariette which carried the main road. Wright worked his way under the bridge and although wounded struggled to set the charges. He was assisted in this work by Sgt. Smith. Wright succeeded in joining up his leads with the local electricity supply in a nearby house, hoping that the current would set off the detonator. However at that very moment the current failed.

B Company of the 1st NF was still holding out at the barricade on the south side of the canal, but the towpath was separated from the barricade by a subsidiary canal, which here spanned the girder bridge 15 to 20 feet wide. Capt. Wright 'bridge-laddered' under this subsidiary canal bridge with extra leads tied on him, and time and time again tried to get at the end of the leads on the towpath. Each time his hands or head appeared above the level of the towpath he was fired at from about 30 yards, so eventually he gave up the attempt. In swinging himself back under the girder across the subsidiary canal, he lost his grip owing to exhaustion, and was pulled out of the water by Sgt. Smith.

The Engineers were almost the last British troops to leave Mons and did not get away until about 17.00 hours. It was a very great pity, despite the heroic efforts of 57th Field Company, that out of eight bridges only the one close to Jemappes station was successfully destroyed.

Two days later men of B Coy. 1st NF who had been particularly impressed by Wright's gallantry, saw him riding past their billets at Bavai and gave him a very enthusiastic cheer. The retreat from Mons began on 23 August and was followed by the Battle of the Marne on 6 September when the Allies began to drive the enemy back towards the Aisne. At this stage 57th Field Company was at Chartres on its way to Lumigny. On the 8th the men crossed the Marne at Nanteuil and marched to Ventelet and later Damard. A few days later they had gone northwards as far as Braine close to the Aisne river.

During the night of the 13th/14th 56 and 57 Field Companies, built pontoon bridges at Vailly, a small town on the Aisne. The 5th Cavalry Brigade crossed the pontoon bridge into the town and then owing to heavy shellfire had to retreat in a hurry. They retired to a wood near Chasseny. Capt. Wright supervised the crossing of the cavalry brigade on their return journey.

An eyewitness, a member of the 2nd Dragoons (Scots Greys), was later to write:

We got across the river at Vailly the day before yesterday (14th Sept.), a bit before our time, and had to get back over a pontoon bridge considerably quicker than was pleasant – under a very unpleasant fire, too. At the head of the bridge was a gallant Engineer officer, repairing bits blown off and putting down straw as cool as a cucumber – the finest thing I have ever seen. The poor fellow was killed just after my troop got across. No man earned a better VC.

The official account said that Wright was mortally wounded while helping an injured man into a shelter. During heavy shellfire, which was affecting both banks of the river, he had made himself responsible not only for the bridge but also for the safety of those who crossed it. Two Sappers and a Sergeant were also killed with Wright.

Wright was buried at Vailly British Cemetery 11, B, 2 and his VC was awarded posthumously on 16 November.

Theodore Wright, known as Dodo, was the son of William Walter and Arabella Wright; he was born in Brighton, Sussex on 15 May 1883. The family lived at Albury, a small village near Guildford in Surrey. Wright was educated at Clifton College and then went to the Royal Military Academy at Woolwich. He played hockey and cricket and on one occasion he was in the Army cricket team against Hampshire. He passed out of the Academy and joined the Royal Engineers in October 1902.

After initial training at Chatham, he was stationed at Aldershot with the Balloon

Section until December 1906. He later served with them in Gibraltar and Cairo. On 21 June 1905 he was made a full Lieutenant. He was appointed to 2nd Fortress Company Cairo in January 1907 and returned to Aldershot in October 1912. He then went to Chatham where he took an advanced course and became Adjutant at Bulford Camp, in Wiltshire, while serving with the 56th Field Company which he was with until the beginning of the war. He was made a Captain on 1 October 1913.

At the start of the war, 57th Field Company was at Bulford Camp and received its mobilization orders on 4 August 1914. It left Amesbury twelve days later for its journey to the front. The men travelled from Southampton to Rouen and then to the Mons area via Aulnoye, Feignies and Cuesmes where they arrived on the 22nd with orders to strengthen the bridgeheads.

A chauffeur who must have been in charge of the car that Wright used to inspect the Mons bridge on 23 August wrote this of him: 'He was the officer who got wounded in the head while I was driving him at Mons. When I was under fire there, I took a wounded soldier to the hospital and returned into the fire for the Captain. It was a bit risky, with eight cases of dynamite on the car. He was a brave man.' After the Mons fighting on 23 August the company moved on to Harmignies south of Mons and entrenched a position at Nouvelles. The next day it was ordered to erect some barricades for the 9th Brigade, in Frameries and lost twelve bicycles when suddenly caught up in the retirement.

L. Cpl. Jarvis (see next chapter), who was also working on destroying the Jemappes bridge at Mons, wrote this of Wright: 'The work on the bridge was done under fire from three sides. Near the bridge I found Captain Theodore Wright, wounded in the head. I wished to bandage him but he said, "Go back to the bridge." It must be done – and so I went . . . '

After Wright's death Lt. Col. Wilson wrote to his mother: 'No one has earned a VC better, and I am truly glad they have given it to him. I have known him so long, and I have always been very fond of him. He was one of the finest officers I have ever had, and I feel his loss every day . . . '

His VC was one of the first to be awarded in the First World War. It is not held in a public collection.

C.A. JARVIS

Mons, Belgium, 23 August

In August 1914 there were a number of bridges over the Mons-Condé Canal which could be raised for canal traffic. The road section of each bridge was secured by light girders.

57th Field Company was in the region of Cuismes and Jemappes guarded by the infantry on the canal bank, and helping to prepare defensive positions. No. 3976 L. Cpl. Jarvis was a member of Field Coy. Royal Engineers and he and Capt. Theodore Wright both received the Victoria Cross for the work carried out on the canal bridges at Mons on 23 August 1914. It was Jarvis who achieved the most tangible results with the successful blowing of the bridge at Jemappes. For various reasons none of the other bridges in the sector covered by the 57th Field Company was destroyed, but it was certainly not through lack of trying. Even to attempt to hold up the German advance under conditions of heavy fire, with the risk of early death or capture, was very risky. The destruction of the bridges would have been a great achievement.

An article published in *The Sapper* of February 1915 tells the story of how Jarvis won his VC on 23 August:

Lance-Cpl. Jarvis and Sapper Neary were detailed with B Company Royal Scots Fusiliers, and ordered to prepare one of the bridges for demolition in case of a retirement. A small boat was procured, and two privates of the RSF were detailed to hold the boat in position. The three girders needing separate charges, required in all twenty-two slabs of gun cotton, which had to be securely fixed to the girders and tamped with clay.

During the work of placing the charges the fire of the enemy gradually increased in violence. L.Cpl. Jarvis sent the two infantrymen back to their company, and despatched Sapper Neary to obtain the exploder and leads, which were in the possession of another party under Corporal Wiltshire. After some considerable time, the amount of fire increased, so that reinforcements had to be sent for. Capt. Traill, RSF, who was wounded in the knee, procured a pony and went to fetch them, and also the ammunition. By this time the firing on the position had become so violent and the casualties were so numerous that a retirement was decided upon. L. Cpl. Jarvis was then called upon to destroy the bridge, but was still without the exploder and leads, as the sapper had not returned. He pulled along the lock to a position where no fire was being directed, crawled out over the bank, and got into the street, where he commandeered a bicycle from a Belgian, and was riding towards the market square to find the exploder himself, when he met Capt. T. Wright, the Adjutant of the RE Companies, 3rd Division, who was then wounded in the head. Capt. Wright told Jarvis to go back to the bridge and be prepared to connect up the leads, as he would fetch them in a motor car, and taking the bicycle from Jarvis, went off to fetch the necessary articles. Jarvis returned to his former position to await the return of Capt. Wright. By this time the infantry had been terribly cut up, and the general order to retire came, which practically meant every man for himself.

After working for about one and a half hours Jarvis did finally manage to successfully fire the charges for the bridge's demolition, which probably saved the lives of many British troops.

In the same *Sapper* article quoted above Jarvis was later reported as saying:

When I got out of my position I saw civilians and soldiers running for their lives, and dropping at the volleys from the Germans. I got into another street, where I found Sapper Neary. The Uhlans by this time were well in pursuit of us. Finding a party of the RSF, we kept together until we were joined by Lieut. Boulnois, RE, Cpl. C. Wiltshire, and Sapper Farmer. The officer decided we 'should make for Frameries to the south of Jemappes . . .

Once at Frameries the group was joined by the section forage cart which was being pursued by a party of twenty Germans. However, owing to the Germans' erratic fire the party was able to get away across open country towards Genly. That night they were fed well by a farmer's wife and barricaded themselves in a barn. At 02.30 hours they returned to Frameries where they tore up stone setts from the road and barricaded the streets. However they were soon shelled out of Frameries and left for a place called Feignies, where they billeted in a theatre and took time off to entertain themselves with some musical instruments they found there.

On the evening of 25 August they moved off again and ended up at Le Cateau. The battle began as an artillery duel between the two armies and the group had an enjoyable time watching the success of the British guns in positions 200 yards to their rear. They were told by a brigade major to retire, much to their consternation; this was about 16.00 hours on the 26th. They then joined the great retreat to the Marne, a column of 6 miles in length, which was to cover a distance of 64 miles in two days.

The 57th Field Company took part in the Battle of the Aisne and was in Vailly in mid-September assisting troops across the river. On the 17th, 18th and 19th the *War Diary* (WO95/1403) noted that they occupied a sandstone quarry at the top of a hill above Vailly and one can safely assume that Jarvis was one of those Sappers who was to spend some time in this deep sandpit, which was made up of a series of tiers. Their work at this time was to support the infantry in cutting communications. The Engineers were suffering from a lack of sleep and continuous exposure to rain and cold. On the 23rd the unit marched to Chasseney and two days later to Brunelle. On the 30th they built a pontoon bridge 250 yards upstream from the railway bridge. A short time later the Field Company began to travel northwards in order to take part in the fighting in Flanders.

Jarvis must have been wounded at some time as there is an account of his being in hospital in November. His VC was gazetted on 16 November 1914 and he was presented with the medal at Buckingham Palace on 13 January 1915. It is said that the winning of the VC was a 'great surprise to him'. His deeds were written up widely in the British Press.

In an edition of the *Fraserburgh Herald* dated 9 January 1917 there is a short article about him under the heading of 'Fraserburgh's VC – Grievance as to Pension':

Corporal C.A. Jarvis the first hero who received the Victoria Cross in the present war, has over 17 years' service to his credit. In ten months (November 1917) he would be entitled to the pension granted to men with 18 years' service. A year ago (January 1916) he answered a call for volunteers for munition work, and as a skilled mechanic he has been so employed since. Last week he was suddenly presented by the civilian manager of the works where he is engaged with his discharge from the army. The effect of that is to deprive him of the opportunity of becoming eligible for his 18 years' pension, and to render him liable to the provisions of the Military Service Act, if he does not remain employed on munition work. Jarvis feels so strongly about his treatment that he declares that he will leave his employment at the munition works to see whether the army will take him on as a conscript.

Corporal Jarvis told a *London Star* representative:

I want to know what I am discharged for? . . . I am 35 years old, perfectly sound, and perfectly ready to go out to the front again if I am wanted. I do not believe that the authorities are acting legally in discharging me in this way.

I have the best possible character from my officers . . . I mean to expose the meanness of the practice, and see whether the public approves such treatment for the men who went through the first and heaviest fighting of the war.

Charles Alfred Jarvis was born on 29 March 1881 at the Admiralty Buildings, Saltoun Place, Fraserburgh, Scotland. The buildings, now in private ownership, are known as the Coastguard Houses. Jarvis' father was the coastguard and had married the eldest sister of Mr Alex Byth of Castle Street. Jarvis attended Carnoustie School, joined the Black Watch at the end of 1899, and served overseas. He left the Army in 1907 and was a reservist until called up in 1914. At some point he transferred to the Royal Engineers.

Jarvis must have had a connection with Essex as after he was awarded the VC he was given a public welcome in July 1915 at Woodford Green and taken for a ride on a fire tender. On 16 September he received another welcome at Chelmsford and was called upon to give a recruiting speech.

Not much is known about his postwar life except that he was a labourer and a 'bit of a loner'. He joined the LDV at the beginning of the Second World War and was on duty at Portsmouth Dockyard. He returned to St Monance around 1943. He died in the Royal Infirmary, Dundee on 19 November 1948, at the age of sixty-seven. On his death certificate his occupation was given as Admiralty

Admiralty Buildings, Saltoun Place, Fraserburgh, Scotland

L. Cpl. C.A. Jarvis at Chelmsford, July 1915

labourer. He was buried at St Monance, Fife, grave number Row G, Plot 176. The inscription on the stone not only mentions Jarvis but also Mrs Jarvis's first husband who died in 1930. It can be assumed that Jarvis married her sometime between 1931 and 1951. Jarvis is also commemorated in Carnoustie where Jarvis Place is named after him.

On 14 December 1947 his VC was sold, and again in July 1953, this time for £105. In October 1961 it was on offer for £600 from Baldwins the medal specialists. At the present time the medal is owned by Birmingham Museum where it is part of a very fine medal collection.

C.E. GARFORTH

Harmignies, France, 23 August

On 23 August the right flank of the 3rd Division rested on Harmignies, 5 miles to the south-east of Mons. It faced the German 17th Division of IX Corps which was attacking from the north-east.

No. 7368 Cpl. C.E. Garforth was a member of A Squadron 15th (The King's) Hussars who were part of the 3rd Division Cavalry Squadron. In a rearguard action on 23 August near Harmignies Garforth's troop was almost surrounded and held up by a wire fence. Ignoring German machine-gun fire Garforth set about cutting the wire which enabled his troop to gallop to safety.

On 2 September at Dammartin, south-east of Senlis towards the end of the retreat from Mons, Garforth was involved in another incident that was to contribute towards his winning the VC. This time he was out on patrol when it came under heavy German fire and was forced to return. Sgt. Scatterfield's horse was shot and fell trapping its rider. Under heavy fire Garforth managed to pull the Sergeant free from under his horse to a place of safety. The next day Garforth was involved in a third heroic incident. Again he was on patrol, this time at Meaux, to the south-east of Dammartin, when Sgt. Lewis's horse was shot from under him. In order to allow his Sergeant to get away from enemy fire Garforth drew the machine-gun fire on to himself for about three minutes and returned fire with his rifle.

The *War Diary* of the 15th Hussars for the last week in August was lost and records were compiled from private diaries. The *Diary* (WO95/1399) lists the places where the cavalrymen took part in patrols and at La Hautemaison they took part in a small flanking action with German patrols. On the 5th they moved on to Chartres and again had a brush with German patrols. On the next day they were part of the Advance Guard and were involved in pushing back a German squadron. On the 7th, at Farmouties, they were involved in protecting the left flank of the division. The next day they moved on to Coulommiers and Rebais. At Bussorres, on the 9th, they had a quiet day and were still advancing. On the 10th, as part of the Advance Guard again, they saw a little action near Bentry.

Cpl. C.E. Garforth in action during early September

On the 11th they acted as escort to the artillery near Dammard. On the 12th they again saw no action and were still acting as part of the divisional Advance Guard. On the 13th, at Braine, they began their involvement in the Battle of the Aisne and reconnoitred towards Vailly where the British were to cross the river.

Garforth's VC was one of five to be gazetted on 16 November, all of them being among the first to be awarded in the First World War. The Battle of the Marne in early September was followed by the Battle of the Aisne in which Garforth took an active part, in particular in patrols at Vailly Bridge on 14 September. At the beginning of October the BEF moved north to Flanders and Garforth took part in the fighting that preceded the first Battle of Ypres. On 13 October near Laventie close to the La Bassée-Ypres line, Garforth's luck ran out. Yet again he was on patrol, this time with Capt. A.E. Bradshaw, at the village of Bout Delville when they were suddenly surrounded and Bradshaw along with seven men were killed. Garforth held out until all ammunition was expended and was then taken prisoner.

During his time as a prisoner of war Garforth was taken first to Hamelin-on-Weser, and then transferred to Bohmte. From there he made three attempts to escape and on each occasion reached the German-Dutch border, only to be recaptured. Once his food ran out and he had nothing to eat for six days and became too exhausted to avoid the frontier guards. He was put on a diet of bread and water as punishment. On 19 March 1918 he was sent to Holland and repatriated to England on 18 November 1918. Two vessels arrived on that day at Hull with 2,000 POWs, one of whom was Cpl. Garforth. The men were met by Maj. Gen. Stanley von Donop who was in charge of the Humber Garrison, and delivered a message of welcome from the King. The men 'cheered lustily and sang the National Anthem'.

Garforth was interviewed by a reporter from *The Times* and his remarks were published in *The Times* and the *Yorkshire Herald* on 19 November. From what he said it appears that the original dates of his winning the VC were not very accurate. This is not really surprising as he had been a POW for four years. From his remark and also from the *War Diary* (which cannot be completely relied upon) his VC action probably took place on 6/7 September. Garforth caught up with his regiment in Kerpen, near Cologne in Germany on 4 August 1919. A few weeks later he returned with the 15th Hussars to Kilkenny, where he served with them as a Sergeant.

On 19 December 1918 Garforth was invested with his VC by the King at Buckingham Palace.

Charles Ernest Garforth was the son of a builder and decorator and was born at No. 19 Chaplin Road, Willesden Green, London on 23 October 1891. He spent most of his childhood in Harrow at the family home at Willow Cottage, Fairholme Road, Greenhill, Harrow.

Garforth attended Greenhill Council School and then briefly Bridge School, Wealdstone between 1906 and 1907. On leaving school he went to work at a local boot shop at St Anne's Road. He was an active member of The London Diocesan Church Lads Brigade and won his first medal as an award for keeping a tidy and clean tent.

In 1907 he left the Church Lads and the following year joined the Middlesex Territorial Battalion at the age of seventeen. Four years later he joined the 15th Hussars as a Trooper and trained at Aldershot before serving with them in Potchefstroom, South Africa. He returned to England with his regiment in 1913. The next year he became a Corporal. On 16 August 1914 he sailed to France with the 15th Hussars and they went first to Rouen before moving north to Mons where he was to begin what was to be a very fine active fighting career but which was to last for less than eight weeks. A day after his VC was gazetted the Middlesex Education Committee, at their monthly meeting at the Guildhall, Westminster said that 'All members would be interested and pleased to know that one of the boys educated at the Greenhill Council School, Harrow, had been among the first to receive the Victoria Cross . . . they all felt it to be an honour to the county . . . It was decided that the achievement should be commemorated by being entered on the records.'

In December 1918, the same month that Garforth received his VC, he was also presented with war savings certificates to the value of £160 and an illuminated scroll from the people of Harrow. In April 1919 he married Lily, a girl whom he had known since he was fifteen and whom he had written to when a prisoner of war. On 11 November 1920 he attended the Armistice Service at the Cenotaph and the burial of the Unknown Warrior in Westminster Abbey. He was one of the recipients of the Victoria Cross invited to attend the ceremonies. Garforth stayed on in the army until 1922 and left with the rank of Sergeant when his regiment was serving in Ireland.

During the rest of his long life he was never to lose his love of the regiment or his pride in having been one of the first VC holders of the First World War. He was also to attend many of the various functions to honour the recipients of the VC. In the early 1920s he and his wife moved to Chilwell in Nottinghamshire and he took a job with the security police at the local Ordnance Depot. He then left that job and worked for a while at Ericson's (later to become Plessey) before returning to the Ordnance Depot for a second spell with the police.

In the mid-1930s Garforth took charge of a local warehouse and in the Second World War he became the Air Raid Precautions (ARP) instructor at British Celanese, Spondon. He finally retired in 1956 when he was sixty-five years of age. In 1959 he was present at Barnard Castle when Princess Margaret presented the 15th/19th Hussars with a new Guidon to commemorate their bicentenary. In 1968 he was back again with his regiment for a very special service and this time a tank in A Squadron was named *Garforth VC* after him.

Famous though Garforth may have been as a VC hero, he did appear to have financial problems from time to time and in 1970 a special pension was confirmed on his behalf. At an earlier period, when he was for a time unemployed, his wife had written to the Headquarters of Scottish Command, seeking employment for her husband. She received a sympathetic reply but it did not lead to any action.

The Garforths had lived in Long Eaton and Bye-Pass Road, Chilwell before moving into a caravan at No. 5 Lock Close, Ryland, Beeston. Charles Garforth enjoyed cycling, walking and gardening – right up to his death he could be seen pottering in his garden. He died on 1 July 1973 in his eighty-second year. Although he had suffered with heart problems and had also had bronchitis, his death in his sleep came as a surprise to his family.

His body was cremated at Wilford Hill (register number 102183) and his ashes scattered in the garden of remembrance. He left a widow and two children. A bungalow now occupies the site of No. 5 Lock Close.

His medals were acquired by the Imperial War Museum, London, in September 1984.

F.O. GRENFELL
Audregnies, Belgium, 24 August

The 9th Lancers, a crack cavalry regiment, was well prepared for war and by 15 August had embarked for France. Among their officers, many of whom were old Etonians, were the Grenfell twins, Francis Octavius and Riversdale Nonus Grenfell. The twins were known throughout English Society circles and especially in the racing and polo worlds. They were over 6 feet in height, with dark hair and full moustaches. Francis was the older of the two by a few minutes. They were born in 1880 and were nearly thirty-four years of age when they set out for France. They were the youngest of thirteen children and their uncle was Lord Grenfell. There was a strong military tradition in the Grenfell family which was to be sorely tested in the war just beginning.

On the eve of embarkation Francis wrote to his uncle, 'that I have always been working for war, and have now got into the biggest in the prime of life for a soldier.'

The unit arrived at Boulogne on the evening of 16 August and passed through Amiens and on to Maubeuge to the south of the Belgian town of Mons. They detrained the next day at Jeunot and moved to Obrechies. They were made welcome by French and Belgian civilians alike as they were the first Allied cavalry to arrive in the area.

The 9th Lancers along with the 11th Hussars and 4th Dragoon Guards belonged to the 1st Cavalry Brigade which was one of four such brigades that made up the cavalry division. The 9th Lancers began by carrying out reconnaissance in order to try and make contact with the Germans and on Friday, 21 August they moved to the village of Harmignies to the south-east of Mons. The next day they moved to Thulin where they dug trenches to the south of the rail crossing. They were behind the left flank of the 3rd Division. It was not the sort of countryside at all suited for cavalry warfare, consisting as it did of small villages, coal mines, railways and wire, etc. They could hear firing to the north-east and were ordered to retire slowly, fighting a rearguard action.

Monday, 24 August was to be the first day of the retreat from Mons which was to last until early September. Capt. Francis Grenfell who was in charge of B Squadron was reconnoitring when his horse was shot from under him. The enemy was massing close to a rail station. The Squadron 'fell back through the regiment' and went into reserve. They were then ordered to support the 18th Hussars to the north of the village of Audregnies. The 5th Division then called on the cavalry to assist as they were in considerable danger of being encircled by the enemy.

The commander of the 2nd Cavalry Brigade, Brig. Gen. de Lisle sent the 9th Lancers and the 4th Dragoon Guards to charge the German gun positions. Beyond a sugar factory were nine German batteries positioned on the south side of the Valenciennes-Mons railway line. The German gunners were protected by many defensive obstacles including fences, hedges and a semi-industrial landscape of slag heaps, railway lines and sunken roads.

The Lancers, with two troops of the Dragoon Guards to their left rear set off down a Roman road which still exists towards the sugar factory. They charged full tilt into the flanks of the advancing German masses, and were met by a hail of machine-gun fire, shelling and rifle fire. Many of the galloping horses fell over the low signal-wires or pitched headlong, breaking their riders' necks. Grenfell

Audregnies, 24 August

later wrote: 'We had simply galloped about like rabbits in front of a line of guns,' and 'men and horses falling in all directions.' Much of their time was spent in dodging the horses.

At the sugar factory the Lancers dismounted and along with some men from the Dragoon Guards under Grenfell and their Commanding Officer Lucas-Tooth, they held on tenaciously. The remainder galloped off to the right and where possible used the protection of various slag heaps. They reassembled with a squadron of the 11th Hussars on the outskirts of Elouges. The small group's position at the sugar factory became untenable and they therefore rode off in a south-easterly direction and fell back on the lee side of a mineral works' railway embankment. There were more than eighty casualties including those wounded or missing. The rail line connected a mineral works to a spoil dump a few hundred yards away to the north-west. A bridge took the line over the road and the remains of the bridge and mineral works line still exist in the 1990s.

Many commentators muddle this former industrial line with a second line which went from Elouges to Quievrain. But it is this one that helped to give vital shelter to the cavalrymen as they swung round to the right after being 'brushed aside' at the sugar factory. Disastrous though the cavalry action may have been in terms of casualties it did give the necessary breathing space to the 5th Division who were able to get away in the retreat from Mons.

The 9th Lancers' second gallant action of the day took place at an embankment to the south-west of Elouges. Here were positioned some detached guns that belonged to the 119 Field Battery (XXVII Brig., 5th Div.) which were in danger of falling into enemy hands. The battery, under the command of Maj. G.H. Alexander, was being attacked by three German batteries and was becoming very short of personnel having lost thirty men and thirty-six horses. Francis Grenfell, who himself had been wounded in the hand by shrapnel, offered his squadron's assistance and called for volunteers among his officers and men. Grenfell had his damaged hand bound up in a scarf, and looked for an exit point for the guns. The dismounted Lancers proceeded to help the battery to manhandle the guns out of trouble despite being under very heavy fire. They had to run the guns by hand as there were no available horses and no rope either. A Squadron under Capt. Lucas-Tooth arrived and he took over command from a dazed Grenfell, suffering from wounds and exhaustion, who was wandering around the battlefield hoping for fresh orders. He was subsequently given a lift by the Duke of Westminster whose Rolls Royce was in the vicinity looking for stragglers. The Duke was a friend of the Grenfell twins and also one of the richest men in England. He and Powell his chauffeur took Grenfell to the nearby town of Bavai where his wounds were attended to by French nuns in a convent hospital.

Overnight Grenfell rested up in the Duke's bed at Le Cateau and felt 'rather done'. Rivy (Riversdale) who was galloper to Gen. De Lisle was with his brother and it was to be the last time that the twins were to see each other. Francis was transferred to Amiens and then to Rouen before being shipped back to England.

Francis, for his prompt action in organizing the saving of the guns and for the earlier dash against the German 'hordes', was recommended for the Victoria Cross along with Maj. Alexander. His was one of the earliest VCs to be won in the First World War and was much written about in the English press with a deal of exaggeration. Furthermore, most paintings that were commissioned to commemorate the deed were not very accurate.

The Grenfell twins were born on 5 September 1880 at Hatchlands near Guildford, Surrey. The family was of Cornish extraction and their parents were Pascoe Du Pré Grenfell and Sofia, who were also cousins. The twins were the last of a family of thirteen children and were doted on by their sisters. They grew up with few cares and learnt to ride almost as soon as they could walk. When they were seven years old the family moved to Wilton Park near Beaconsfield in Buckinghamshire where their father had spent his childhood. At the same time they began their education at a private school at East Sheen. When they were fourteen they followed the family tradition and went to Eton. They became popular and dominant figures at Eton where Francis ran the College Hounds with Rivy's help as Whip. In the summer of 1899 Francis scored a vital and unbeaten eighty runs at Lords against the old adversary Harrow School.

Although the boys enjoyed Eton immensely they clearly did not spend enough time on their studies, something they were to regret in later years. Their father died in 1896 and their mother in 1898, and subsequently they left Eton and the family home at Wilton Park. Their uncle, Lord Grenfell, became their guardian; he was Francis' godfather. Lord Grenfell was himself a distinguished soldier and was to lose some of his own sons in the First World War.

The twins both dearly wanted to join the Army but the money was not available. It was decided, however, that Lord Grenfell would pay for Francis to enter the Army while Rivy would pursue a business career. Francis began his service career with the Seaforth Militia in December 1899 but caught typhoid at around the same time and went on a sea voyage to recuperate. He did not fully recover for a year. In Egypt, with the Seaforth Highlanders, he began to study for his Army examinations. He then left for Malta where he was commissioned in May in the 60th Battalion (The King's Royal Rifle Corps). While there Rivy paid him a visit.

In the autumn of 1901 Francis sailed from Cork to South Africa to take part in the latter stages of the Boer War but he saw little of the fighting. He did, however, make a little money in diamond speculation which went towards his considerable expenses as an army officer. At the time Rivy was not doing very well with his financial affairs. It seems that there was an understanding that he should try and make enough to keep them both. This included the buying and selling of horses for racing and of polo ponies. They had both taken to polo with considerable success.

In 1903 Francis was back from South Africa and the twins spent the summer attending society balls and playing polo. Later Rivy went to America on a business trip, while Francis left to join the Army in India. He was desperately keen to get into the Cavalry. He enlisted the help of Douglas Haig and Lord Kitchener who both said that he would have to study hard and that he would then eventually achieve his ambition. The Cavalry was the top branch of the Army 'tree' at that time and much sought after by men of means who were well connected. Francis particularly wanted to join the 9th Lancers because it was a unit containing many old friends.

Polo had become a passion with the twins and in 1904 Rivy was able to visit his brother in India where they were much taken up with sport. Rivy won the Kadir Cup, a famous Indian pig-sticking event. Francis had been promoted to Lieutenant and in May 1905 realized his great ambition of joining the 9th Lancers. He had studied hard and had done well at languages.

The year 1907 was spent back in England with more polo playing. In April 1908 Francis sailed for South Africa to re-join his regiment. He was studying for his Staff College exams. Rivy was badly injured in a riding accident and Francis, back from South Africa, was also injured before going on to Germany to study the language. While there he observed German military manoeuvres.

Of this time, a friend of the twins, John Buchan, wrote of them in a memoir as being 'the most conspicuous figures in English society. They knew everyone and went everywhere.'

Rivy's business career seems to have been a precarious affair and one feels that he would have much preferred the life of a soldier. He had joined his brother Arthur's firm. Arthur had recently lost his wife and took a long time to recover. He was unable to keep a tight hold on the business which subsequently collapsed in May 1914. Both the twins had invested heavily in the firm and the polo ponies had to be sold off. The coming of war was to solve their financial problems and also to give them both a purpose in life enabling Rivy to 'redeem private failure in public service'.

Rivy had annually trained with the Bucks Hussars and on the outbreak of war quickly obtained a transfer to his brother's regiment, the 9th Lancers, as a reserve officer. He 'sat at his brother's feet' in order to learn the ropes in the shortest possible time, which included the buying of equipment that would be needed. The twins decided to take six horses with them and they borrowed an additional groom from their friend the Duke of Westminster.

After Francis won his Victoria Cross he left Rivy behind in France while he recuperated in a hospital at No. 17 Belgrave Square, London. He received visits from Lord Grey, Lord Grenfell and Lord Roberts who wanted to know all about his exploits. From there he went to his uncle's home at Overstone Park in Northamptonshire and it was there that he received the tragic news of his brother's death.

Rivy was killed on 14 September to the north of the River Aisne, near the road between Troyon and the Chemin des Dames when directing the firing onto a German piquet. On stepping out from behind a haystack in order to observe the situation he was shot in the mouth and died soon afterwards. His body was left behind as the Lancers had to retire but it was recovered a short time after in a subsequent advance. He is buried close to where he fell, in the civilian cemetery at Vendresse. He had been 'in the field' for just twenty-five days.

It was Lord Grenfell who had the task of breaking the news of his brother's death to Francis and his uncle later wrote: 'From that moment he was a changed man in everything but his enthusiasm for his regiment and his desire to get back to the fighting line.'

In October 1914 Francis was sufficiently recovered from his wounds to be able to return to France, and to resume as B Squadron Commander of the 9th Lancers. The position of the British Army was now on the left of the Allied line and Francis re-joined his unit at Strazeele. They were about to go into action. It was 'a day of

heavy rain and thick steamy fog', and Francis noted in his diary that: 'I could not help observing on my return that the war was affecting the spirits of all a little: there was much more seriousness than when I left.'

Francis assumed his squadron command on 15 October and the unit marched through rain to Locre and through Ploegsteert Wood. He wrote in his diary: 'We have had five of the hardest days of the war in trenches repelling German attacks . . . I am afraid all the cavalry traditions are for ever ended, and we have become mounted infantry pure and simple, with very little of the mounted about it . . . '

The Lancers were involved in trying to force a crossing of the River Lys. On 22 October they moved further north to the Wytschaete area where the 5th Cavalry Brigade of the 2nd Cavalry Division needed support. They were in a support line close to the town of Messines, which was fought for between 12 October and 2 November, and eventually captured by the Germans.

At the end of October the Lancers were still being used for such tasks as digging trenches but by now they had moved to the east of Kemmel. The enemy had made his main assault thrust for the winter and had not cracked the Allied defence line. It was at this time that a shell fell into the middle of B Squadron, causing several casualties. Francis himself was wounded again and this time he had a serious injury in the thigh. He was taken in an ambulance to Bailleul and was shipped to Dublin.

He read of the confirmation of his VC in the gazette of 16 November and in a letter to his uncle he wrote: 'I also feel very strongly that any honour belongs to my regiment and not to me . . . '

Francis was a very changed man and possibly had a premonition that his own death was not very far away. He was very miserable at being absent from his regiment and frustrated that his latest wounds were taking a long time to heal. He was not able to come to terms with the death of so many of his friends, let alone the death of his twin brother. He made a new will with his friends John Buchan and Lord Grey as executors.

Slowly he made a physical recovery and took up hunting and shooting once again. On 7 April he gave what was to be a farewell dinner at Claridges, guests included his brother Arthur, Lord Grenfell, Winston Churchill and John Buchan. A fortnight later he rejoined his regiment in billets at Meteren where they had been training for several months. The regiment's role was to support the French to the north-east of Ypres in the Second Battle of Ypres, where gas was used for the first time on the Western Front. According to the Lancers' regimental history, on the morning of 24 May the gas 'drifted into trenches and hung about in full density for over an hour'.

Despite the British respirators becoming saturated with the gas the dismounted cavalrymen were still able to resist the strong German divisional attack. It was the last phase of this particular German assault but as the regimental history noted, 'the regiment underwent its greatest day of glory and sorrow of the whole war.'

In the early hours of the 25th a small party stumbled in the half light along the Menin road. John Buchan wrote: 'Those who passed them saw figures like spectres, clothes caked with dirt, faces yellow from the poison gas. They were all that remained of the 9th Lancers. Their Brigadier General, Mullens, met them on the road, but dared not trust himself to speak to them. "Tell them," he told the Colonel, "that no words of mine can express my reverence for the 9th."'

The party continued through Ypres and out towards Vlamertinghe, and they brought with them the body of Francis Grenfell. At Hooge, south of the

Ypres–Menin road, he had been shot in the back at about 10.30 hours and his wounds were bandaged up by a Corporal. But Francis ripped the bandages off as he knew the bullet had entered his heart. He died after half an hour and his last words were said to have been, 'I die happy. Tell the men I love my squadron.'

In his notebook Francis had written of 'the bad situation of the trenches and emphasized the necessity of a relief arriving'. A colleague wrote: 'We carried him back the five miles; he looked so calm and peaceful in the moonlight. I shall never forget that walk back – everybody done to a turn.' Another man wrote: 'Francis Grenfell has left a memory which will never fade, a braver soul never stepped . . .'

He was buried at Vlamertinghe alongside Capt. Algy Court, a brother officer. On 24 May the 9th Lancers had suffered 208 casualties out of 350 men who had gone into the line that day.

The American journalist Frederic Coleman had become a friend of the Grenfells during the war and wrote the following in his book *With Cavalry in 1915*:

> As the sun went down that evening their comrades of the 9th Lancers buried the bodies of Francis Grenfell and Algy Court. Court's face wore a smile, as though he was quietly sleeping. Grenfell, shot through the heart at the height of the battle, bore, too, a look of deep peace, as if at last he had cheerfully gone to a better country, to join his beloved brother 'Rivy', from the shock of whose death, on the Aisne, Francis had never recovered.

The Grenfell twins were much written about after Francis' death in the English newspapers in 1915. A memorial service took place in Eaton Square, London, on 2 June and Lord Grenfell received telegrams from the King and Sir John French. Lord Grenfell himself was able to visit Francis' grave in the early 1920s.

In his will Francis left an estate worth £40,569 gross. His medals he left to his regiment and various bequests were left to former friends and servants. He paid

Beaconsfield parish church

the following tribute to his uncle: 'I should like to express my deep gratitude for his kindness to me during my lifetime, ever since the day when he decided I should go into the Army at his expense. I have endeavoured to base my career on his example. He has, since the death of my father done everything that a father could do for me.'

He also thanked the Duke of Westminster for his 'great generosity and kindness to me on many occasions – no man ever had a better friend.'

In 1926 The Hon. Ivo Grenfell was killed at Hawkhurst, Kent in a car accident. He was the son of Lord Desborough and brother of Gerald and Julian who had both been killed in the war. They were cousins of the Grenfell twins.

Francis is commemorated at St George's chapel, Ypres and the twins are remembered at Canterbury Cathedral and Beaconsfield parish church which has a stained glass window in the north wall of the nave where they are portrayed as Saul and Jonathan. The inscription below the two figures is particularly apt: 'They died for England . . . They were lovely and pleasant in their lives and in their death they were not divided: they were swifter than eagles, they were stronger than lions.'

Francis' medals are in the ownership of the Lancers' Museum.

E.W. ALEXANDER
Elouges, Belgium, 24 August

The 5th Division as part of 11 Army Corps under Lt. Gen. Sir H. Smith-Dorrien arrived in France in August; Brig. Gen. J.E.W. Headlam was the CRA. On 22/23 August at Mons the 5th Division was responsible for the line along the Condé Canal to the west of the city, and the 3rd Division was responsible for the line as far as Mariette. The position was not at all suitable for artillery, as it lacked a field of fire and observation.

Right from the start the ground to the south of Mons was surveyed for suitable gun positions, south of the Haine river but north of the line between Dour and Wasmes. The landscape was criss-crossed with railway lines, most of them industrial ones, and there were several mining spoil heaps and Fosses.

The XXVIII Brigade RFA was deployed to the left of the line and the XXVII Brigade RFA to the right. The latter was behind the 15th Infantry Brigade and consisted of 119 Battery (Maj. E.W. Alexander), 120 Battery (Maj. C.S. Holland) and 121 Battery (Maj. C.N.B. Ballard) and 37 Howitzer Battery (Maj. E.H. Jones) of VIII Howitzer Brigade.

We are mainly concerned here with the story of 119 Battery which on 23 August, had been in position near d'Hamme Wood. It fired on the enemy at Ville Pommerouel and in the afternoon 'searched' for enemy gun positions. It was joined in this work by 108 Heavy Battery in position near the village of Dour. On the 24th, later to be nicknamed 'Shrapnel Monday', the Germans having suffered a great many casualties the day before were planning to cut off the British Army with a massive enveloping movement from the west as well as attacking from the north and east. The 8th Division (IV Army Corps) was the main force used and nine German Batteries were in position on a line from Valenciennes to Mons to the north-east of the village of Quievrain.

In the morning Gen. Allenby, General Officer Commanding of the Cavalry Division, had sent out units of the 1st Cavalry Division to make contact with the enemy but they failed to do so as the Germans were already too far to Allenby's left. As the Germans advanced, the Commander of the 5th Division ordered a rearguard to be set up consisting of the 1st Cheshires, the 1st Norfolks and 119 Battery. The commander of this force was Lt. Col. C.R. Ballard of the 1st Norfolks. The infantrymen were positioned to the north-east of the road between the small towns of Elouges and Audregnies. They were facing north-westwards and were on slightly higher ground than their opponents.

At 12.30 hours the enemy began to move forward from the area of Baisieux and Quievrain and Brig. Gen. De Lisle in charge of 2nd Cavalry Brigade ordered the 9th Lancers and two troops of the 4th Dragoon Guards to make a mounted charge from Audregnies against the enemy. They reached the outskirts of a sugar factory adjacent to a Roman road and were covered by the guns of L Battery who were in positions to the north-east of Audregnies close to an industrial railway. The attack was very foolhardy but despite the considerable number of casualties it did manage to 'buy time'. There is a full account of this charge in the

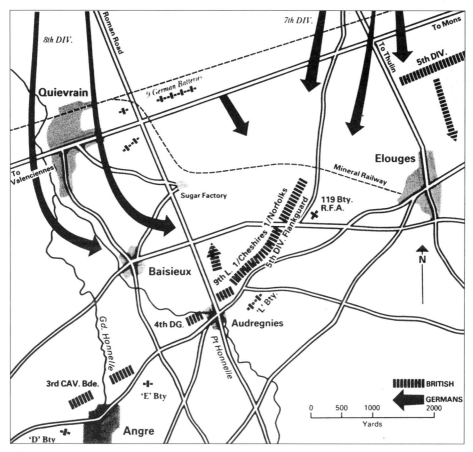

Elouges, 24 August

section on Francis Grenfell. Although the cavalrymen did not do much damage to the advancing Germans and their gun positions, L Battery was able to inflict considerable damage and was seen to be firing 'as if on an exercise'. In addition the Cheshire and Norfolk Regiments inflicted heavy casualties with rifle and machine-gun fire. One section of 119 Battery close to the railway station in Elouges itself, under Lt. C.O.D. Preston, had to withdraw as it came under heavy fire. After half a mile Preston halted the section and brought it into action against German cavalry. Later, Preston once more took on the enemy infantry and machine guns until they were only 800 yards away. He was wounded four times.

However, 500 yards to the left of Elouges station there were two other sections of the battery in operation, close to a mineral-works' railway line. Alexander was trying to keep the guns firing to the last minute. The mineral works was to the east of the Elouges-Audregnies road with its own railway line running along an embankment. The line took away spoil to a dump a few hundred yards away to the north-west. A bridge carried the line over the road, and the protection afforded by the embankment was to become crucial in the saving of the remaining four guns which were under considerable threat of being overrun by the German advance. As the battery had lost so many of its horses in the fighting Alexander gave instructions for the guns to be moved back by hand to the shelter of the embankment. Unfortunately the ground was very heavy and only one gun could be manhandled at a time. The situation was grave as Alexander was running short of men to do the work. At this point Capt. Francis Grenfell, with the remnants of the 9th Lancers and 4th Dragoon Guards (eleven officers and forty men) came up on horseback and offered their assistance. Grenfell was already wounded. Their offer was quickly accepted and the dismounted cavalrymen worked hard with the remaining gunners running the four guns by hand to a place of safety. They were under ceaseless fire from the enemy with shells and bullets flying around in all directions. At least three German Batteries were concentrating on destroying 119 Battery. The guns were limbered up and taken away at great speed just as the enemy reached the mine dump at the end of the mineral-works line.

During the battle 119 Battery lost forty-two men and forty-three horses, but this figure paled beside the casualty figures of the Cheshires and Norfolks who between them had 800 casualties. Despite these high casualty figures, together with those of the Cavalry, the left flank of the British Army had been saved from almost certain capture. Both Grenfell and Alexander were awarded the Victoria Cross and Sergeants Turner and Davids the Distinguished Conduct Medal (DCM) for their work on this day. Grenfell had been wounded a second time and was picked up by his friend the Duke of Westminster in his Rolls Royce and taken to Bavai to have his wounds dressed.

Alexander's decoration was to be the first of no less than eighteen VCs that were won by the Royal Artillery in the First World War.

Woolton Heyes, Woolton, Liverpool, which was demolished in 1938

The 119 Battery was involved next in the Battle of Le Cateau on 26 August when it fired all day at the enemy from a well-protected position alongside 121 Battery. They were in positions to the north-east of Troisvilles, south of the Le Cateau-Inchy road. Maj. Alexander was still in charge of 119 Battery and they were again in support of the 15th Infantry Brigade. The artillery was behind a ridge about 1500 yards to the north-east of Troisvilles, with its observation post (OP) to the north-east of the village. The guns could only fire at long range owing to difficulty in clearing the immediate hill to the front. At about 15.30 hours orders were received for the batteries to fall back. At first 15th Brigade and 119 Battery covered the withdrawal of 121 Battery and then it was 119's turn to move back to the rear.

After their role at Le Cateau 119 Battery fought at Crépy to the east of Nery on 1 September and on the Marne in the early part of September. They also fought in the First Battle of Ypres in mid-October. A year later Alexander used the method of the 'creeping barrage' for the first time at the Battle of Loos. Alexander received his VC at Buckingham Palace on 12 July 1915. In 1922, seven years later, 119 Battery was disbanded.

Ernest Wright Alexander was born in the southern suburbs of Liverpool on 2 October 1870. His home was at Woolton Heyes, a mansion with a large estate that was situated between Out Lane and Watergate Lane. The main entrance was in Woolton Street. Alexander's father was Robert Alexander, a director of the Suez Canal Company and a prominent shipowner. Ernest's mother was Annie Alexander, a daughter of James Cranston Gregg of Belfast where the family had its roots.

The firm of Robert Alexander & Co. had formed the Sun Shipping Company and their offices were at No. 17, Water Street, Liverpool in 1868. The firm later became the Hall Line of Steamers and in 1901 the business was sold to J.R. Ellerman for the sum of £434,000. The name of the Hall Line was retained until the 1960s.

Alexander went to school at Cherbourg House, Malvern before moving to public school at Harrow. He then went direct to the Royal Military Academy at Woolwich. He was made a Second Lieutenant in the Royal Artillery on 27 July 1889, when he was not yet nineteen. From 23 September 1892 to 13 November 1900 he was stationed in India. He married Rose Newcome, daughter of the late Major H.G. Newcome, RA (retired), HM Bodyguard to the Royal Household, on 1 September 1903. The marriage took place at Aldershot Manor, Hampshire and a month later Alexander returned to India, with his wife, where they remained until 25 June 1906. By this time he had been made up to Captain with the RFA on 26 December 1899 and to Major with the Royal Artillery on 25 April 1906.

After Britain declared war on Germany in early August 1914 Alexander left for France as Officer Commanding (OC) 119 Battery RFA, 5th Division. After he had gained the VC on 24 August he became the Commander of XXII Brigade RFA on 5 October 1914. He then became Commander of the XXVII Brigade RFA, and later Commander of RA 15th Division, and then Temporary Brigadier-General on 25 August 1915. On 22 March 1917 he became Commander of the Royal Artillery of the 11th Corps. He left this position when he became Major-General, RAHQ, 1st Army under Lord Horne. Later he became Commander of the Royal Artillery, Southern Area, Aldershot Command with the temporary rank of Brigadier-General. He was promoted to Lieutenant-Colonel on 30 October in the same year. During the First World War he had been in France from August 1914 to March 1917 and from May 1917 to 1919, and altogether he was mentioned in despatches nine times. He remained with the 1st Army until the end of the war and became CRA, 2nd Division at Aldershot and retired as a Major-General in 1920. He was created Companion of St Michael and St George (CMG) in 1915, and awarded the Military Order of Savoy (Cavalier) in 1918. In 1919 he received the Croix de Guerre and CB. He was also made Grand Officer, Military Order of Avis. In 1919 he was promoted to Colonel on 2 June and purchased Horswill House, South Milton in South Devon.

Alexander became very involved with local affairs and became a Justice of the Peace (JP), a member of the Kingsbridge Guardians Committee, a member of the local Rural District Council, and also the President of the local branch of the British Legion. He also became vice-president of numerous clubs and groups. If a man in the village was without employment Alexander endeavoured to find work for him on his estate.

In the summer of 1934 he underwent an operation but did not recover and died in hospital in Kingsbridge, Devon on 25 August almost exactly twenty years

Horswill House

after he won the VC. His ashes were placed in the family grave at Putney Vale. Six months later his wife also died and in 1936 their house in South Devon was put up for sale. The South Milton parish hall commemorates Alexander where a portrait of him is on display.

A particularly endearing quality of Alexander was his loyalty to his former Army servants: he employed three of them on his estate. Thomas Williams, who had been his batman, was made his gardener, and employment was found for Thomas Doyle, his former groom, and William McCullen, his trumpeter. On Alexander's death he left them cash or annuities to the value of £52, £50 and £50 respectively. All three men had taken part in the battle at Elouges on 24 August 1914.

On their deaths the Alexanders left three surviving children: their eldest son, Robert who became a Lieutenant in the Royal Navy, Annie, Robert's twin, who had married Lt. Col. W.P. Akerman in 1925, Mary their youngest daughter was still at school, and Gear a younger son had died aged three in 1914. Alexander also left a brother, Mr F. Alexander, OBE, who lived in Lancets, Cornwall.

Horswill House has had its own ups and downs; a few years ago it was acquired by a property developer who began to turn it into flats without touching the servant's quarters on the top floor under the roof. The developer then went bust and the house was left empty with the usual dire results to the fabric. However in the early 1990s the house was bought by a family who plan to restore it to its former glory. While they work on its restoration they are living in the former servant's quarters.

G.H. WYATT

Landrecies, France, 25/26 August

The Battle of Mons took place on 23 August 1914 and the British Army began its retreat the next day. However, without Sir John French's support Gen. Sir H.L. Smith-Dorrien, General Officer Commanding of 11 Corps decided to stand and fight on the uplands to the east of Le Cateau. Sir Douglas Haig, Commander of 1 Corps planned to set up his headquarters and billet his troops in the town of Landrecies, a few miles to the north-east of Le Cateau. A main road to Paris ran between the lines of the neighbouring Corps.

By late afternoon on the 25th, the 4th (Guards) Brigade of the 2nd Division (1 Corps) under Douglas Haig reached the outskirts of Landrecies. The day's march had begun in the small hours and had continued through a very hot day.

In Landrecies there were many rumours circulating about the coming approach of the Germans, and what the Guardsmen did not know, was that it was also the German intention to spend the night in Landrecies where the British were already being billeted.

The Germans were from the 7th Division (IV Army Corps) who had fought at Mons. The 27th Regiment was their advance guard and had instructions to occupy the Sambre Canal crossing in Landrecies. At about 17.30 hours some French civilians rushed into the town, declaring that the Germans were already in the Forest of Mormal and Englefontaine, to the north of the town. The Guardsmen were ordered to fall in but as there was no apparent sign of the enemy, they were subsequently dismissed. This acted as a sort of dress-rehearsal for the Guardsmen came to know their positions in the event of an enemy night attack.

The 3rd Coldstream Guards were one of four Guards Battalions of the 4th (Guards) Brigade, and the 2nd Grenadier Guards, 1st Irish Guards and the 2nd Coldstream Guards were the other three battalions.

North-west of Landrecies, beyond the Sambre Canal and the railway line, was a narrow road called the Faubourg Soyères. After a couple of hundred yards the road split, one part went to the north-west to Englefontaine and the edge of the Forest of Mormal, and the other went due north into the forest itself. This was thought to be where the main enemy threat would come from.

The 3rd Coldstream Guards set up an outpost with a machine-gun section under Capt. C. Heywood in a ditch close to the fork. The other Guardsmen took up their positions to the south of the fork under their company commander Captain the Hon. C.H. Monck. The eastern and western approaches to the town were also covered by other Coldstream Guardsmen. Darkness fell early on the evening of the 25th and a thunderstorm followed the extreme heat of the day. A report soon came in that the Germans were approaching the town with an estimated thousand men together with guns. At 19.00 hours a German patrol reached the crossroads and was immediately fired on by the Coldstream Guardsmen, which resulted in a few casualties and a swift withdrawal down the Forest road. Number 2 Company of the Coldstream Guards was then replaced by Number 3 Company and the defensive positions were moved forward in order that the straight road to the forest should be covered.

It was then reported that the French Army was also in the immediate vicinity on its way from the direction of the Englefontaine so the next group of men were expected to be French. The men at the outpost could indeed hear the sounds of French singing. When the group approached the British positions, they were challenged and a light was suddenly flashed in Capt. Monck's face. The order to fire was immediately given but before he was bayoneted, the man firing one of the machine guns was able to send a hail of bullets down the road and into the oncoming mass of men and horses. A whole gun team was knocked out which caused chaos in the narrow road. In the fight Capt. Monck and Lt. Bingham were swept aside and desperate hand-to-hand fighting ensued. The Guardsmen were forced to fall back because they had lost the use of one of their machine guns which was later recovered. Gradually, with the use of revolver and bayonet, the Germans were pushed back.

At the Faubourg Soyères the enemy had set up a field gun, and attempted

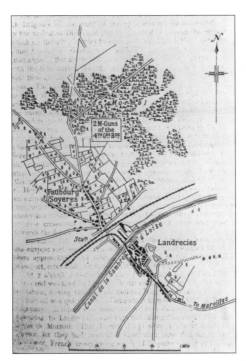

Landrecies, 25/26 August

to fan outwards from the road and to work their way into the town from the east and west. Maj. T.H. Matheson then came up to reinforce Number 3 Company and brought up more Guardsmen. The 1st Irish Guards barricaded the streets and generally placed Landrecies in a state of defence.

The fight between the Guardsmen and the enemy continued through the night and the advantage kept swinging from one side to the other. The Germans were trying to get around the back of a barn behind the cover of a hedgerow at the end of the street in order to set up a machine-gun post, to enfilade the right of the British positions. They were prevented from achieving their aim and the barn was shelled with incendiaries. This resulted in a haystack catching fire illuminating the British positions, which could have been disastrous had the fire continued to burn. No. 5854 Pte. G. Wyatt heard Maj. Matheson shout out 'put out that light,' and decided to obey this order. The haystack caught fire a second time and again Wyatt put out the flames. He was not more than 25 yards from the enemy but his actions encouraged the Coldstreamers to hold their ground. At 01.00 hours on the 26th a howitzer was sent up by Col. Feilding of 54th Brigade which put the German field gun out of action. The attack subsequently died down with the resulting casualties of 14 men of the 3rd Coldstream Guards being killed and 115 either wounded or missing. The 2nd Coldstream Guards lost one officer killed and six men wounded. The 4th Guards Brigade evacuated Landrecies before dawn.

The action of Pte. Wyatt was the first of two such incidents which were to gain for him the Victoria Cross. A few days later, at a rearguard action in the forest to the north of the small town of Villers Cotterêts, he was involved once more in an action. To paraphrase his citation: 'After being wounded in the head, Lance-Corporal Wyatt continued firing until he could no longer see owing to the blood which was pouring down his face. The Medical Officer bound up his wound and told him to go to the rear, but he at once returned to the firing line and continued to fight.'

Pte. Wyatt's VC was the first awarded to a member of the Coldstream Guards since the Crimean War. It was gazetted in November 1915 and presented to him at Buckingham Palace on 4 March 1916.

George Harry Wyatt was the son of Mr Arthur Digby and Sarah Ann Wyatt and was born in Britannia Road, Worcester on 5 September 1886. At the time of George's birth his father was working as a groom to a local veterinary surgeon, and three years later he became coachman at Hindlip Hall, in the employ of Dowager Lady Hindlip. He worked for her for twenty years. George Wyatt went to school at Hindlip and then he and his parents moved to Hadzor. George, who used to sing in the local choir, then attended Holloway School at Droitwich. It was always his ambition to join the Army. He was a strongly built man and over six feet tall. He enlisted in the Coldstream Guards at the age of eighteen on 23 November 1904, at Birmingham. He served in the 2nd and 3rd Battalions for nearly four years, spending two and a half of these in Egypt and was discharged on 23 November 1908.

After leaving the Army he joined the Police Force in Barnsley, South Yorkshire on 9 January 1909. He served there for six years and won numerous swimming prizes. On 19 May 1914 he was transferred to the Doncaster force where he was trained as a mounted officer but ten weeks later, on the outbreak of war, he was recalled up as a reservist on 5 August.

He was posted to the 3rd Battalion Coldstream Guards who embarked on the 14th as part of the BEF. He was promoted to Lance-Corporal on 18 December 1914.

In 1915 his parents were living at the Pear Tree Inn, Hindlip and it was the local newspaper, the *Berrow Worcester Journal*, that broke the news of their son's VC to them. They were overjoyed.

At first Mrs Wyatt was under the impression that the Victoria Cross meant the Russian Cross, which her son had won some months previously, but when she realized that in addition to the Czar's decoration her son was to receive the most coveted decoration in the British Army, her eyes welled with tears, and she remarked, 'Bless the lad. He is such a good boy.' Immediately she went outside to an adjoining field, where her husband was working, in order to break the news to him. He was equally delighted. Wyatt's mother was asked to say more about her son, 'He was always a good lad, and never gave any trouble.' But his father said something more illuminating, 'He was always a willing lad, and willing to help others, and he was always up to some devilment or other.' Interviewed by a local paper about his exploits Wyatt himself said the following:

Well, there's not much for me to say about it. I just did as I was told. During the retirement from Mons the 3rd Coldstream Guards reached Landrecies. It was dark at the time, and there we were attacked by a large number of Germans who must have been rushed up in motor lorries. We lost our machine gun, and had to rely solely upon rifle and bayonet. Suddenly something flared up between us and the enemy, and Major Matheson, of 'Ours' shouted, 'Put out that light'. So I did it. I never thought it would bring me the Victoria Cross and the highest Russian decoration which can be given to any man in the ranks.

How did I put the fire out? Oh, I jumped on it and dragged some equipment over it. After a while it burst out again, and I ran back and extinguished it. Yes, there was heavy fire from the Germans when I first obeyed the order. That affair at Villers Cotterêts. I got hit on the head and went on firing. That's all.

When he had recovered from his head wound Cpl. Wyatt returned to the battalion and in February 1915 Wyatt was shot in the head once more.

A few months later Wyatt received the Cross of the Order of St George 3rd Class as well as the VC. In April 1916 he was greeted at Doncaster station by the Chief Constable and his former police colleagues. He was driven in an open car to the Mansion House where a reception was held for him and he was presented with a gold watch. His wife was given a silver cream jug and sugar bowl.

On 28 February 1917 he was promoted to Lance-Sergeant, and left the Army with this rank on 14 January 1919. He returned to police service and in June 1924 he bravely stopped a runaway horse. He was awarded a guinea. He retired from the Yorkshire Police Force on 10 February 1934 and took up farming, owning a smallholding. He died on 22 January 1964 at the age of seventy-seven in Sprotborough, near Doncaster and is buried at Cadeby Cemetery. His grave has a headstone.

Wyatt's medals are in his family's possession and apart from the Victoria and Russian Cross he was also awarded the 1914 Star with clasp, BWM 1914–20, and the VM 1914–19 with Oak Leaf (mentioned in despatches). Unfortunately he lost his original Russian Cross while attending a remembrance service in London. However, in August 1988 his family were presented with a replica by the regiment.

C.A.L. YATE

Le Cateau, France, 26 August

The 2nd King's Own Yorkshire Light Infantry was part of the 13th Brigade of the 5th Division. The battalion arrived in the Mons area on 22 August and took part in the fight to defend the town from the Germans on 23 August. The 5th Division was on the left flank of the British 11 Corps and men of the 2nd KOYLI were in positions close to the railway bridge over the Condé Canal at Les Herbières. The next day they were involved in fighting a rearguard action to the south-east near the town of Wasmes.

On 25 August the 2nd King's Own Yorkshire Light Infantry, as part of 5th Division, must have marched at least 30 miles before reaching the town of Le Cateau, to the south-west of Mons, and was looking forward to a good night's rest and a decent meal. The news of the arrival of the 4th Division from England also cheered the men up.

It was at Le Cateau that Sir H. Smith-Dorrien, Commander of 11 Corps, after consultation with his commanders, planned a holding action against the advancing German Army. Smith-Dorrien did not have the full support of Sir John French, Commander of the BEF, or the assistance of Sir Douglas Haig's 1st Corps either, after the latter's dawn withdrawal from Landrecies on the morning of the 26th. In fact, Haig was so worried about the position at Landrecies during the night that he had asked 11 Corps to spare some troops. Fortunately the situation improved enough for the units of 1 Corps to make their escape.

For evidence of just how heroic the stand at Le Cateau was to be, we need to look no further than the tally of five Victoria Crosses which would be awarded as a result of the day's fighting. Two were won by members of the 2nd KOYLI and three went to the Royal Artillery.

The 5th Division decided to take up positions to the south of the Le Cateau to Cambrai road and the 13th and 14th Brigades were also heavily involved. The 13th Brigade consisted of the 2nd KOYLI, along with the 2nd Dukes, 1st RWK and the 2nd KOSB. Companies of the KOSB and A, C and D Companies of the KOYLI were close up to the main Cambrai road. But half of B Company of the KOYLI was ordered by Brig. Gen. G.J. Cuthbert, the Brigade Commander, to dig trenches along the side of the Bavai–Reumont road and at right angles to it. These positions were also just to the south of the road to Troisvilles. The rest of B Company was on the other side of the Reumont road, together with the battalion's machine-gun section. This section's two guns were intended to give some enfilading protection to the 2nd Manchesters and 2nd Suffolks of the 14th Brigade to the east. Divisional field batteries made the situation more complicated as they occupied the line of company supports. Gun teams and limbers crowded the narrow road to Troisvilles. In addition Battalion Headquarters was close to B Company on the west of the road near a position held early in the day by part of B Company. A culvert under the road was used for communication between the two firing lines. The 1st RWK was to the rear of B Company as Brigade Reserve.

At about 06.00 hours Cuthbert, who was in the sunken road leading to Troisvilles, to the left of the artillery teams, issued an order to the Battalion Headquarters to the effect that there would be no retirement for the fighting troops and they were to fill up their trenches with as much ammunition, water and food as possible. In order to ensure this order was received a Staff Officer also came around to the positions to give the instructions verbally.

The Adjutant, Capt. C.H. Ackroyd, when riding back from the left flank drew enemy fire which seemed to act as a signal for the battle to commence. Within minutes whistling shells came pouring down on the British positions. Communication became impossible and telephone lines were soon destroyed.

The town of Le Cateau fell into enemy hands at about the same time as the battle commenced, and the ridge where the 2nd Suffolks were in position was exposed to fierce fire as it was to the east side of the battlefield where enemy guns were concentrated. The Suffolks were under considerable pressure, being attacked from the right flank as well as from the front. They were assisted by companies of the 2nd Manchesters and 2nd ASH.

It was not until 11.00 hours when the Germans emerged from the direction of Montay Spur to the north, that Maj. Yate, in charge of B Company of the 2nd KOYLI, had the target that he wanted for his machine gunners. B and D Companies opened fire and from then onwards they were continuously involved in the action.

Until noon the German artillery concentrated on destroying the British guns, which they outnumbered by a ratio of six to one. Slowly the number of guns able to reply was reduced. At about 12.45 hours orders were given to pull out any gun that could be saved. This led to an even fiercer response from the enemy artillery, until about 13.20 hours when there was a lull in the fighting, enabling some of the remaining guns to be taken away.

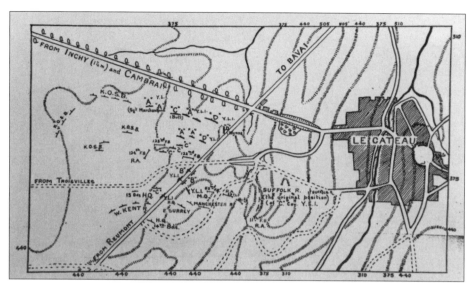

Le Cateau, 26 August

The shelling and rifle fire was now directed on the infantry positions and all the time the Germans were gaining ground. Of the two KOYLI machine guns, one fired for about six hours while the other was eventually knocked out.

Between 14.30 hours and 14.45 hours the end came for the Suffolks: they were overwhelmed from the front, right flank and right rear. They had been under continuous bombardment for nine hours.

Two German battalions swept over the Suffolk's ridge and down the beet field on the western slopes. The range for the KOYLI platoons and machine guns came down to 600 yards. B Company held their fire to the very last moment and then opened fire. This caused havoc and the Germans retreated for a short period, leaving their casualties behind them.

It was, however, only a matter of time before the enemy returned. At about 14.00 hours Sir Charles Fergusson (5th Division) had given the order for the retirement, which had reached some of the front line battalions.

At about 15.00 hours reserve battalions began to fall back to the rear covering the retirement of the front line troops who were running out of ammunition. Yate's company, along with companies of the KOSB decided to stay and fight it out. They became surrounded on three sides and were continuously shelled and subjected to concentrated rifle and machine-gun fire. The end came at about 16.20 hours when Yate, in charge of the remnants of B and D Companies in the second line of trenches, gave an order to the nineteen men who remained. They refused German calls for their surrender and charged the enemy. Yate fell wounded and his gallant band of Yorkshiremen

Maj. C.A.L. Yate as a prisoner-of-war

was overwhelmed. The enemy had got round the right hand flank of the battalion and the KOYLI casualties were at least 600 on the day, of whom just over half were prisoners. The total British casualties for the day were 7,812 men and 38 guns, but the enemy had suffered heavily as well and had not managed to disrupt the retreat towards Paris.

By 16.30 hours it was all over and the Germans who captured Yate's part of the line were identified by their badges as being from the 26th, 66th and 72nd Regiments.

Most of the captured prisoners were taken to Le Cateau, and then on the 31st to Cambrai before being transferred to Germany. Yate, with his fluency in German, made a statement that he would never consider himself a prisoner of the Germans; he subsequently became a marked man. He was sent under a strong escort to join other officer prisoners at Torgau. Once there, he tried to escape three times and in the third attempt on 21 September he was shot by his captors while trying to struggle through barbed wire. It is said that he fled wounded into a river from which he never emerged alive. The British *Official History* states that he had his skull smashed on attempting an escape.

He was buried in Berlin South-West Cemetery, Stahsdorf, Germany. The German pastor who officiated at Yate's burial service sent a wire to Mrs Yate, confirming his death and burial.

One of his officer colleagues quoted in the book *In the Hands of the Enemy*

described Yate as follows: 'He was a great loss to us, being a fluent German speaker. His memory was prodigious; he learnt up the names and addresses of all his fellow-prisoners in order to notify their relatives in case he succeeded in his attempt.' The Germans allegedly kept his clothes, perhaps as some sort of evidence of his death.

Cpl. F.W. Holmes VC also of the 2nd KOYLI wrote this of Yate in *The London Magazine* in April 1915:

Major Yate was a very fine officer. He joined us and took command of B Company just before we went out to war. On this day he was in the trenches on our left, not very far from where I was. When we went into action he had 220 men, but they caught so much of the hot fire which was meant for the battery behind that he lost all his men except nineteen when he was surrounded and captured. The day before this happened the Major declared that if it came to a pinch and they were surrounded he would not surrender – and he kept his word. Reckless of the odds against him he headed his nineteen men in a charge against the Germans – and when the charge was over only three of the company could be formed up. All the rest of B Company were either killed, wounded, or taken prisoner, though very few prisoners were taken. The Major was one of them; but he was so badly wounded that he lived only a very short time, and died as a prisoner of war. His is one of the cases in which the Cross is given although the winner of it is dead. He was always in front, and his constant cry was 'Follow me!'

Yate's VC was gazetted on 25 November 1914. He was an outstanding soldier on all counts. However there is a note in the War Office File WO32/4993 about his award and the following caption was sent back from the War Office to Sir John French: 'Was his company covering a retreat and was the maintenance of the position in the trenches necessarily continued so long? Also can you say where the latest reliable information is . . . Is it a fact that he was taken prisoner and has since died?'

This query was soon answered satisfactorily as Yate's VC was confirmed in the second batch of the war.

A branch of the Yate family moved from Berkshire to Madeley Hall, Madeley, Telford, Shropshire in the middle of the eighteenth century.

Charles Allix Lavington Yate was the son of the vicar of Madeley, Prebendary George Edward Yate, and was born on 14 March 1872. He was to be known as Cal throughout his life, this being an abbreviation of his initials.

Yate went to school at Weymouth College, where he remained until December 1890. In 1891 he went to the Royal Military College at Sandhurst and passed out in the ninth position of 1,100 candidates. After his two-year course, Yate was commissioned on 13 August 1892 and joined the 2nd King's Own Light Infantry, then stationed in Bombay. Yate saw active service for the first time in the Tirah Expedition of 1897–8 on the North-West Frontier and was subsequently awarded a Medal with clasp. By this time he was a Lieutenant and was made up to Captain in 1899. Yate then moved to Mauritius where he studied for entrance to the Staff College. Almost as soon as he had achieved this qualification the Boer War began and the KOYLI were picked up in Mauritius and taken by ship to Cape Town in South Africa, where they were in the vanguard of British troops. During the war Yate was badly wounded in the Battle of Graspan on 25 November 1899 and he took little active part thereafter. Nevertheless, he was one of the deputation sent to General Botha in order to arrange the start of peace negotiations. He was awarded the Queen's Medal with four clasps for his service in South Africa.

Yate graduated at Staff College and married Helen Brigg of Greenhead Hall, in the Yorkshire West Riding. The ceremony took place at St George's Hanover Square, London on 17 September 1903. There were no children of the marriage. Shortly after his marriage Yate went to Japan as a member of a British Army Mission. Later he reported on military tactics used by the Japanese during their war with Russia. He was one of the first men to enter Port Arthur with the Japanese at the end of 1904. Yate was presented with two medals by the Japanese Emperor, one of which was later to cause some amusement to his colleagues. It was called the Order of the Sacred Treasure, 4th Class. The second was the Japanese War Medal for Manchuria (Port Arthur). Yate returned from Japan, arriving at Liverpool on 22 March 1906 and later went back to South Africa for two years, serving as Captain of General Staff, in the Cape Colony District. He then returned to London and was seconded to work on the staff of the War Office between 1908 and March 1914. He had been promoted to Major in 1912 and when he left the War Office he re-joined the 2nd KOYLI and sailed with them to France in August 1914 with the BEF. He turned down an offer to work on General Joffre's staff, preferring to take the more active role of Company Commander.

Four years after the war ended a memorial to the memory of nine British officers was unveiled by the then Prince of Wales at St Andrew's Church, Shiba, Tokyo on 14 April 1922. Yate's name was at the head of the list but the memorial was subsequently destroyed in the Second World War. An article by Yate was posthumously published in *Blackwoods Magazine* in September 1914 entitled 'Moral Qualities in War'.

In his spare time Yates had been fond of riding and from an early age had hunted with the Albrighton hounds. He was also a fine polo player and a good skier, as well as an accomplished linguist.

He is commemorated at St Michael's church, Madeley, Telford, Shropshire. His medal is owned by his regiment and is on display at the Regimental Museum at Pontefract in West Yorkshire.

F.W. HOLMES

Le Cateau, France, 26 August

The second man from the 2nd King's Own Yorkshire Light Infantry Battalion to gain the Victoria Cross on 26 August 1914 was 9376 L. Cpl. F.W. Holmes, a member of A Company. At about 02.00 hours on the morning of the 26th A Company's positions were south of the Le Cateau–Cambrai road in a right angle formed by this road together with the one running south-west towards Reumont.

After the extremely hazardous fighting in the morning and early afternoon the order to retire was given by Gen. Sir H. Smith-Dorrien in mid-afternoon. Not all the units received this order but A Company did. To carry it out, however, was going to be a very dangerous business. After about 16.00 hours each man from the Company attempted to run across the zone of land to safety, under the close fire of the enemy.

The following is based on Holmes' version of what happened: When it was his turn to escape he heard someone call out, 'For God's sake, Freddie, save me!' On looking around he saw Bugler H.N. Woodcock who was lying close to the path with both of his legs broken at the knee. Without considering his own safety Holmes quickly picked up the injured man and giving him a fireman's lift made off as quickly as he could. Woodcock cried out in pain and after about a hundred yards Holmes was finding it very difficult to carry a 12 stone man as well as his own equipment. He therefore took off his equipment and put the injured man over his shoulder. Finally Holmes came across some stretcher bearers in a small village about two miles from the trenches and handed over his burden to them. Holmes then ran back towards his previous lines, all the time dodging the German shells. He came across a scene of carnage where an unattended British 18-pounder gun with six horses was standing idle surrounded by dead and dying artillerymen. However on seeing him one of the men, a young Trumpeter, began to crawl towards him (on all fours). The wounded man asked Holmes whether he could ride a horse as the gun team had to be got away and all the drivers were dead. Holmes placed the young men on one of the horses and mounted the leading horse himself. At this same moment the enemy was beginning to close in on all sides and according to Holmes he used his bayonet to good effect. He desperately urged his horses on to the gallop and described what happened next in one of several articles written by him that were published in the popular magazine *Tit-Bits*.

> It is impossible to describe exactly what took place; all that I can picture is flying along the roads and making terrible patterns when turning corners, bumping over hedges and ditches, and hearing the noise the gun made every time it flopped down on to the road from the hedge sides. I looked back once to see if the young trumpeter was all right, but failed to see him. I have no idea how long this was after we had started, but it was nearly dark when I looked back.

After travelling about three miles they were finally out of the range of the German shelling when it began to rain. The artillery team came to a stream where the horse stopped to drink. By this time Holmes had absolutely no idea where he was. It was not until the following evening that the horses finally brought him into the rearguard of a retiring artillery column. At first the artillery Major was suspicious but after a while Holmes' story was verified and he became an honoured guest of the battery. On the 30th he was directed to a certain crossroads where he was told that his battalion would soon be passing, which they did, and Holmes met up with some of his old friends once more.

Six days later Holmes' unit reached Coulomniers. The next day, 7 September, they received orders that the retreat was over and that they were now to press forward and advance against the enemy. Holmes recorded that their position was south of the River Aisne for thirteen days, where they were exposed to German artillery. Then on the 28th they finally moved across the river and reached the village of Missy where they were to remain for four days. Here they were not safe either, for there were German snipers just outside the village.

On 2 October the Battalion re-crossed the Aisne and by a devious route eventually ended up in St Pol close to Arras on 8 October. The BEF was in the process of transferring to the left of the line. 11 Corps marched to the area of Compiègne where it entrained for Abbeville and from there advanced towards Béthune.

At about 17.45 hours on 14 October the KOYLI heard the sounds of rapid firing on the left in the positions of the KOSB. Cpl. Holmes was ordered to investigate. He returned quickly having seen a party of Germans charge in their direction. The KOYLI Maxims were brought into action quickly which slowed the Germans down and they promptly fell to the ground. The KOYLI decided to rush the enemy in a bayonet charge. In the first moments of this scrap Holmes was hit in the left ankle preventing him from walking. He crawled away and taking a rifle from a dead colleague began to fire in the dark in the direction of the German rifle flashes. After a while he became unconscious.

He was picked up and taken to a dressing station where the doctors wanted to amputate his left leg. But Holmes refused. He was sent back to England to hospital at Weybridge in Surrey and was then taken to Aldershot where he began to recover from his wounds, although he was unable to walk properly for a long time. It was during this period that he was to receive the French Médaille Militaire and then on or about 25 November he was brought news of his Victoria Cross which had just been gazetted. He then went to convalesce at Millbank in London where he could be visited by his wife. On 13 January 1915, three months after being wounded, he went to Buckingham Palace to receive his VC from the King.

Frederick William Holmes, the son of T.G. Holmes, was born in Abbey Street, Bermondsey in south-east London on 27 September 1889. He went to school at the London Board School. On 28 September 1907 he joined the Army at the age of eighteen and served for seven years. He then joined the reserve but two weeks later he was called up for active service in August 1914.

After he had received the VC from the King he was invited by the mayor of Bermondsey to a reception for their 'Bermondsey VC'. A procession was organized through the streets from Warner Street via Abbey Street, Holmes' home, to the Town Hall. Holmes presented with an illuminated address and also with a purse of gold. In addition, a sum of money, which had been raised by public subscription, was held on his behalf by the Town Hall for his future use – perhaps to start up a business.

In his reply Holmes made a short speech: 'Ladies, gentlemen and comrades. I only did my duty at the best. If Bermondsey is proud of me, I am proud of Bermondsey.' He was wearing his new VC and the French Médaille Militaire with its yellow, green-edged ribbon.

In the VC files at the Imperial War Museum there is a short note about Holmes' VC written by a Major H.E. Trevor of D Coy. 2nd KOYLI, who wrote in a letter to his wife dated 4 April 1915: 'I regret recommending the VC as Holmes had been inaccurate in his account and had "caused a nuisance in Bermondsey and others did equal work".' It is not entirely clear just what he meant. Maybe Holmes had been a bit of a line shooter and Trevor did not approve of the account of the deed being written up in such a journal as *Tit-Bits*. We shall never know, nor shall we ever know what the trouble in Bermondsey was.

On 6 October 1915 Holmes joined the 1st Green Howards and was promoted to Sergeant on the 10th. In December he left for India where they were to be stationed. He was commissioned on 14 March 1917 as a Second Lieutenant with the Green Howards and attached to the 9th Worcesters. He went to Mesopotamia in July

1917. There he had a serious accident in which he fractured his skull and as a result was sent home in January 1918. He was promoted to full Lieutenant on 14 September 1918 and was employed in the Infantry Record Office from October 1918. In addition to the VC and the French Médaille Militaire, Holmes was also awarded the 1914 Star with clasp, the BWM, and the VM.

Harry Norman Woodcock, the man who had cried out to Holmes for help on 26 August 1914, survived for nearly another four years after Le Cateau but was killed in action on 19 August 1918. He was still serving with the 2nd KOYLI, then part of 32nd Division on the Somme.

After the war Holmes served in Ireland during the rebellion and eventually left the Army on 20 August 1921 when he went to work in London. In February 1954 Holmes wrote to the *Daily Mail* from an address in Watford Road, Croxley Green, Rickmansworth, Hertfordshire about the meagre size of the special pension awarded to holders of the VC.

A few years later he left Britain to live in Port Augusta, South Australia. In the early 1960s he broke one of his legs and just when it healed he fell again breaking the other. In 1968 he wrote to his regiment: 'I have been through the hoop for the past two years all due to a brain injury in Mespot in 1918 which has only begun to work its tricks since I came out to Australia. I am practically a cripple and have not left the house for a year and a half and can only hobble a dozen yards.'

Holmes died in Port Augusta on 22 October 1969 and was cremated at the Stirling North Garden Cemetery. His medals are not in public ownership.

D. REYNOLDS

Le Cateau, France, 26 August

No fewer than five Victoria Crosses were awarded for heroism in the battle of Le Cateau on 26 August. The experiences of two infantrymen from the 2nd King's Own Yorkshire Light Infantry, namely Maj. Yate and L. Cpl. Holmes, have been written about in a previous chapter. It is now the turn of the men from an artillery unit, the 37th Howitzer (H) Battery.

At 02.00 hours on 26 August Brig. Gen. Sir H. Smith-Dorrien conferred with Maj. Gen. Hubert Hamilton (3rd Division) and Maj. Gen. Allenby of the Cavalry Division at his headquarters at Bertry. Allenby advised that his men and horses were widely scattered and that both were pretty well played out. Hamilton stated that he could not possibly get his Division away until 09.00 hours and Smith-Dorrien realized that it would taken even longer to extricate 5th Division from its congested positions to the south-west of Le Cateau. These were the main reasons for Smith-Dorrien's decision to stage 'a stopping blow, under cover of which we could retire'. In making this decision he was assuming that he would have the assistance of Sir Douglas Haig's 1 Corps and it was not until 05.30 hours that he heard of Haig's decision to leave Landrecies and to continue the retreat. By this time it was too late to change the plan.

The main British units that took part in the battle were from right to left: the 5th, 3rd and 4th Divisions, all of 11 Corps. This force totalled about fifty thousand men. Opposing them from right to left were the German 5th, 7th, 8th and the 4th and 9th Cavalry Divisions of their IV Corps. Each side had the full support of their respective artilleries, and the Germans used about 600 guns to the British 225.

Undoubtedly the 'hottest spot' was in the slightly sloping land to the south-west of Le Cateau, divided by the main road leading to the village of Reumont, headquarters of the 5th Division. To the east was the river valley of La Selle.

After serving at Mons the 37 (H) Battery later withdrew with the rest of the 5th Division along the hot dusty roads towards Bavai where briefly the battery acted as a covering rearguard, to the north-east of Le Cateau. The Division arrived at Le Cateau in the evening of the 25th. The instructions to the artillery of the 5th Division were to reinforce the right of the Division, on a gently sloping ridge. The plan for the guns was to place an artillery brigade with each infantry brigade. The artillery was to be as close up to the infantry positions as possible, to give them maximum support. The proximity of the guns to the infantry made it even harder for them in their exposed positions, as the enemy guns sought them out for destruction.

The batteries supporting 14th Infantry Brigade were from XV Brigade and a Howitzer Battery from VIII Howitzer Brigade. In line they were from right to left: the 11th, 80th, 37th (H) and the 52nd. Together they made up a group of twenty-four guns. The four batteries were positioned between the 2nd Suffolks who were in the front line to the north-east and their supporting infantry on a forward slope.

At first 37th (H) Battery was astride a road which led to the main road to Reumont and was camouflaged in a covered position. They dug entrenchments as well as they could in the short time available in soft ground where corn had recently been harvested. Close by there was a small stream and beyond that was part of B Coy. of the 2nd KOYLI (13th Brig.) with two machine guns. The Observation Post for the XVth Artillery Brigade was on the top of a small rise from which there was a good view.

The Germans, who had been chasing the British for three days, occupied the high ground to the west of Le Cateau, and could use the valley of the La Selle river as an approach along the eastern edge of the battlefield. They had entered the town before 06.00 hours. This left the British right flank to the east of the high ground at Le Cateau in German hands.

At 06.00 hours the enemy guns began firing from close to a forest at a position 3 miles north-east of the town. Their main targets were the positions of the 5th Division, to the west of the town. The guns of XV Brigade with 37th (H) had some success in silencing the enemy batteries, by firing at the enemy gun flashes. The Howitzer Battery in particular quickly silenced two guns. They soon discovered, however, that it was very difficult to carry out counter-battery work when the guns were so close to the infantry.

Driver J.H.C. Drain (69960) kept a diary of 37 (H) Battery and to paraphrase his words he wrote:

There was little cover or hiding place and when the battle began there were 18-pounder batteries on either side, with a siege battery to the rear of them and hundreds of infantrymen were going up to meet up with the enemy. Terrible shells came over in sixes and were bursting all over the place and over the tops of our guns and wagon lines with plenty of bullets flying about. Man after man was becoming wounded and horses were being killed and batteries were being smashed to pieces. I just don't think there was a man on the field who did not say his prayers for a general retirement to be ordered.

The 2nd Suffolks suffered many casualties simply because their positions were so close to their 'protective guns'. Maj. E.H. Jones in charge of 37 (H) Battery was wounded just before 07.00 hours. After 10.00 hours 37 (H) Battery along with XVth Brigade began to shell the German infantry who were advancing on the 2nd Suffolks and 2nd Manchesters of the 14th Brigade. The battery inflicted many casualties among the enemy infantry who came forward in small groups and who sometimes used corn-stooks for cover. Later the batteries began to run out of ammunition and although they had been told that they were to fight to the finish, the order was changed at about 13.30 hours to one 'of retrieving the guns and of leaving the battlefield'. The guns, however, did not withdraw until almost all their ammunition had been used up and they could no longer sustain action. It became quite obvious that it was only a matter of time before the British would be forced to retire. The artillery units were the first to begin to leave the field as the result of a further order from the Brigade Major. This was at about 13.45 hours when 80 and 37 (H) were still firing. All morning and early afternoon they had behaved in a heroic fashion and one by one the guns were brought out. On the other side of the Reumont road were 52, 123 and 124 Batteries who had been especially close to the front line. It was decided to abandon the guns and to take out their breech-blocks and smash their sights.

Of XVth Brigade's twenty-four guns fourteen were eventually brought out and the teams of the 80 and 37 (H) were among the last to leave the field having moved forward in order to take away the last five field guns and four Howitzers.

Capt. D. Reynolds of the 37th searched for spare limber teams in order to move two of the Howitzers away before they fell into enemy hands. However no such teams were available so he put the guns out of action and withdrew with his men down the road to Reumont which was about 1½ miles to the south-west. Once there he did find two limbers and promptly asked permission from the CRA to call for volunteers to rescue the remaining Howitzers which had been left behind. He was accompanied by Lt. E.G. Earle, who was already wounded, Lt. W.D. Morgan, Drivers Cobey, Luke and Drain, along with another team. The horses were harnessed in pairs with one driver for each pair.

Capt. Reynolds and the two other officers led the two limbers up the road from Reumont, at first at a slow trot, towards the two remaining Howitzers. As the teams under Earle and Morgan, with Luke as 'Wheel', drew near to the positions they were ordered to gallop. The artillerymen stretched themselves forward and with their limbers bouncing moved right up to the astonished German infantry who were moving in on three sides of the position, and in the process overwhelming the 2nd Suffolks on the right flank. The limbers moved through a wall of shrapnel although the CRA gave orders for a brief battery ceasefire for a short time while the guns were rescued. When Driver Luke with great skill was bringing Morgan's limber out with one of the guns, the centre driver, Ben Cobey, between Luke and Drain was shot dead. Cobey's whip was flung up into the air but Reynolds galloping alongside managed to catch it and urged the horses on. This left Drain, Luke and Capt. Reynolds along with two other artillerymen on the limber. They charged past the Germans to safety. The British onlookers were incredulous at the sheer speed and audacity of the operation, as the retrieving of the guns appeared to be a hopeless task. The wounded Lt. Earle was not as successful as Morgan; having hooked in with the other gun, he only managed to get 50 yards away before his two centre horses were killed. Earle and Sgt. Bower quickly unhooked the centre and lead horses but by then the two Wheelers were shot and not surprisingly the Howitzer had to be abandoned. Bower helped Earle, who had been wounded again, this time in the eye and forehead, back to safety at Reumont.

Only four of the eighteen officers in the Brigade were left unwounded. Maj.

Capt. D. Reynolds, Drivers J.H.C. Drain and F. Luke at Le Cateau, 26 August

E.H. Jones, Commander of 37 (H) Battery was wounded and also taken prisoner on the day. For their heroism Capt. Reynolds, Driver Luke (71787) and Driver Drain were all awarded the Victoria Cross. Reynolds' was gazetted on 16 November and that of the two Drivers on 25 November. Driver Cobey, who some thought should have been posthumously awarded with the VC, became the central subject of several artistic reconstructions of the famous incident. Lt. Earle was recommended for the VC but the War Office turned down the claim as he was 'under the orders of a superior officer', and instead he received the DSO. Sgt. Bower and Trumpeter S.F.G. Waldron both received the DCM. Throughout the day Waldron (the Captain's trumpeter) had carried on heroic work as the chief link between the battery guns and their limbers and ammunition. The wagon line was about 2,000 yards behind the gun position. Waldron remained at his post with German shells firing all around him and once took a horse up to the firing line through very heavy fire. During the day he was wounded, not surprisingly. Much later 37th (H) Battery was to be given the honorary title of 'Le Cateau', which they thoroughly deserved.

The battery continued the retreat from Mons, marching towards the town of St Quentin. Driver Drain wrote about the continuous marching in the heat which was very harsh for man and horse. This heat often killed the horses, some of whom just dropped down on the road while others became lame and had to be shot. Exhausted men also fell out on the march. They were 20 miles from Paris before the pushing back of the enemy began in early September.

On 9 September, the fourth day of the Battle of the Marne, Capt. Reynolds was at Pisseloup, just north of the River Marne, where he spotted a German battery which was holding up the advance. He ordered 37 (H) Battery to destroy it. This incident was included with his VC citation. A few days later, during the Battle of the Aisne the battery crossed over the River Aisne to the village of Bucy le Long as part of the artillery support to the 5th Division. Drain wrote of being billeted at a farm close to Soissons and on the 14th the guns fired all day. On the next day the battery advanced over the river using a pontoon bridge. The battery was in action for four days between Soissons and Missy and remained there until about 8 October when it went by train to Flanders to the north.

During this period Capt. Reynolds was seriously wounded in the side by shrapnel from a bullet which passed up to his chest and lodged there. After his recovery, Major Reynolds, as he had now become, was involved in training a new Howitzer battery which he was later to command. On 13 January he received his VC at Buckingham Palace.

In the First Battle of Ypres a section of 37 Battery was in action near Annequin and again on 24 April 1915, this time with the Canadians near Frezenberg. The

Second Battle of Ypres had recently begun. A couple of days later the battery helped destroy the German infantry emerging from the Gravenstafel Ridge.

In December 1915, just before Christmas, the hearts of Reynolds and several of his men were affected by the explosion of an asphyxiating bomb near their positions. They seemed to recover but Reynolds died of septicaemia from gas poisoning on 23 February 1916. He was buried at Etaples Military Cemetery, grave I, A, 20.

❖❖❖

Douglas Reynolds was the son of Lt. Col. H.C. Reynolds and his wife, Eleanor. He was born in Clifton, Bristol on 20 September 1882. His mother was daughter of Wildman Goodwyn of the Indian Civil Service.

Reynolds went to Cheltenham College as a day boy in September 1892 and later went into the military and civil side of the college. In 1898 he went on to the Royal Military Academy at Woolwich and was gazetted to the Royal Artillery at the end of the following year. Although he volunteered for the Boer War when it began, he did not get to South Africa until a few months before it ended. He served with the mounted infantry which was attached to the artillery. Later he served mainly in India where he was in charge of an ammunition column at Nowshera. He was a keen sportsman and an excellent shot. When war broke out he was in Ireland and immediately left for France with 37th Howitzer Battery. He was mentioned in

The Reynolds' family home in Clifton, Bristol

despatches for gallantry during the operations in the last few days of August and again in 1915.

In January 1916 Reynolds' son was born, shortly before his father died. Mrs Reynolds remarried Major J.C. Bulteel DSO after the war. Her son joined the Army himself in later years. He became a Lieutenant but was posted missing in May 1940 during the Second World War.

Reynolds is commemorated at the family grave at St Peter's church, Leckhampton in Cheltenham. He is also commemorated at Cheltenham College and Cheltenham War Memorial.

His medals became part of the collection of Sir John Roper Wright of the Territorial Army. In the early 1940s Sir John presented them to the Royal Artillery.

J.H.C. DRAIN

Le Cateau, France, 26 August

Job Henry Charles Drain was born on 15 October 1895 and attended a Church of England school in Barking. He enlisted in Stratford on 27 August 1912 in order to escape unemployment. He served for seven years with the colours and five with the reserve. He was decorated, together with Driver Luke, by the King in the field at Locon, France on 1 December 1914. He was welcomed back to his home town of Barking and presented with a purse of gold, an illuminated address and a watch. The ceremonies took place at the municipal buildings and local park.

Drain went through the war without being wounded and was demobilized with the rank of Sergeant on 28 August 1924. His father also served in the First World War.

Drain junior found employment difficult in civilian life and was a Whitehall messenger, then a fish porter at Billingsgate and later a London bus driver. In 1926 he went to court charged with a driving obstruction offence but the case was dismissed. On 5 October 1931 he was a special guest at Barking's Charter Day Celebrations and was presented to Prince George, the Duke of Kent. He was wearing his bus driver's uniform.

On 7 July 1956 he was photographed for *The Sphere* with F. Luke; both men wore civilian clothes and a long row of medals. They were described as 'Old Contemptibles' and had recently attended the VC Centenary Service at Westminster

Abbey on 25 June. Drain was a local celebrity for many years. Frederick Luke and Job Drain remained the best of friends until Drain's death. He died at home at No. 42 Greatfields Road, Barking on 26 July 1975 at the age of seventy-nine. He was buried at Rippledale Cemetery. His widow Patricia, then aged seventy-five, had married him in 1919 and they had two children. In his retirement Drain was a keen gardener.

In 1983 Drain's career was featured in an exhibition mounted by the local library service on winners of the VC from Essex. The exhibition was a great success. Drain's medals are now with the Royal Artillery.

F. LUKE

Le Cateau, France, 26 August

Frederick Luke was the third man from 37th (H) Battery to win the VC on 26 August. He was born at Lockerley, near West Tytherley, Romsey, Hampshire. His father William Luke was a mill worker at Elwood Mill and his mother was named Kete. The family consisted of five brothers and eight sisters. Two of the sisters died in infancy. The Luke family lived at Top Green and Frederick went to Lockerley school. He was later employed as a farm worker at East Dean Farm and enlisted, when he was seventeen and under age, at Winchester in January 1913. He was only eighteen when he won the VC. He served for the rest of the war, but was wounded and spent some time in hospital at Todmorden, where he met Jenny Husband, his future wife. After leaving hospital he was then transferred to D180 Battery RFA of 16th Division.

After the war he married Jenny on 4 April 1919 and they were to have one daughter and three sons. Luke became a school janitor at the Glasgow High School for Boys. He was discharged from the Army reserve in 1929. In the Second World War he joined up with the RAF regiment as a ground gunner. After the war he became a gauge and tool storeman with Weirs of Cathcart, Glasgow, and remained there until about 1960. His address in Glasgow was No. 208, Allison Road, G42.

In 1962 he was present at Le Cateau for a ceremony and service to mark the 48th anniversary of the Battle of Le Cateau. He was accompanied by Brig. Earle who received the DSO in 1914 in the same battle. Luke also received the Freedom of Le Cateau and was back in the French town two years later for the fiftieth anniversary along with the battery which had replaced the 37th (H) Battery. It had been re-named the 93 (Le Cateau) Battery as an honour and two troops had been named after Drain and Luke. Eventually Luke became the oldest man living to hold the Victoria Cross. At a dinner held at Buckingham Palace for surviving VC winners it was Luke's duty to present the First World War veterans to the Queen. He regularly attended the various VC ceremonies. At the age of

Top Green, Lockerley, former home of Driver F. Luke

seventy-two in 1967 Luke resumed work for a short while as a petrol-pump attendant. In an interview with the *Scottish Newspaper* in 1976 Luke said that when he and Drain were fighting together in the trenches near Bethune on 1 December 1914, a field officer informed them that the King wanted to see them. With no time to clean up they were pushed into the King's inspection line in Locon. It was there that they were informed they were to receive the VC. The King told Luke not to lose his medal in the mud but to give it to his commanding officer to send it home. At a garden party in 1920 the King remembered Luke and recalled the incident.

In February 1981 Luke was invited to spend a week with the Le Cateau battery at Paderborn in Germany. The unit had become a part of 25th Field Regiment, Royal Artillery, and was commanded by Maj. Gen. Gerry Middleton. Luke was escorted by Sgt. Inglis who had been at Le Cateau in 1964. He fetched the elderly veteran from his Glasgow home and returned him there at the end of the week. During the visit a champagne lunch was laid on in Luke's honour at Le Cateau, and at Paderborn he took the salute at a special parade in his honour. He was also introduced to the GOC of the 4th Division, Maj. Gen. Richard Vickers, who expressed the hope that 'We would never have to go to war again.' Luke's reply was 'Well, if you do and you need any help, just give me a call.' During his stay with the battery Luke was entertained and also interviewed on Forces'

Radio. He participated in numerous photographic sessions and answered hundreds of questions. In the Officers Mess Luke was pictured under a dramatic painting reconstructing the famous deed at Le Cateau, painted by Terence Cuneo. Luke was described as a 'bird like' figure.

Frederick Luke died at his Glasgow home at No. 597 Castlemilk Road, Croftfoot, on 11 March 1983 at the age of eighty-seven. He had held the VC for a record breaking sixty-nine years. In 1969 a duplicate medal had been put into circulation by a fraudulent dealer, but in September 1983 his VC Trio medals were listed by the London Stamp Exchange for £12,450.

One has the distinct impression that Luke basked in the fame that his heroic action had brought him and that he had been spared to enjoy it all, unlike so many of his colleagues among the 1914 VC winners.

E.K. BRADBURY, G.T. DORRELL AND D. NELSON

Néry, 1 September

Capt. Bradbury

BSM Dorrell

Sgt. Nelson

After a short action at Mons the Allies retreated. The British were so exhausted when they reached Le Cateau that Gen. Sir H.L. Smith-Dorrien, commanding 11 Corps decided to stand and fight. Douglas Haig, General Officer Commanding 1 Corps, believed the British should have pushed on and saved both men and equipment. But Smith-Dorrien knew his troops were exhausted and he also wanted to open up a gap between his troops and the German enemy which he was subsequently able to achieve. However, on 31 August, five days later, the gap was once more closing. After Le Cateau the BEF retreated towards the Marne and Paris. The 1st, 2nd and 4th Cavalry Brigades were acting as rearguard, and as left flank, to Smith-Dorrien's 11 Corps.

On 1 September, a curious incident took place which is always described as The Affair of Néry.

On the afternoon of 31 August the cavalry division under Gen. Allenby was to the south-west of the forest of Compiègne and west of the town of Soissons, at a village called Verberies. Allenby himself was at the village of St Vaast to the north-west of the small village of Néry in which units of the 1st Cavalry Brigade were to billet, having journeyed from Choisy au Bac near Compiègne. It was reported that a large body of German cavalry was getting close but their division had moved further southwards. The French cavalry was retiring through the

Compiègne Forest with the idea of billeting on the line of the River Autonne. Later they were ordered to move closer up to their Allies.

In the story of Néry it is important to try and remember the cavalry units and where they were ordered to spend the night, after another hot and tiring day. The plan was that they were to continue their retreat towards Paris early next morning. The enemy was not thought to be close by, and by this time had completed his westerly movement and was turning south towards the line of Noyon-Compiègne.

Néry today is a very quiet agricultural village with solidly built houses together with small gardens and orchards. The fields yield beet and corn. It is probably not very different from the time of the First World War. On entering the village from the north there is a civilian cemetery, and then two main streets which are roughly parallel to one another, running north to south. The church is in the north-east part of the village.

The most important geographical feature of the village is a ravine which runs parallel to the east side. To the east of it is a plateau. In 1914 the ravine was not only steep but also full of scrub. At the bottom was a stream which had almost dried up during the summer. Prior to the war there had been plans to continue a north-south railway through the ravine bottom.

The Commander of 1st Cavalry Brigade was Brig. Gen. Briggs, and under his command were the 2nd Dragoon Guards (Queen's Bays), 5th Dragoon Guards, 11th Hussars and L Battery with its six 13-pounders. The 5th DG were billeted in and around the northern part of the village close to the church and school area. The 11th Hussars were spread over two farms and some houses on the eastern side of the village and they faced the ravine and plateau. Briggs' Brigade Headquarters was in a house in the main street which was the western side of the two parallel roads that ran through the village.

A and B Squadrons of the 2nd DG were billeted in buildings opposite and to the south of Brigade HQ and C Squadron was further to the south-west of the village in a small field on the side of a road which formed a deep cutting. They had to picket their horses in orchards and fields close to their billets. L Battery which had already earned its keep in its brief time in Belgium and France at Mons, Audregnies and Le Cateau, was in a position on open ground nearly opposite the 2nd DG. As the battery was at the southern end of the village the men were able to spread themselves and lay down good horse lines. They made their HQ at the local sugar factory which was then a building of some size, with the usual tall chimney. There was a water supply there which was vital to the cavalry as well as to the artillery for watering their horses. The factory's foundations can still be seen today. The 2nd DG had an advanced post opposite.

On 31 August L Battery was the last unit into billets and on the way they had watered their horses at the river in Verberie. It was harvest time and the corn had been cut and was standing in stooks waiting to be harvested. Although their Intelligence showed that the enemy was nowhere close to the village, the various units did send out patrols in the early hours of 1 September but they reported nothing except that it was very misty. At 04.15 hours the 11th Hussars sent out 2nd Lt. Tailby who was relatively inexperienced in patrol work. His small party did, however, include Cpl. Parker who was an experienced hand. Tailby was ordered to take a north-easterly route and then make for the east side of the plateau before taking a southerly

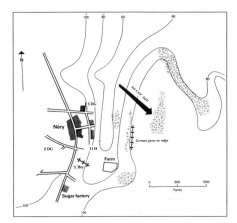

Néry, 1 September

sweep. The morning was very misty and the patrol could not see further than 100 yards. At one point the patrol did see a small group of dismounted Uhlans who appeared to be lost, and one of Tailby's scouts could not resist letting off a rifle shot which, of course, encouraged the Germans to move. The patrol's way back to Néry was now barred and the Germans charged towards Tailby's group, who galloped off in a north-easterly direction. Despite having an accident with his horse Tailby and Parker escaped from the German patrol and at the bottom of a hill they came across an *estaminet* where they discovered a discarded German cloak and rifle. The cloak was draped over the back of a chair. A woman said that three Germans had just run out of her house. Tailby asked for directions to the Néry–Bethisy road as he was by now some way from Néry.

The party returned to base at about 05.30 hours and Tailby ordered Parker to warn the 5th DG while he rushed to see Col. Pitman of the 11th Hussars. His report was received with some scepticism until he produced the German overcoat. Immediately Pitman gave orders to Maj. Anderson to get the men of the 11th Hussars into battle readiness. The cavalrymen and the artillerymen had woken at dawn ready for the early start. They were washing, breakfasting and getting the horses and equipment ready. L Battery was watering its horses at the sugar factory where they may have been joined by some of the cavalry. The battery officers were grouped at two haystacks behind the guns and were shaving.

The first shell, which came as a complete surprise to the billeted troops, was followed by hundreds more, many of which fell among the Bays' horses and L Battery's positions. The shelling was accompanied by shrapnel and rifle and machine-gun fire, which resulted in total destruction. The horses from the Bays were terrified and stampeded down the main street. The men in that confined space suffered badly; L Battery and 2nd DG were especially vulnerable. Those cavalrymen billeted on the eastern side and north of the village had considerable protection. Such was the accuracy of the German artillery, or maybe it was luck, that a shell dropped on the roof of the building in which Cavalry HQ was housed. Briggs, Brigade Major Cawley and Battery Commander Sclater-Booth were all in residence at the time, along with Col. Pitman of the 11th Hussars. Briggs retrieved the timer belonging to the shell and this recorded the distance of fire as being about 550 yards. Col. Pitman had only just made his report. A few minutes earlier Col. Wilberforce (Commanding Officer of the Bays) had been walking up the street on his way to HQ to find out if there was any prospect of an immediate move. He then heard the first gun report and hurried back to organize his defence positions. This was at about 05.40 hours.

Maj. Sclater-Booth, in command of L Battery, hurried out of Brigade HQ and was on his way to L Battery. On crossing a field, before reaching their positions, a shell exploded near him and he fell unconscious and was also blinded. He was not picked up for five hours. The story of what follows might have been very different had Tailby been able to re-enter the village from a southerly direction and give more warning.

The positions of what turned out to be twelve German guns, consisting of three batteries of four guns each, could only be guessed at in the morning mist by the gun flashes. Fire was being concentrated on the positions occupied by the 2nd DG and L Battery. The enemy was to the south-east of the village and south-west of Feu Farm. This farm, the German battery site, and the sugar factory formed an arc. The German range of fire was about 400 yards. Early in the action one German battery had been brought round from a position facing the village in the west across the plateau to be in line with the other guns to the south-east.

The German cavalrymen had been as exhausted as their British counterparts the previous day, and they, together with their artillery, had been attempting to meet up with the left flank of the French Army. Instead, by a quirk of fate they now faced a whole English cavalry brigade.

There was continuous mayhem in the L Battery and 2nd DG positions. Initially the horses of the rear left section of the guns were taking water at the sugar factory and when the shelling began the battery was caught in a hailstorm of shells, shrapnel and bullets. It quickly tried to get at least some of its guns into action from B and D sub-sections. Some horses had been secured to the gun limber wheels and other animals became wild and terrified. Simultaneously machine guns had quickly been set up by the Bays and the 11th Hussars in their positions in order to return fire. Individuals also joined in with accurate rifle fire. The L Battery guns were in columns of sections and three guns were quickly brought into action, with officers and men frantically working alongside one another. The other three guns were already damaged by the shelling and out of

No. 6 gun of L Battery

action. Capt. Bradbury was second in command of the battery after Maj. Booth and had been standing about 50 yards north of the guns with brother officers when the first shell had burst. He had called out, 'Who's for the guns?' He and Sgt. Nelson took over one gun and Lt. Giffard another and Lts. Campbell and Mundy the third. This third gun was soon silenced when it received a direct hit. Lt. Giffard was then severely wounded and his detachment either killed or wounded too. This left only Bradbury's gun in action and Campbell and Mundy went to assist him. Gunner Darbyshire and Driver Osborne served the gun with ammunition from a wagon 20 yards distant, continuously crossing the shell-torn ground. Campbell was killed after only firing a couple of rounds and the duties were then shared out between Capt. Bradbury as layer, Sgt. Nelson as range setter and Lt. Mundy as observer. By 06.30 hours Lt. Mundy was mortally wounded (he died two days later) and Sgt. Nelson was hit. At about 07.15 hours BSM Dorrell reached the gun but then Bradbury himself was hit and had both his legs taken off by a shell. He had himself propped up against a gun and continued to give orders. He had been hit when he had left the gun to seek ammunition. When he was carried off he is reported to have said to Lt. Col. Wilberforce of the 2nd DG, 'Hullo Colonel, they've hotted us up a bit, haven't they?'

Another account which appeared in the contemporary *Great Deeds of the War* states that Bradbury had asked the Medical Officer for heaps of morphia in order that the men should not hear him screaming and that he should be quickly taken to the rear. This left Dorrell and the wounded Sgt. Nelson to fire the last round, the gun having in all accounted for three of the German guns.

Sgt. Nelson and BSM Dorrell at Néry, 1 September

In a lurid diary account Sgt. Nelson wrote:

During the awful carnage the moaning of dying men and horses audible amidst the terrific thundering of cannon; the scenes in most cases beyond description. One man in full view of me had his head cut clean off his body. Another was literally blown to pieces, another was practically severed at the breast, loins, knees and ankles. One horse had its head and neck completely severed from the shoulders.

Though wounded himself Sgt. Nelson, after a brief visit to a dressing station, still had a role to play and as the L Battery guns no longer existed he decided to help the Bays with refilling their ammunition belts for their machine guns. Earlier an order had been issued to send despatch riders to inform Allenby of what was happening and to ask for reinforcements as soon as possible. The positions of the 5th DG near the church and the 11th Hussars were not precarious as much of the shelling passed over their heads, and as a result the two units hardly suffered. The 5th DG was also slightly protected by its position in the village which gave extra cover. The dragoons also managed to prevent their horses from stampeding. There was a feeble attempt by the German cavalry to attack the village from the north-east but it came to nothing. A lot of rifle and machine-gun fire was built up along the eastern side of the village. Gen. Briggs had quickly made a plan of a counter-attack and had sent one squadron of the Hussars into Brigade Reserve and 5th DG to make a turning movement. A large number of their horses were collected and Col. Ansell organized two fairly strong squadrons: one to the north of the village and one to make contact to the south-east with the right of the German lines. It was during this fighting that he was to lose his life. Two other squadrons of the Hussars were used to barricade the southern edge of the village and to help the 2nd DG in the vicinity of L Battery who had been even more exposed than the artillery. The Bays had been employed in 'loop-holing' the village walls on the western side. A squadron led by Maj. Ing did excellent work at the sugar factory. One troop under Lt. de Crespigny reached a position to the east of the factory, almost on the German flank but he was mortally wounded. He was buried in France but was later exhumed and taken home for burial in Maldon in Essex. The machine guns under the Bays and 11th Hussars had fired effectively at the German batteries.

One man in the 11th Hussars kept a diary and his picture often appears in current histories of the period. His name was Lt. 'Deafy' Arkwright. He was apparently so deaf that he did not even hear the first shells – it is hard to believe this as he would not have passed a medical. Nevertheless he had rushed out to help and in a gap on a bank on the side of the road he found Maj. Cawley who was mortally wounded. On the other side of the road was a gunner corporal firing away, quite regardless of bullets all about him.

The ravine worked in the Allies' favour for it would have been very difficult for the German cavalry to cross it without being 'picked off'. During a temporary break in the mist the Uhlans were seen briefly massing on the plateau opposite the Hussars' position but a French liaison officer identified them as French so the opportunity to fire was lost.

The 4th Cavalry Brigade at Verberie and Gen. Allenby the Divisional Commander at St Vaast, had received news of the trouble in Néry from Gen. Briggs. Parties of a composite battalion consisting of men from the Royal Dublin Fusiliers and the Middlesex Regiments quickly marched off to assist the cavalrymen at Néry. In addition, a squadron of the composite regiment of the Household Cavalry was to work its way further round towards the sugar factory. Lt. Heath who was in front of the leading troop was killed charging the German guns. At about 07.00 hours Cavalry Division HQ had been established about three quarters of a mile to the west of the sugar factory and just before 08.00 hours two German machine guns began to fire from the factory but were soon silenced. At about the same time the 4th Cavalry Brigade had reached La Bardé Farm to the west of the village and reinforcements arrived from the south-west and the north-east simultaneously. The Germans were in danger of being surrounded. In addition the artillerymen of I Battery were arriving from St Vaast and entered the village over rising ground from the south-west of the village to set up their gun positions. Initially they began to fire at the flank of the German artillery by 'lining up' with the tall chimney of the sugar factory. The mist began to clear and the Germans became visible. One battery of the German guns was turned round towards I Battery but they lined up against a cultivator pole and never got their range correct. Some of the enemy had reached the sugar factory at some point and had captured a few civilians who were later set free. The sight of the British reserves beginning to swarm encouraged the Germans to return to their colleagues. Even the ravine had been tried as a way in to capture the village but all the German Uhlans fell and the mere sight of a battery limbering up on the horizon discouraged any further such attempts. The enemy withdrew after about 20 minutes at around 09.00 hours. They were pursued vigorously by parties of the Hussars as far as the village of Le Plessis Chatelain, to the east of Néry.

The Allies took about a hundred prisoners, and the enemy left eight guns behind, five of which were useless. The four guns that they did manage to make off with were found next day in the forest in Ermenonville. Their total force with the three batteries consisted of a cavalry division of six regiments with machine guns. Perhaps the cavalry brigade should have been more alert with their picketing arrangements and generally quicker but it seems that the Germans were just as surprised to see the British as they were to see them. The enemy subsequently came into action in a somewhat haphazard fashion, but then they had no idea of the real strength of the force they had stumbled upon. They were also worn out themselves. They could, I suppose, have carried out a stronger frontal attack and smashed their way through the Bays and L Battery lines.

The Affair of Néry had lasted barely four hours but the heroism of the British horse battery had saved the lives and equipment of a whole cavalry brigade. Their action will be forever remembered in the annals of the Royal Artillery.

The scene in Néry after the short but bloody battle was chaotic with guns destroyed, the wounded to attend to, and the dead to bury, including 300 or 400 dead horses. One of L Battery's horses, No. 53, was tied to a gunwheel with eight wounds in his side and yet was still enjoying his nose bag. Many of the carcasses were subsequently buried by the villagers. In this they were not hindered by the Germans who entered the village the same evening and who treated the inhabitants well. The wounded had all been collected up before the British left. Those casualties too ill to move were cared for in neighbouring farms. The French Army returned to Néry a few days later to reclaim it.

Casualty figures vary, but the British lost about 135 officers and men of whom five were officers from L Battery along with forty-two men from the same unit. The proposed attack of the German 4th Cavalry Division had been covered by their twelve artillery guns along with the Guard Machine Gun Battery on their left. Under this cover of fire the 3rd Cavalry Brigade was to advance from the Bethisy direction to attack the British left. The other flank was to be taken care of by the 17th Cavalry Brigade. In this attack the 18th Dragoons were to be used while leaving the 17th Dragoons in reserve at Le Plessis Chatelain. The 18th Cavalry Brigade was kept back as part of divisional reserve. However, the firing from L Battery combined with a stubborn defence of the village slowly brought the German advance to a standstill. German ammunition was in short supply as well because an ammunition column had been left behind in the forest at Laigue. In addition, the attacking force knew that British reinforcements might arrive at any time. The Germans were to suffer roughly the same number of casualties as the British.

There are two other incidents during the action worth noting. Prior to the war Feu Farm had been bought by a German but at the time of the Affair it was empty. A French girl on holiday from Paris in the village was caught up in the battle and had helped out with the wounded, in particular with Maurice Hill of the 5th DG whose body had been laid next to that of Lt. Col. Ansell. Hill was seen to have life in him still but his identity disc had been removed. He was treated for wounds as well as for loss of memory and a brother officer had to travel from Paris in order to identify him.

In Néry Civilian Cemetery there is a memorial to the men of L Battery where seven of them are buried in a single grave. Also buried here is the chief hero of the day, Capt. Bradbury, along with Brigade Major Cawley. At Verberie, a few

The graves of five men of L Battery, at Verberie Cemetery

miles away is another memorial and grave to L Battery where five men are buried. In the same French cemetery lies the body of Col. Ansell, Commander of the 5th DG.

Three men from L Battery were to be awarded the VC: Capt. Bradbury (25 November 1914), BSM Dorrell and Sgt. Nelson (both on 16 November 1914). There was some delay over Bradbury's award as Brig. Gen. Briggs, his commanding officer, was unaware that the medal could be awarded posthumously as, indeed, those for Dease and Wright had been. Darbyshire and Osborne whom the Press had expected to receive the award were given the Médaille Militaire instead, a less prestigious award.

The guns of L Battery were partly repaired by I Battery, assisted by men of the 2nd DG, before being sent on to the Ordnance Department at St Nazaire on 3 September. L Battery was then sent home for a refit to Woolwich and there was controversy about who should have been awarded the VC. The L Battery survivors (according to Canon Lummis' files) thought that Dorrell should not have been given the award but that Gunners Darbyshire and Osborne, who were both to die during the Gallipoli campaign, should have been. However, as the Canon reminded us it was Dorrell and Nelson who were firing the gun at the end of the action and surely they did deserve the VC for such heroism? There was also controversy when L Battery was amalgamated with I Battery for a time. In 1926 the battery was, however, re-named L (Néry) Battery, RHA.

There was an official commemoration in 1954 at Néry and at various times additional memorials have been erected. One interesting inscription is the one that states, 'The Battle of the Marne was won at Néry.' If any reader is keen to visit the village of Néry I advise them to go in late August in order to feel the atmosphere of the harvest season. Tailby's epic ride is described in full in an article in the *Cavalry Journal* and Lt. Arkwright's diary entry is also in print in full. It is a fascinating incident and one which inspired several artistic reconstructions which were so popular between the world wars and which are now regaining their former appeal.

Edward Kinder Bradbury was born at Parkfield, Altrincham, Cheshire on 16 August 1881. He was son of His Honour the late Judge Bradbury and Mrs Bradbury. He was educated at Marlborough College, and then entered the Royal Military Academy at Woolwich. He joined the Royal Artillery in May 1900 when he was nineteen. He was made a Lieutenant in April 1901. Between January and October 1902 he served with the Imperial Yeomanry taking part in the South African War and was present at the operations in Cape Colony. He gained the Queen's Medal with two clasps. During 1905 and 1907 he was a member of the King's African Rifles and was made up to Captain in February 1910. At the start of the First World War he went to France with the BEF and was to earn undying fame at Néry on 1 September 1914.

Before the war Bradbury had been a keen fisherman and used to spend his leave in County Cork fishing and hunting.

George Thomas Dorrell was born at 23 G Street, Queen's Park Estate, Paddington, London, on 7 July 1880. He was the son of a cab driver, who eventually lived at 70 Kilburn Park Road, Carlton Vale, London. On 2 December 1895 he was attested Gunner with the Royal Horse Artillery and gave his age as nineteen when he was only fifteen. He served in South Africa in 1899 and received Long Service and Good Conduct Medals. He was promoted Bombadier Royal Horse Artillery (RHA) on 2 January 1900. On 18 June he was made up to Sergeant. He served throughout the second Boer War (1899–1902) and received the Queen's Medal with six clasps and the King's Medal with two clasps. On 2 December 1908 he was made Battery Quarter Master Sergeant (BQMS) with the RHA and Battery Sergeant Major on 29 November 1911.

In August 1914 he went to France with L Battery and the BEF and was later awarded the Mons Star with clasp. During the action at Néry he became senior officer after the L Battery officers were either killed or wounded. He was commissioned from the ranks on 1 October 1914, the same month he married his wife, Lucy. His Victoria Cross was gazetted on 16 November. He was promoted to full Lieutenant, RFA on 9 June 1915, and to Temporary Captain on 2 May. On 25 September 1916 he was appointed Acting Major while in charge of A/122nd Brigade RFA and as Acting Major while commanding B/190th Brigade RFA on 19 March 1917, the day before he was mentioned in despatches. In 1921 he retired from the regular Army and served for a further term with the Territorial Army. He was a Company Commander in the Home Guard between 1940 and 1945. He was made a Member of the British Empire (MBE) in 1925. He became Brevet Lieutenant Colonel and in 1956 he was present at the Néry Day celebrations at Hildesheim, Germany. He was one of fourteen veterans from the First World War who had travelled from Britain to attend the ceremonies.

Three of these men had been wounded and captured at Néry. Alongside Dorrell at the Battery's march-past stood Mrs D. Nelson, the widow of Acting Major Nelson. During the ceremonies she presented her late husband's Victoria Cross to the Battery. Dorrell handed over Capt. Bradbury's VC on behalf of Maj. A.J. Creudson, MC, a nephew of Bradbury, who was unable to attend the ceremony. In 1970 Dorrell celebrated his ninetieth birthday but died six months later on 7 January 1971. His home was at No. 30 Bray Road, Cobham, Surrey. His wife, Lucy, had died on 13 September in 1969.

He was cremated at Randalls Park in Leatherhead on 15 January 1971. A gun carriage and two trumpeters were provided for the service by The King's Troop RHA and L (Néry) Battery was in charge of the military arrangements for the service. The procession formed up in the cemetery car park and travelled half a mile to the crematorium at Randalls Park. The 'Last Post' and 'Reveille' were both sounded. After the service Dorrell's medals were presented to Capt. C.B. Daw on behalf of L (Néry) Battery to whom they had been bequeathed. L (Néry) Battery now held all the VCs won at Néry on 1 September 1914.

David Nelson was born at Deraghland, Co. Monaghan, Ireland on 3 April 1886. He enlisted in the RFA in 1904 – his number was 34419. He was made a

Bombadier with L Battery on 18 May 1910 and Corporal on 7 January 1911. On 5 August 1914 he was promoted to Sergeant, the rank he held at Néry. After the battle was over his wounds began to bleed again and he was assisted into an ambulance with four other men and taken to a temporary field hospital at Baron. In the hospital were about eighty British soldiers, four French and twelve German. At about 17.00 hours on 2 September the enemy arrived in the village and the Allied hospital patients were made prisoners of war. The Germans also helped themselves to the hospital food. The next day the contents of the hospital were packed up into French farm carts before being evacuated to Germany. A couple of days later Nelson decided to try and escape. He succeeded and met up with a French patrol riding near the hospital. He was lent a horse and reported to the French General Plailly and told him of the situation at the hospital at Baron. The French officer promised to send a relief the next day. Nelson then went on a 30-hour journey in motor ambulances to Dinan where he was operated on in order to remove a piece of shrapnel touching his right lung.

Nelson was commissioned from the ranks on 15 November 1914, the day before his Victoria Cross was gazetted, and posted to Shoeburyness Gunnery School in January 1915. In October 1916 he was appointed Temporary Captain and then Acting Major in command of D Battery, 59th Battery in March 1918. He died of wounds at 58 CCS at Lillers on 8 April 1918 and is buried in the Lillers Communal Cemetery (No. V, A, 16). In 1971 his widow was living at No. 34 Cowper Street, Ipswich.

W. FULLER
Near Chivy, 14 September

The retreat from Mons demoralized the men of the BEF who were getting fed up with continuously marching away from the enemy. They would much rather stand and fight. They were to have their wish fulfilled after the German Army crossed the River Marne to the north of Paris in early September. The Germans were pushed back across the river and then pursued to the valley of the River Aisne where they had already made defensive positions.

On 14 September, the 3rd Infantry Brigade of the 1st Division was acting as a reinforcement on the left of the 1st (Guards) Brigade in conditions of mist and torrential rain. Their adversary was the right flank of the German 25th Reserve Infantry Brigade, which was advancing in a south-easterly direction towards the village of Vendresse, between the hamlets of Chivy and Troyon. These small hamlets were little more than a collection of buildings, which today are even smaller. Soon the mist lifted and two artillery batteries numbered 46 and 113, in a position to the south-west of Vendresse, were able to check the German advance with their accurate fire. Once the advance was slowed the 2/Welch and 1/South Wales Borderers of the 3rd Brigade moved north-west against a high ridge which sheltered the village of Chivy. The SWB's progress was impaired by dense woods but the 2nd Welch had a simpler task as they approached through open ground and dug themselves in on the south-eastern slopes of the Beaulne Spur. Beaulne was a small village to the south-west of Chivy. The SWB were to the rear of the Welch Regiment between Chivy and Beaulne.

The enemy began to counter-attack on the right of the British line and successfully drove the 2nd Brigade and 1st (Guards) Brigade of the 1st Division back from the sugar factory near Troyon to the west of Chivy. The Germans thus exposed the right of the 1st Cameron Highlanders, who were with the 1st (Guards) Brigade upon whom the Germans were then able to turn a devastating machine-gun fire. Later in the day, however, the 2nd Welch were able to capture over a hundred prisoners as well as a machine gun.

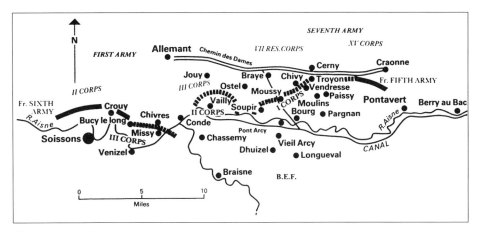

The Aisne battlefield

In a newspaper account dated 24 November 1914 L. Cpl. Fuller of the 2nd Welch described the events of the morning of 14 September:

We were supposed to be the advance party for the South Wales Borderers, but instead formed a bit to the left and made an advance ourselves. We marched from a wood in the direction of a ridge, and on the way we came across a wire fence.

Instead of waiting to use our wire-cutters, Captain Haggard pulled one of the posts out, and we continued our advance to the top of the ridge.

On reaching that point we saw the enemy and Captain Haggard and myself and two other men who were in front, started firing. On proceeding a little further we were faced by a Maxim gun. There was a little wood on the top ‛and a hedge about 50 yards long. It was not long before the men on Captain Haggard's left were both shot, and the man on the right was wounded.

At the same time Captain Haggard was struck in the stomach, and he fell doubled, the shot coming out through his right side. Thus I was the only one uninjured. Our company was met with such an enfilading fire that the right part of the platoon had to retire back and make an attack towards the right.

That left Captain Haggard, myself, and the wounded man below the ridge, and it became necessary for me to carry Captain Haggard back to cover.

This was done by him putting his right arm around my neck, while I had my right arm under his legs and the left under his neck. I was only from 10 to 20 yards behind him when he was shot, and as he fell he cried 'Stick it, Welch!'

With the shots buzzing around us I bandaged him, the while our fellows were mowing down the Germans, and Captain Haggard asked me to lift up his head so that he could see our big guns firing at the Germans as they were retiring from the wood. . . .

Haggard, in charge of B Company, had made a solo advance to the top of the ridge and on seeing the German Maxim, which had already caused much havoc, he shouted out to his men to, 'fix bayonets'. Haggard then shot and killed three Germans who were serving the gun but not surprisingly in view of the odds he was soon hit. The air was full of rifle and machine-gun bullets and shrapnel shells were bursting among the Welshmen.

It was some time before Fuller was able to set off to try and rescue his wounded Captain and he risked being killed by shrapnel, rifle or machine-gune fire. Fuller dressed his officer's wounds as well as he could, and then removed his kit to make it easier for him to lift Haggard's body. Even then they had to wait for about an hour as conditions were too hazardous. Finally they set off when enemy fire slackened. Eventually an officer, Lt. Melvin and a Private called Snooks came to Fuller's assistance and the three men got Haggard to a barn which adjoined a farmhouse that was being used as a dressing station. This was about three quarters of a mile from the spot where Haggard had been wounded. The barn, used as a temporary hospital, was later flattened by German shelling. In his account Fuller also mentions two other officers, Lt. the Hon. Fitzroy Somerset and Lt. Richards, being treated there before they were taken away by ambulance. Here Fuller helped with the patients but also became temporarily responsible for sixty women and children from the neighbourhood who were sheltering in the farmhouse. This building was soon to be destroyed along with the barn and the other farm buildings.

It seems that Fuller was almost an orderly to Capt. Haggard and spoke of him with the highest regard and admiration. It was a great shame that Haggard's wounds were so serious. He had been shot in the stomach at about 10.30 hours on the 14th and died the next day at 16.30 hours. His last words were, 'Stick it, Welch', a phrase he had always used to encourage his men in times of danger and on the march. He was buried at night in Vendresse and the burial service was read by Col. Morland of the 2nd Welch.

A few days later during the night of 20/21 September according to the *Official History*, the posts of the Welch and South Wales Borderers of the 3rd Brigade were withdrawn from their advanced positions at the head of the Chivy Valley. They were moved to a less-exposed position on a spur to the south of the village. Free access to the valley was therefore available to the enemy but any German advance would lead them into trouble especially with British artillery. On the 25th the Welch assisted the SWB in repelling an enemy attack – this is the last mention of their involvement in the Battle of the Aisne.

Capt. Mark Haggard was a nephew of Henry Rider Haggard, the novelist who lived in Ditchingham near Bungay in Suffolk. Mark came from Kirby Bedon a couple of miles from Ditchingham. On 18 September, three days after Mark died of his wounds, his uncle wrote the following in his diary:

Capt. Mark Haggard

> I have just heard over the telephone from my daughter Angie that her brother-in-law, my nephew Mark Haggard, died of wounds on the 15th. It is a great shock for I was very fond of him. He was a good officer and a very gallant man. He said before he left that never would he live to be taken prisoner by the Germans. Well, he has not lived. All honour to him who has died the 'best and the greatest of deaths'. But his poor young wife, whose marriage I attended not a year ago! [Mark had married Doris Elizabeth Vaughan, a daughter of Colonel J. Edwards Vaughan of Rheola, near Neath.]

A week later Rider Haggard wrote again in his diary:

> I have heard more details of Mark's death, supplied to his mother by an officer of his regiment, Lieutenant Somerset, who was in the next bed to him at the hospital in France. [That is, the barn near Vendresse.] It seems that he got ahead of his men and killed three gunners serving the gun, he was charging with his own hand and was then struck down . . .

'A few weeks later Fuller himself was to be wounded on 29 October in the Battle of Gheluvelt in Belgium. In a Welsh newspaper he described what happened: 'We were advancing across a mangold field when a shrapnel burst hit a comrade named Tagg, an officer's servant, who was wounded in the leg. I stopped to bandage him up, and was just getting a safety pin to hold up the bandage when over came half-a-dozen shrapnel shells in succession.'

Fuller was wounded in his right side and a bullet travelled up his body and lodged behind his neck. He was sent home and was taken to Manchester Hospital. When he returned to Swansea, his home town in South Wales, he went into the local hospital for an operation where the bullet in his body was discovered. He kept it as a souvenir.

On 7 November Henry Rider Haggard wrote more about his nephew in his diary: 'In the papers appears a statement from Lance-Corporal Fuller, who, it seems, carried Mark back from the trenches. He describes him as "a brave man and a fighting soldier from his head to his feet." He adds, "He never complained of his wounds. Always he said he was alright."'

Fuller's VC was gazetted on 23 November and although Swansea was not his birthplace he was claimed by the people as their own VC. He was, in fact, the first Welshman to win the medal in the First World War. He lived at Charles Court, which was in the front of Jones' Terrace. Fuller had been spending the evening at the opening of the Free Soldiers' and Sailors' Club at the Albert Hall in Swansea. He was unaware of the impending award and naturally became 'the hero of the evening'. In the rush to congratulate him his bandaged right arm was slightly injured. He still had a month's sick leave to spend at home but was also called upon by the authorities to help with recruiting. When asked about his heroic act, Fuller told a local reporter, 'What I did anyone else would have done in my place.'

Rider Haggard had a visit from the artist Caton Woodville on 5 January 1915. He required background information for a large drawing that would illustrate Mark's rescue and which would be published in the *Illustrated London News*. Eight days later Haggard had another visitor, this time Cpl. Fuller himself who had just received his VC from the King at Buckingham Palace. The following describes Rider Haggard's version of the talk with Fuller:

> He described Mark as a man who would 'fetch you a clout' if you didn't do what he told you . . . a circumstance which seemed to endear him to Fuller. He says that there was no hand-to-hand struggle between Mark and the Germans, so as such a struggle is clearly described by others, I can only suppose that either Fuller did not see it or that it occurred elsewhere. The study of the hero at home is rather amusing, for it appears that in private life Fuller is interested in breeding canaries, and he has no yearning desire to return to mingle in the joy of battle. In short, he seems to have had enough of it, and informed me that his nerve is not what it was, nor his weight either. Like myself he has been enjoying the influenza, and lay awake all last night at the lodging which was given him at Scotland Yard, coughing as I do, with this difference, that there, as he remarked pathetically, he was not allowed to spit. He showed me his Victoria Cross, which he had just received from the King, in a little white cardboard box, but objected that they had put Corporal Fuller on the back of it, when at the time of Mark's rescue he was Private. [In fact Fuller had been made up to Lance-Corporal on the morning of 14 September.]

Although Fuller assisted in the recruiting drive as a Sergeant, his military career did not last much longer. His last day in the Army was 31 December 1915 when he was judged unfit for future military service. He was to receive a pension of £10 a year made to all holders of the VC.

William (Bill) Fuller was born at Newbridge, Laugharne, Carmarthenshire, West Wales on 24 March 1884, the son of William and Mary Fuller. The family moved to Swansea when William junior was about four years old. He attended at Rutland Street School, which was later destroyed in the Blitz, and Swansea Truant School which no longer exists. Fuller was inclined to play truant. His father was a sailor and later a prominent local butcher. On 31 December 1902 Fuller enlisted in the Welch Regiment, and served in South Africa and India. He was discharged to the Reserve and recalled at the outbreak of war. In 1909 he married Mary Elizabeth Philips at Swansea, and became caretaker at the Elysium Cinema in High Street, Swansea. Previously he had worked as a timber handler at John Lewis and Sons, a local timber merchant. By August 1914 he and his wife had two children, aged four and thirteen months. He went to France with the BEF on 11 August.

One day in 1915 when he was home from the war he visited a circus at Fishguard. News of his presence reached the proprietor who challenged him to appear in the same cage as the circus lions. Fuller accepted the challenge, took off his cap and walked fearlessly into the cage where he stroked the lions' heads, while chatting to the trainer. He was presented with a gold medal and used the occasion to appeal for more recruits for the Army.

Haggard's widow had presented Fuller with a Hunter watch while the inhabitants of West Wales contributed to a gift of Exchequer Bonds at Tenby in 1916. It was clear that Fuller was a pretty fearless individual as on 7 June 1938 he saved the lives of two boys who had fallen into the sea, having been marooned on a sandbank near the Slip. Fuller, at some danger to himself, waded into the water fully clothed to save the boys. He received the Royal Humane Society Medal for Lifesaving for this action.

His occupation after the First World War was as proprietor of a horse-drawn fish cart in Swansea. He was a well-known personality at Swansea Docks. He also liked to breed greyhounds as a pastime. He also used to take a regular part in Armistice Day commemorations – he was Swansea's only VC holder.

In the Second World War he served as an air-raid warden in Swansea. In 1969 there was a report in the *Swansea Evening Post* that the 85-year-old VC holder along with his 81-year-old wife were not fit enough to attend a ceremony at Cardiff Castle. The two regiments that were to take part in the big parade were the Welch Regiment and the South Wales Borderers. On 11 June they were to amalgamate into The Royal Regiment of Wales. The Prince of Wales, as Colonel-in-Chief was to present the colours to the 1st Battalion.

On 29 December 1974 Bill Fuller died at his home 55 Westbury Street, Swansea aged ninety. He left four daughters as well as several grandchildren. After a small private service at his home he was buried at Oystermouth Cemetery, The Mumbles, Swansea on 2 January 1975. More than a hundred

mourners attended the ceremony and the coffin was draped with the Union Jack on which were placed his medals, military belt and cap. The coffin was carried from his house by members of the 3rd and 4th Battalions of The Royal Regiment of Wales. The cortège had a police escort through the streets of Swansea and 'The Last Post' was played by a bugler of the 3rd Battalion. Fuller's grave, which at the time of writing is still unmarked, is numbered as 373 Section R.

In 1984 the curator of the Welch Regiment Museum wrote to Fuller's family as it was thought that it was time that his unmarked grave at Oystermouth had a memorial erected on it. The regiment was willing to contribute to the costs of such a memorial. Apparently the museum had written to Fuller's grandson but he had recently died and his mother, one of Fuller's daughters, 'didn't want to know'.

Meanwhile the regiment decided in 1985 not to pursue the matter as Fuller had been commemorated in the Regimental Chapel at Llandaff Cathedral and at The Welch Regiment Museum. One cannot believe that Fuller's grave will remain unmarked for ever.

Besides the VC, Fuller's other medals included the 1914 Star with clasp, and the British War and Victory Medals. He later received the George VIth and Queen Elizabeth 2nd Coronation Medals of 1937 and 1953 respectively. The regiment also wished to acquire Fuller's medals. They are presumably still with his family.

Mark Haggard is commemorated in the village church at Ditchingham, and in Shipdham, Norfolk. His name is listed on two other war memorials in Wales at Rosolven in the Neath Valley and at Ammanford.

W.H. JOHNSTON
Missy, France, 14 September

W.H. Johnston (second left) is presented with the Victoria Cross by the King, 3 December 1914

Under very heavy fire the 5th Division continued its efforts to cross the River Aisne during the night of 13/14 September between the bridges at Venizel to the east and Missy to the west. The bridges at these two crossings had not yet been adequately repaired by the Royal Engineers. In addition, at night the Germans were using strong searchlights to illuminate the scene.

On 13 September the 14th Brigade (5th Div.) had crossed the river between the Venizel and Missy bridges, close to a mill called the Moulin des Roches, and made progress on a line from St Marguerite to Missy. The 15th Brigade attempted to link up with them. All day on the 14th men and ammunition were taken across the swollen river on rafts. In places the Aisne was 170 feet wide and in the middle it was often as deep as 15 feet. On the return journeys from the north bank the wounded were brought back on the rafts.

On 14 September 1914 no fewer than four Victoria Crosses were won in the Aisne battle. One of them went to a member of the 59th Field Coy. Royal Engineers, Capt. W.H. Johnston, who together with Lt. R.B. Flint worked all day until 19.00 hours, in ferrying men from the 15th Brigade over the Aisne, at the Moulin des Roches. The two men had worked from dawn to dusk carrying out this crucial work under heavy fire. During the afternoon German Howitzers (8 inch and 5.9s) came into play from the strongly held north bank. Throughout the day the area had become a deathtrap from the German guns on the opposite heights, which rose as high as 400 feet. The situation on the north bank became untenable and on the 15th the men had to be brought back. Flint was awarded the Distinguished Service Order (DSO) for his role. He was killed the following year in January 1915. He was also mentioned in despatches.

The 3rd Division had crossed the river to the right of Missy at Vailly and the 4th at Venizel to the left. It was important that the gap between these two divisions should be filled as soon as possible. The 14th Brigade were to remain

Capt. Johnston ferrying men across the River Aisne

between St Marguerite and Missy, until Fort de Condé was in British hands. The fort overlooked the British advance to the north-east. All this took place down stream from Missy and today the site of the Moulin des Roches is close to a large factory complex. The real progress of the day, however, occurred to the right where Sir Douglas Haig's 1 Corps was advancing between Chavonne and Moulins on the north bank of the river.

Johnston's Victoria Cross was published in the *London Gazette* on 25 November and he was presented with the medal at General Headquarters, France, by the King. A photograph of the ceremony shows Johnston towering above the King in height. In the War Office file WO32/4993 there is a query regarding Johnston from the War Office to Sir John French which asks, 'What were the operations around Missy which more show how far his actions would contribute to success?'

In March 1915 Capt. Johnston was appointed to the command of 172nd Company and on 2 May became Brigade Major of the 15th Brigade. He was given his Brevet for this rank on 3 June but was killed only five days later.

Johnston was an infantryman at heart and had a strong contempt for enemy fire. He was killed by a sniper on the St Eloi front on 8 June 1915. It may be that his audacity and his height contributed to his death. He was buried at Perth

Cemetery (China Wall), Zillebeke, Plot 111, Row C, Grave 12, to the south of Hooge. It was a premature end for a man who was clearly a brilliant soldier and who would have progressed far in the Army hierarchy.

William Henry Johnston was born at Leith on 21 December 1879 and was the son of Major William Johnston (RA). He entered the Royal Military Academy at Woolwich and was awarded a commission in the Royal Engineers on 23 March 1899. He went overseas to Gibraltar where he spent five years working in Intelligence. He had been made a Lieutenant on 19 November 1901. When he returned to England he was employed in the Survey Department. In 1908 he left this position for service in China, as a GSO where he was made up to Captain on 23 March 1908. He served in China for three years, and travelling widely, was once more working in Intelligence. He was also involved in surveying the boundary between China and the recently acquired New Territories of the Colony of Hong Kong. In 1911 Johnston worked in South China. At the end of July 1912 he returned to England to work in the War Office for eleven months, this time in the Geographical Section. He entered Staff College in 1913 and began his course there in January 1914.

At the beginning of the war he joined 59th Field Company and went out to France with the BEF in August 1914 taking part in the retreat from Mons, where he was in charge of a mounted section of the company. Here his section was responsible for building a pontoon bridge over the Haine in order to allow infantry to retire. His colleague, Lt. Flint was responsible for blowing up a bridge in the same area on 23 August 1914. A couple of days later the company was involved in infantry fighting for the first time. At 07.15 hours on the 26th the men were assembled outside their billets at Reumont, near Le Cateau and were about to move off when their Commanding Officer, Maj. Walker was summoned to a meeting at 14th Brigade HQ at Le Cateau.

Meanwhile, Johnston went into the town briefly in order to look out materials suitable for shelter. He also searched for Brigade HQ but was unable to find it. He and his party did, however, meet up with the enemy when a German ammunition column dashed up the road from Le Cateau and went through the company's lines, causing some confusion. The company then assisted 19th Brigade which was on the right flank of the 5th Division. A few hours later they too joined in the retreat, and their tasks from then on until reaching the Aisne consisted mainly of blowing up bridges.

After Johnston's death Count Gleichen wrote of him in his memoirs *The Doings of the Fifteenth Infantry Brigade*:

> He never spared himself an ounce. He was occasionally so nearly dead with want of sleep that I once or twice ordered him to take a night's sleep; but he always got out of it on some pretext or other . . . he seemed to like getting shot at. One night he got a ricochet bullet over his heart, but this only put him in a furious rage . . . he was a wonderful fellow all round, always full of expedients and never disheartened by the cruel collapse of his plans by the wet weather.

Johnston had married on 6 June 1897 at Emmanuel Church, Attercliffe, Sheffield. His wife was Mary Florence Edwards, daughter of Thomas Edwards. They had two sons, born in 1903 and 1907 respectively. After the war Johnston was commemorated at St Luke's in Kew Gardens, Surrey. It was here that his parents lived in a house called Hurstleigh. His Victoria Cross is in the Museum of the Royal Engineers at Chatham, Kent. He was mentioned in despatches on four occasions.

G. WILSON

Near Verneuil, France, 14 September

The 2nd Highland Light Infantry of the 5th Infantry Brigade was part of the 2nd Division. It participated briefly in the fighting at Mons in August 1914 and a few days later at Etreux where the men were involved in repairing roads. On 14 September during the main Battle of the Aisne, the HLI was involved in the fighting in a line roughly parallel to the Oise and Aisne Canal, with the village of Braye to the north-west and Moussy Verneuil to the south-east.

The 1st Royal Berks and 1st King's Royal Rifle Corps of the 6th Brigade were pushed back by the Germans to a position abreast of Beaulne, a small village to the south-west of Chivy, which was just under half a mile from Moussy-Verneuil. However the KRRC was then reinforced by men of the 2nd Worcestershires and 2nd HLI of the 5th Brigade who were able to stem the German advance until the British artillery in the form of 46 and 113 Batteries, began to operate. Later in the day, according to the *Official Historian*, these three battalions were able to advance up the eastern slopes of the Beaulne Spur, where they managed to hold on.

During this period of fighting a remarkable deed of heroism took place. The two companies of the KRRC fell back and were then assisted by the Worcesters and the HLI who with the KRRC then went forward to try and take a small wood near Moussy-Verneuil in which the Germans had established a machine gun. This attack by the British left an exposed left flank on the edge of the wood. The enemy then proceeded to take a heavy toll of the HLI and the KRRC. It was at this stage that Pte. George Wilson (HLI) took a hand in the battle.

At Verneuil, adjacent to Moussy the 2nd HLI came into action for the first time since Mons according to Pte. Wilson. They had been involved for an hour only when he spied a couple of Germans and informed his officer. The officer was incredulous and took up his glasses to take a closer look but he was shot dead immediately. Wilson quickly avenged his killing by taking aim and shooting the two Germans. He then advanced about a hundred yards and saw eight more

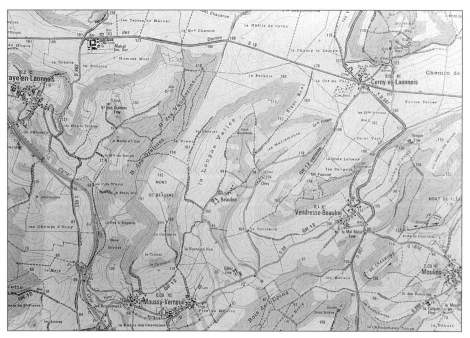

Moussy-Verneuil, 14 September

Germans. He charged them at once making noises as though he was accompanied by a strong group. The Germans immediately surrendered and in doing so gave up two prisoners from the Middlesex Regiment. Wilson shouted for assistance and handed over the captured Germans. It was then when he was going forward that he came across the scores of wounded and dead who had previously been part of the attacking left flank and who had been caught by German machine-gun fire. Wilson was so incensed by the terrible massacre that he virtually went berserk and together with a volunteer from the KRRC he set out to destroy the German machine-gun position. After only a hundred yards Wilson's colleague was shot dead by the machine gun. Wilson took steady aim and killed the machine gunner, his third German that day. In fact, Wilson wiped out the whole of the enemy position by his careful and accurate shooting until he got as close as 10 yards from the gun. At this point the officer in charge of the Maxim emptied his revolver in the direction of the Highlander but missed. It was a costly error as Wilson quickly plunged his bayonet into him and killed him. But even then Wilson was not satisfied and turned the gun round against the enemy and fired 750 rounds. Throughout this time he was a victim of heavy shellfire which eventually forced him back to his own lines where he promptly fainted. When he came round he discovered that no one had thought of retrieving the

'One man against seven – how a Highlander won the Victoria Cross'

Maxim so he set off again to bring back the gun. It took two more trips to carry back the remaining two and a half cases of ammunition as well. He still had once more task to carry out and this was to fetch the body of his colleague from the KRRC who had been shot seventeen times. Wilson's action must rank as one of the most effective and courageous in the early months of the First World War.

Pte. Wilson wrote out his account by hand and gave it to Lt. Col. J.C. Jameson, the Commanding Officer of the Field Ambulance to which he was sent after being wounded in the action. On the same day Lt. Sir Archibald Gibson Craig, Wilson's platoon commander, was killed leading his platoon in an attack on another machine gun.

Wilson's Victoria Cross was gazetted on 5 December, although he had received it already from the King who visited the regiment on 3 December. There is a note in the War Office file WO32/4993 that Wilson's name had been accidentally omitted from the list of those recommended for the VC – but the omission did not last for long. Unfortunately Wilson was wounded more seriously later, and then gassed and wounded once more at Loos. He was subsequently discharged from the Army in 1916 and resumed his former occupation of selling newspapers in the streets of Edinburgh. He was known as the 'Newsboy VC'.

George Wilson was born in Edinburgh on 29 April 1886 and joined the Army as a Private. He was a small man in stature and the war wore him out and he never fully recovered. The Lord Provost of Edinburgh discovered that he was not at all

well and offered him employment on a farm in order to build up his health and strength. He also arranged for him to work with the Edinburgh Corporation. Despite this assistance Wilson's life continued to be burdensome. He became dependent on alcohol and in order to raise extra cash he tried to pawn his VC for £5 which was then the equivalent of two weeks' wages. Local shopkeepers were sympathetic to the 'fallen hero'. He used to live in an area called The Close, which was a small alley of tenements off the Lawnmarket in the poorer part of Edinburgh. 'Lawn' was a type of fine fabric made from flax. The site has been replaced with student residences.

Wilson died a few days short of his fortieth birthday on 22 April 1926 at Craigleith Hospital (now the Royal Victoria). He became another victim of the First World War, only seven years after it came to an end. Craigleith Hospital at that time was a tuberculosis (TB) hospital. George Wilson was buried at Piershill Cemetery, Edinburgh, on 25 April with full military honours, consisting of a single piper and a small bearer party. The comparative lack of ceremony prompted a spate of letters in the Scottish Press.

He was the first Edinburgh man to gain the VC in the First World War and it was the highlight of an otherwise tragic life.

His medals are held by the Royal Highland Fusiliers.

R. TOLLERTON

Aisne, France, 14 September

On 8 September the 1st Cameron Highlanders had been involved in the forcing of Le Petit Morin as their contribution to the counter-offensive in the Battle of the Marne. They had replaced the 2nd Royal Munster Fusiliers in the 1st (Guards) Brigade in the 1st Division. The Munsters had virtually been annihilated at Etreux during a rearguard action on 27 August.

A few days later on 14 September the Cameron Highlanders were heavily involved in the Battle of the Aisne. Their day began at Paissy where they had breakfast at 04.00 hours before moving off through Moulins and into the village of Vendresse from which they advanced uphill in a north-easterly direction to their battle positions. The 1st Black Watch was to their right and the 1st Scots Guards to their left. Behind the three battalions was the 1st Coldstream Guards, at Vendresse, who advanced later.

The aim of the 1st (Guards) Brigade was to fight its way to the Chemin des Dames, the main highway which ran parallel to the Aisne Valley and which dominated it. Once captured the Allies would have command of the country between Berry-au-Bac to the east and Soissons to the west. At this time the ridge was held by the Germans. The brigade was supported to the right by 2nd Brigade who were to be heavily involved in the fight for possession of the sugar factory at Troyon. The factory was just south of Cerny crossroads and was nearer the latter than Troyon. The ruins of the factory can still be seen today. Troyon itself was merely a small hamlet and today is little more than a collection of farm buildings. The village of Chivy was to the south-west of the 1st (Guards) Brigade's position.

The morning of 14 September was very wet and misty. The enemy endeavoured to push back the British 2nd Brigade at the sugar factory, and in doing so they managed to expose the right flank of the 1st Cameron Highlanders upon which the Germans concentrated a withering machine-gun fire. This resulted in losses of 600 officers and men. No. 7281 Pte. Ross Tollerton had been in a reserve position and advanced with part of B Company under Lt. Matheson in support of A Company. They managed to reach the three haystacks which are frequently mentioned in accounts of the action, to the south of Troyon and attacked in a north-westerly direction. Shell and machine-gun fire was very heavy.

Matheson was now in control of his platoon and of a large section of A Company. But in the act of getting up off the soft ground he was shot and fell flat on his face. He could not move and was nearly suffocated because his nose pressed down into the mud. He signalled to Tollerton to move him onto his back but this was not possible. The Private had words with L. Sgt. Geddes who helped to get the officer onto Tollerton's back, although he was shot dead through the head in doing so. Tollerton, who was over 6 foot in height, carried the officer back to a place of safety. He then returned to the fighting but was soon wounded in the hand and head. The order to retire was given and Tollerton returned to Lt. Matheson's side to try and carry him back to the British lines.

The enemy, however, surrounded them and Tollerton had to bide his time until he had the opportunity to carry the wounded man to safety. It was three days before Tollerton thought it safe enough to move when he saw the Germans retreating. During this time shells had been continually whistling overhead and Matheson was hit once more by a shrapnel bullet. His main wounds were now in his head and back. During this time the two men had enough water but quickly ran out of food and all Tollerton could find when searching bodies nearby were cigarettes. A short time later he saw some British soldiers digging a trench and made contact with them. They arranged for a stretcher to be brought for the officer while Tollerton was directed to a dressing station.

The records of the Cameron Highlanders describe where the incident took place in the following way: 'Half B and part of C Companies crossed the eastern part of the Chivy Valley and moved northwards up on to the small spur which divides it from the western branch . . . '

It was on this small Chivy Valley spur that Matheson was wounded. His wounds were dressed in the village of Chivy but by this time he was very weak. It soon became clear that his spinal cord was badly damaged. His clothes were cut from his body and he was subsequently put into a French ambulance and transported by train to Paris where he was admitted to an American hospital.

A few days later the 1st Cameron Highlanders moved up to relieve the Black Watch in the trenches to the west of the village of Beaulne. A shell hit the top of the cave in a quarry where Battalion Headquarters was situated and buried the staff. A couple of the men were rescued but the shelling was too heavy for a prompt rescue attempt and it was not until evening that a party of Royal Engineers was able to dig out the bodies. Five officers were killed including Capt. Miers, the acting Commanding Officer, Capt. A.G. Cameron of Lochiel, Lt. N. Cameron and Lt. Meiklejohn. Meanwhile, seventeen officers had become casualties on the 14th. In addition thirty other ranks were killed in the Battalion HQ disaster.

Pte. Tollerton was invalided home and returned to Irvine to recover from his wounds – one in the hand caused by a bullet and another on his scalp on the crown of the head. He had lain wounded for a day and a night before being sent to a dressing station. Seven months later on 19 April his VC was gazetted for saving Matheson's life. The medal was presented to the kilted Highlander by the King at a ceremony attended by 50,000 people on Glasgow Green in Scotland on 18 May 1915.

Tollerton continued to serve in the regiment until the war ended in November 1918, by which time he had been made up to Sergeant. When he came back to Irvine by train, a horse and landau awaited him to take him to the local landmark named the Cross. However, such was the enthusiasm of the crowd that they unhitched the horse and a willing band of volunteers hauled the carriage together with its passenger up the hill.

Ross Tollerton was born in Hurlford, Ayr, Scotland on 6 May 1890. While still a child he moved to Irvine and was educated at Laurieknowe Primary School which was originally Maxwelltown School. The name was changed when the new school, Maxwelltown High School, was built.

It was always Tollerton's ambition to join the Army. He was the son of James Tollerton, a Sergeant in the Police, and brother of R.S.M. Jas. Tollerton, also of the 1st Cameron Highlanders. He enlisted in 1905 and served with the regiment for seven years. In 1906 he was sent to South Africa and later served in Hong King, North China and India. In 1912 he was placed on reserve and worked in the Irvine Shipyard. He was recalled at the outbreak of war in August 1914, and posted to the Queen's Own Cameron Highlanders. In May 1915 he visited Montgomery School, Irvine, which he might have attended along with Harry Ranken who also won a VC on the Aisne. The children were delighted at the visit and even more delighted with a half-day holiday from their studies.

When he was demobilized Tollerton joined a Territorial unit, the Irvine Company of the Royal Scots Fusiliers and became its Company Sergeant Major. Later he worked as janitor at Bank Street School. After his death it was alleged that his ghost used to haunt the school buildings. The school was subsequently demolished and houses were built on the site.

About 2,000 men from the town of Irvine served in the First World War and 238 of them died. When the town war memorial was unveiled in April 1921 Tollerton laid the first wreath upon it.

In 1930 Tollerton became ill and died on 7 May 1931 after an illness which lasted several months. It is certain that his war experiences contributed to his premature death at the age of forty-one. At the time of his death his home address was No. 15 High Street, Irvine. His military funeral

Memorial at Knadgerhill Cemetery, erected to the memory of Sgt. Tollerton

took place on 9 May where a bearer party, a firing party, pipers and buglers were supplied by the Royal Scots Fusiliers. There were many wreaths including one from Maj. J.S.M. Matheson, the man whose life Tollerton had saved sixteen years before. The funeral took place at Knadgerhill Cemetery and was a very impressive affair. The pavements from Irvine High Street to the cemetery were crowded with the sad townspeople. The coffin, covered with a Union Jack, was taken on a gun carriage to the cemetery with the boy pipers playing 'The Land O' the Leal'. Tollerton's father then aged seventy-eight also took part in the procession.

One obituary described Tollerton as having a fine military carriage as well as exceptional strength. In addition he was friendly, sociable and very modest.

On 11 September 1932 a memorial was unveiled to Sgt. Tollerton's memory at Knadgerhill Cemetery and despite severe stormy weather over 3,000 people turned out for the ceremony. Brig. Gen. J.W. Walker gave the address. The memorial was erected by the British Legion and the people of Irvine, and took the form of a rustic obelisk of silver-grey Creetown granite. The Tollerton family, including Ross's widow who wore her late husband's medals, was present at the

Tollerton Drive

ceremony. Wreaths were laid and a firing party was supplied by the Royal Scots Fusiliers. Apart from the VC Tollerton had also been awarded the 1914 Star (with clasp), the BWM and the VM. His medals are held by The Queen's Own Highlanders.

Maj. J.S.M. Matheson of Alchany, Lairg, Sutherlandshire died in February 1933, less than two years after Tollerton. He was a prominent landowner. He had obtained his commission in the Cameronians in 1900 and served in the South African War. His medals included the Queen's Medal and five clasps.

The town of Irvine also became associated with another man who won the VC early in the First World War. This was Capt. H.S. Ranken RAMC, son of the local minister. Both Tollerton and Ranken are commemorated locally with streets named Tollerton Drive and Ranken Drive. Tollerton Drive consists of council houses close to playing fields but today although some of the houses have well-tended gardens, many houses are boarded up. This part of the town was built to receive overspill from the slums of Glasgow.

E.G. HORLOCK

Vendresse, France, 15 September

On 14 September the 3rd Brigade of the 1st Division was sent by the Divisional Commander to support the left flank of the 1st (Guards) Brigade In mid-morning it found itself on the eastern flank of the German 25th Reserve Infantry Brigade. The enemy was pushing in a south-easterly direction towards the village of Vendresse, between the small hamlets of Chivy and Troyon. The early morning mist was lifting and the 46th and 113th artillery batteries unlimbered to the south-west of Vendresse, close to the village of Moussy, in a quarry where there were several batteries already in position. They opened fire with deadly effect. The range was about 900 yards and considerable slaughter was inflicted upon the enemy. Not surprisingly the German advance was checked and two machine guns were damaged and eventually captured. The 2nd Welch and 1st South Wales Borderers of the 3rd Brigade 1st Division were thus clear to attack the enemy in a north-westerly direction. It was during this fighting that Pte. Fuller gained the Victoria Cross when attempting to save the life of Capt. Mark Haggard (see earlier chapter). The weather had been very wet and misty and the British had to fight an enemy who concentrated hard on pushing the British back to the River Aisne.

The next day, 15 September, witnessed a series of savage German counter-attacks. It was on that day that No. 42617 Bombardier Ernest George Horlock, a member of the 113th Battery of XXV Brigade RFA won the VC for his gallantry under heavy shellfire. Despite being wounded he returned twice to lay his gun, after having his wounds dressed, although he had been ordered by the Medical Officer to go to hospital. By the end of the day the British line had been consolidated but the positions of the 4th and 5th Divisions were still precarious.

Two days later Horlock was promoted to the rank of Sergeant by the General Officer Commanding 1st Division for 'gallantry in the field'. The Royal Artillery Institution has some notes on the life and career of Bombardier Horlock. These were published in the book *The VC and DSO* by O'Moore Creagh and E.M. Humphris. They are as follows:

Bombardier E.G. Horlock returned twice to lay his gun despite being wounded

We were in action in an open field, and it was hot, I can tell you. Jack Johnsons and shrapnel. When a Jack Johnson burst in the ground there was a shrapnel shell burst overhead simultaneously and they kept on coming. Then one burst right under Horlock's gun, and that shell fell in two, clean, and killed No. 1. Horlock got splinters in his right thigh, not severe, you know, just enough to keep him in hospital for two or three weeks; so he went to the dressing station, and the doctor dressed him and told him to go in the ambulance and go to hospital. Well, Horlock goes outside, but he doesn't look for any ambulance, but comes back to the battery. Hang me, he hadn't been there five minutes before he got hit in the back. Down he walked once more to the dressing station, and the doctor wanted to know why he hadn't gone to hospital. Horlock says he couldn't see the ambulance; so when he was dressed the doctor puts him in charge of an orderly, and says that as he was able to walk to his battery, he can . . . well walk to the hospital. So the pair set out, but Horlock pointed out to the orderly casualties who wanted the orderly's attention more than he did, and if the orderly went back to the dressing station he could find his way all right. The orderly agreed about it, but says to Horlock, 'No jokes, mind, or you'll get me into trouble. You go straight to the hospital.' Horlock said, 'Good morning,' and then changed the doctor's words around, and thought if he could . . . walk to the hospital he could just as easily go back to the old 113th. So back he came again, and he hadn't been with us five minutes before he got some splinters in his arms. It was rotten luck, and he was afraid to go back to the doctor again, so he just stayed there till he went out of action in the evening. Some of our officers saw the doctor that night and told him about Horlock, and then they had him down and reprimanded him. But I think that they had their tongues in their cheeks when they did it . . .

Horlock's VC was gazetted on 25 November and he was presented with it by the King at General Headquarters in France on 3 December. He was awarded his Sergeant's stripes on the same occasion – these became known as The King's Stripes.

The Royal Regiment of Artillery had a tremendous record in the early months of the war and the infantry came to have considerable faith in their gunner colleagues. Horlock was one of eight artillerymen to gain the VC within a short space of three weeks in 1914.

In August 1915 he returned to his home in Langrish in Hampshire and was given a very enthusiastic reception both in Langrish and in Petersfield, a nearby larger town. At Petersfield station he was met by his family and by members of the Urban Council and was driven to his home in a motor car. The next day he was driven in a decorated motor car with his parents from their home in Langrish and met by members of the local council together with members of the Horlock family. He took his seat in an open carriage and the whole procession moved off to the Square. There was a bugle band and many local organizations took part. The Guard of Honour was supplied by members of the local Police Force, and a gaily decorated truck had been drawn up into which Horlock and his parents were ushered as it was to serve as a platform. Horlock's war record was read out to the cheering crowd and a purse containing £20 was presented to the local hero. Horlock thanked the Chairman of the Urban Council for his kind gift and used the occasion to drum up support for the war effort. The procession then re-formed and the Horlock carriage was taken to Langrish where it drew up at the local post office. This time the local Vicar, the Revd H.L. Bashford, made a long speech of welcome to which Horlock replied. The proceedings ended with the National Anthem. A few days later Horlock was given another official reception in East Meon, a nearby village, where a presentation took place in the grounds of the local vicarage. The soldier and his family were installed on a wagonette and taken to a platform which had been especially erected. Lord and Lady Peel were to take part along with the deputy vicar. Lord Peel made a stirring speech praising Horlock and his deeds and mentioned the local contribution to the war effort. Horlock was then asked to step forward for a presentation. The gift was a gold signet ring which had been subscribed to by the local inhabitants. The outside of the ring was inscribed EM which stood for East Meon, and on the inside the inscription was E.G. Horlock, 113th Battery, RFA, VC. The ring was placed on Horlock's wedding finger. Before the ceremony finished a reference was made to the fact that there were still some young men in the village who ought to join up.

Horlock had been treated like royalty for a few days and went back to his unit the next day. The whole welcome home period had been a very light-hearted affair but once again a winner of the nation's highest military honour had been used for propaganda purposes.

Horlock served with 113 Battery until February 1916 when he was promoted and posted to D Battery, 119th Brigade RFA where he was not happy. He thought the battery 'an unruly mob' and was keen to get back to his old battery even if it meant losing his rank. In September 1916, Sgt. Maj. Horlock was sent to Salonika with 301 Brigade SAA Column 60th (London) Division and in July was posted to the Base Depot in Egypt. By now, one of his brothers who had been serving with the Dorset Regiment had died at Kut in the Middle East.

On 13 October 1917 Horlock was married in the town of Littlehampton, Sussex. His bride was Miss Ethel May Hasted of Climping who was described as 'winsome' by a local reporter. Houses and streets were decorated and in the Congregational church the pulpit was covered with a huge Union Jack; there

were also flags hanging from the church galleries. A large body of wounded soldiers, dressed in their hospital blues, was present. When the couple emerged from the church the wounded soldiers formed an archway with their crutches. The reception took place at No. 60 High Street, and the couple left for East Meon for the start of their honeymoon.

Horlock returned to Egypt at the end of November travelling by land to Marseilles where he boarded RMS *Aragon*. On 30 December within 10 miles of Alexandria the ship was hit by two torpedoes and after thirty minutes she capsized and sank. A large number of people were saved by local minesweeping trawlers and torpedo boat destroyers although a destroyer was also torpedoed. Horlock was one of the 610 casualties out of a total number of 2,500 people on board. His body was retrieved and buried at the British Military Cemetery at Hadra, close to Alexandria.

Ernest George Horlock (usually known as George) was born at Beech Farm, Alton, Hampshire, on 24 October 1885. He attended Hartley School near Alton. The family later moved to Langrish and lived in Laundry Cottage. His father worked on the Talbot-Ponsonby Estate and his mother was laundress to the family. He enlisted on 22 February 1904 using the name of Harlock and this was the spelling that the Army used; it is assumed that he tried to join up under the name of Horlock but was rejected. His service records were destroyed in the Second World War

Laundry Cottage

but it is assumed that he probably joined 113 Battery as early as 1907; the Battery had been formed in 1900 in Colchester. He was made up to Bombardier by 1914 and prior to the Battle of the Aisne the battery had been involved in the retreat towards the River Seine. In September, after he had won the VC, he was made up to Sergeant.

In 1920 Mrs Horlock attended the unveiling and dedication of the Royal Artillery Victoria Cross Memorial at the garrison church of St George's, Woolwich. Unfortunately Horlock's name had been left off the memorial but this error was soon rectified and apologies made to Mrs Horlock. The church was hit by a V1 in 1944 but the memorial was saved.

In 1967 attempts were made to find out more about the life of Ernest Horlock and Mrs Horlock was traced by the Royal Artillery. She presented many of her husband's possessions to the 10th (Assaye) Battery and three of her husband's medals, including the mention in despatches on 8 October 1914. This handing over took place at the Napier Barracks, Dortmund. Mrs Horlock flew there for the ceremony; at the age of eighty it was to be her first flight. She was accompanied by her 76-year-old sister. The 10th (Assaye) Battery was formerly the 113th Battery.

A great deal of this short biography would not have been possible without painstaking detective work by Maj. A.S. Hill whose findings were published in *The Gunner* in January 1969.

In 1974 Mrs Horlock of Hillsboro Road, Bognor Regis, gave her husband's VC to the Royal Regiment at a special ceremony. At the luncheon she said, 'I have been told that the Victoria Cross alone would be worth over £2,000 to collectors, but I am not interested in money. My husband was a regular, and very proud of his regiment.'

In 1982 the wording on Horlock's grave was changed. The Commonwealth War Graves Commission had printed his name as Harlock. Horlock is also commemorated at Langrish church in Hampshire.

H.S. RANKEN

Hauteavesnes, France, 19/20 September

After Bombardier Horlock had earned his Victoria Cross on 15 September the next to gain the coveted award was Capt. H.S. Ranken of the RAMC. Unfortunately there is conflicting evidence about his activities in September 1914. He was attached to 1 KRRC and was given the medal of the Chevalier of the Legion of Honour (France) for gallant conduct during the operations of the retreat from Mons in the last part of August.

On 10 September Ranken was at a place called Hauteavesnes which is a few miles to the south-east of Villers Cotterêts. The official VC citation says that he was here on 19 and 20 September tending the wounded in the trenches under rifle and shrapnel fire. Ranken was certainly here according to the battalion *War Diary*. He tended the wounded at Hauteavesnes but ten days earlier than the VC citation records. The simplest explanation is that there was a clerical error at some point which changed 9/10 September to 19/20 September. An alternative suggestion is that the citation should have read 'close to Soupir' on the Aisne and not Hauteavesnes.

The action at Hauteavesnes came at the end of the Battle of the Marne which began on the 6th and ended four days later. The Allied retreat ended on 5 September and the enemy was driven back to the Aisne heights where the Germans made a stand. The 2nd Division History tells the story of the action on 10 September in the following way:

The 1st Royal Berks. (6th Brig. 2nd Div.) were ordered to make good the northern exits of Hauteavesnes, whilst the 50th Battery came into action immediately south-west of the village. The time was about 9.30 a.m. A second column of German infantry was then discovered moving northwards along the Vinly road, evidently acting as rearguard. The guns immediately opened fire at 1,500 yards, and the 1st KRRC at the head of the main guard deployed to attack. The enemy lined the side of the road, which at this point ran through a cutting forming a natural trench. C Company was ordered to attack, starting with their left on the right of 50th Battery, and advanced across an open stubble field to a position about 400 yards in front, on the slope of a hill. B Company was deployed on the left of C Company, and D Company kept in reserve in a sunken lane until another battalion was deployed on our right. As soon as our guns opened fire, the enemy brought four guns into action from high ground just north of Brumetz.

Casualties in the KRRC were four officers wounded, ten other ranks killed and sixty other ranks wounded, whom Ranken tended.

The KRRC *War Diary* (WO9/1358) for 12 September shows that the battalion had got as far as the village of Braine close to the River Aisne. They halted there for an hour in order to obtain supplies and to bury the dead the Germans had left behind after earlier fighting.

On the 14th the battalion left their billets at 03.30 hours and marched via Pont D'Arcy, crossing the Aisne by pontoon bridge near Verneuil. The battalion was then split up with C and B Companies being sent to the right to get in touch with 5th Brigade. A and D Companies were sent to the left of La Bouvette Wood in order to make contact with the 4th Guards Brigade; they thus became flanking units. La Bouvette Wood was to the east of a farm called La Cour de Soupir to the north of the village of Soupir. A and D Companies of the KRRC suffered casualties from German snipers and subsequently re-formed halfway down La Bouvette Wood. They were on the right and their former colleagues, the 1st Irish Guards, were on their left. They advanced through the wood driving the enemy out on the far side. However, they became so far ahead that they were shelled by the British artillery. A little later the Irish Guards retired halfway down the wood and the Rifles followed them, leaving behind them frontal posts. The KRRC spent the next four days very exposed at the edge of La Bouvette Wood, receiving support from 1st Royal Berks. and 2nd O and BLI (of the 2nd Division). Early in the afternoon of the 19th the enemy began to shell the whole line much more vigorously and began a regular attack bringing up infantry and machine guns. Lt. Alston was wounded and while tending him Capt. Ranken had his leg shattered by a shell from the British artillery. Another officer was also hit by a 'friendly' shell but he escaped with only a bruise. The enemy attack petered out at nightfall and in the small hours of the 20th A and D Companies of the Rifles were relieved and went down to Soupir and on to Verneuil. Their casualties in the previous week had been 27 killed, 141 wounded, and 18 missing.

Capt. Ranken, by all accounts, had done marvellous work in tending the wounded in exposed positions. In newspaper accounts he was said to have had to cross a ravine in order to reach the wounded and in time was mortally wounded by a shell from a Jack Johnson which shattered his leg. As he was tending the wounded he bound up his own wounds and arrested the bleeding but refused to leave the trenches; he went on with his work until he was too weak to continue. He was later taken away by stretcher-bearers to a dressing station at Braine where he died of his wounds.

There is an anonymous account of an operation carried out on Ranken which was quoted in the Press in 1914: 'Only last night I amputated poor Ranken's leg above the knee-joint, a terrible shell wound it was, but he will probably get a VC for his behaviour. Although the leg was only hanging on by a very little, he continued to dress the wounded in the firing line.'

A little-known diary kept in the PRO (WO95/1407) throws further light on Ranken's final hours. It was written by Lt. H. Robinson RAMC serving at the time with No. 8 Field Ambulance. The date was around 23 September:

It was one of those days at Braine that I came across Captain Ranken RAMC. When I saw him he was lying on a stretcher at Braine Station platform, he was smoking a cigarette and talking with animation. He had recently had his leg amputated somewhere above the knee and said he was in no pain and was quite comfortable and well. We were all horribly shocked to hear a day or two later that he had died suddenly of an embolism but he had already received the award of the VC for his work at the time when he had received his injuries.

Ranken was buried in the Braine Communal Cemetery in grave A 43. He is in a group of four officers and he was one of many doctors who were to give their

lives in the Aisne fighting. His VC was gazetted posthumously on 16 November and was presented to his father on 29 November.

❖❖❖

Harry Sherwood Ranken was born in Glasgow on 3 September 1883. He was the eldest son of the Revd Henry Ranken, who was the minister of the parish church at Irvine, Ayrshire, and Helen, daughter of Mathew Morton, who lived at The Manse. Harry Ranken went to school at the Irvine Royal Academy and later attended Glasgow University where he graduated as Bachelor of Medicine (MB ChB) 'with commendation' in 1905. He was appointed House Physician and House Surgeon to the Western Infirmary, Glasgow. Later on he became the assistant medical officer to the Brook Fever Hospital in London. He entered the RAMC on 30 January 1909, gaining top place in the entrance examination. He was particularly interested in tropical medicine and won the Tulloch Prize in Military Medicine. His real inclination was towards research. He became a member of the Royal College of Physicians and passed his examination for Captaincy in 1911 and took that rank on 30 July 1912. He then entered the Egyptian Army serving in Sudan and carried out research into sleeping sickness. He made a study of his patients while researching at the

Irvine war memorial

same time. He also wrote several scientific papers based on his researches. He was a great favourite of all who knew him. He was a big-game hunter, a scratch golfer and a member of the Automobile Club.

Ranken returned home in July 1914 and immediately volunteered for active service with the British Army in August 1914. He went to the front in France with the 1st KRRC as part of the BEF. Within a month he was awarded the Cross of the Legion of Honour by the French for his gallant behaviour during the retreat from Mons. Just a few weeks after he had left for France he was mourned not only as a hero and saver of life but also as a friend and scientist.

Ranken was the very first war casualty to be reported in the *Kilmarnock Standard* on 3 October

Ranken Drive

1914. Like Ross Tollerton (see earlier chapter) he had a road named after him in the town. It is called Ranken Drive. It was a considerable coincidence that two men from the same Scottish town should win the VC within two weeks of each other. Today Ranken Drive, like Tollerton Drive, has houses with well-tended gardens but some houses are derelict and boarded up.

There is a plaque to Ranken's memory in Irvine old parish church with a likeness of him incorporated into the design. His medals are held by the RAMC.

F.W. DOBSON

Chavonne, Aisne, France, 28 September

The 2nd Coldstream Guards was one of four battalions in the 4th (Guards) Brigade that in turn was part of the British 2nd Division. It had been involved in the rearguard action at Villers Cotterêts on 1 September 1914 and a week later at Le Petit Morin after the German Army had been turned back on the River Marne to the north of Paris. On the 13th the Guards were at Chavonne with the aim of crossing the River Aisne. They crossed by way of a trestle bridge and advanced towards the northern heights. Unfortunately they came under very heavy artillery fire and had to return to the south bank of the river. During the next two weeks the Guards were heavily involved in the attempt to win command of the heights of the Chemin des Dames. They had a particularly hard time fighting for the farm called La Cour de Soupir, to the north of Soupir and close to the ridges which the enemy tenaciously hung on to. Both sides suffered heavy casualties.

The main Battle of Aisne took place in the middle of September and by the end of the month the operation was petering out. In early October the BEF moved northwards for what was to be known as the first Battle of Ypres, as the line extended towards the sea.

The seventh VC award of the Battle of the Aisne was gained for saving life by No. 6840 Pte. F.W. Dobson. At the front or eastern part of the sector allocated to the 2nd CG the ground was very exposed and sloped gradually upwards towards the enemy. The range or field of fire varied from 50 to several hundred yards and there were three dense woods, which at one point came as close as 20 yards from the British trenches, opposite Tunnel Post, near La Cour de Soupir Farm, not far from the village of Soupir.

Monday, 28 September, began with a thick mist. A patrol of three men from Capt. Follett's company was sent out towards the German lines. The mist suddenly lifted and the three men became an easy target. One of them got back to his lines with only a scratch, and Pte. Dobson immediately volunteered to go

out across the exposed battlefield by crawling over the ground, under heavy fire
to see if he could help the remaining two men. When he reached them he found
Pte. Haldenby dead and Pte. S. Butler wounded in three places. He rendered first
aid with First Field Dressing and then returned for a stretcher and assistance,
crawling back the entire way. This time Dobson was accompanied by Cpl.
A. Brown and using a stretcher they brought the wounded Private back to safety.
Fortunately the mist had partially returned giving them some protection. These
two men from the patrol were the only casualties of 2nd Division that day.
Dobson was recommended for the Victoria Cross and Brown the Distinguished
Conduct Medal (DCM). However, in WO File WO32/4993 there is a note from
Sir Douglas Haig dated 30 September: 'I am not in favour of this coveted award
being created for bringing in wounded officers or men in European warfare.'

Haig, therefore, recommended the DCM instead. He was, however, overruled
by the King. Dobson's award was gazetted on 9 December. He was decorated by
the King at Buckingham Palace on 3 February 1915.

Frederick William Dobson was the son of Thomas and Elizabeth Dobson and was
born at Nafferton Farm, Ovingham, near Newcastle-on-Tyne on 9 November
1886. The farm is just off the eastbound carriageway of the A69, west of Horsley
between Newcastle and Hexham. It is now managed by Newcastle University.

Nafferton Farm, birthplace of L. Cpl. Dobson

Dobson joined the Army at the age of nineteen on 7 July 1906, and was discharged on expiration of his service on 7 July 1909. He was called up on 6 August 1914 and posted to the 2nd Battalion on the 14th of that month. He went with them to France as part of the BEF. After he won his VC he was promoted to Lance-Corporal but on 1 July 1917 he was discharged as 'No longer physically fit for War Service'. He had sustained several injuries in the war and was to spend months in hospital. He suffered constant pain for the rest of his life for he had been permanently maimed by shrapnel.

He found that his VC was a hindrance when he tried to seek employment working in the mines. His colleagues claimed that he received special treatment from the management. He said that 'the miners made it tough for me'. For a time he became a commissionaire in a local cinema and lived in Leeds where his address was Abbey Terrace, Hunslet. Finally, he lived in rooms at Westgate Road, Newcastle and died at the General Hospital on 13 November 1935 at the age of forty-nine, after a lengthy stay. He was buried at Ryton and Crawcrook Cemetery with full military honours. For fifty years his grave was unattended and obscured until the local branch of the Coldstream Guards Association was alerted. On 15 March 1986 the Association held a service of thanksgiving at the graveside and dedicated a headstone on the site.

Dobson had left his medals to his regiment but three of them, including the VC, turned up in a pawnbroker's shop in Newcastle in 1936. In agreement with his family the medals were retained by the Regimental Collection. He had been awarded the Cross of the Order of St George, Fourth Class (Russian), the 1914 Star, the British War Medal 1914–19 and the Victory Medal. The two missing medals were in the possession of Dobson's eldest son. In May 1988 his widow wrote to the regiment asking if they would like them. She said that her late husband had always intended to present the medals to the regiment but had never got round to it.

So Frederick Dobson was yet another of the men who, although he had won the nation's highest military honour in 1914, was to subsequently lead a very short and tragic life.

H. MAY

Near La Boutillerie, France, 22 October

Twenty-three Victoria Crosses were to be recommended by Sir John French during the initial fighting of the first five weeks of the First World War. It was to be over three weeks before another such award was made. It was not until 1918, the last year of the war that the distribution of these coveted awards was again so widely made. The Allied and German Armies were fighting a very different type of war in those first few weeks – something which is often overlooked in the endless photographs of mud and trenches that sum up the popular image of the '1914–18' War. In 1914 from October onwards, the battle area became much wider and less confined than it had been in August and September.

L. Cpl. F.W. Dobson (see previous chapter) won the VC close to the village of Chavonne on the Aisne on 28 September at the same time as the Battle of Aisne was beginning to peter out. The plan was for the French to take over the British positions which they began to do at the beginning of October. The British then made their way by train to the northern part of the battlefield. During October there was fighting around Arras and the Germans were determined to try and capture the Belgian ports including Antwerp in a dash towards the Belgian coastline. In addition the Kaiser was desperate to capture the Belgian town of Ypres. The First Battle of Ypres began on 19 October. On 22 October the Germans took the town of Langmarck and on that day the battle around the industrial town of La Bassée also began.

Pte. Henry May was a member of the 1st Battalion Cameronians (Scottish Rifles). His battalion, along with the 2nd RWF, 1st Middlesex and 2nd ASH was formed into the 19th Infantry Brigade commanded by Maj. Gen. L.G. Drummond. The Cameronians had landed in France on 15 August and joined up with the other three battalions on 22 August at Valenciennes. The next day the 19th Brigade was ordered to join up with Gen. Sir H. Smith-Dorrien's 11 Corps. The Cameronians moved to Mons on the extreme left on the left flank of the Mons-Condé Canal. However, they withdrew before encountering the enemy. On the 26th at Le Cateau the 19th Brigade had a supporting role to play before retreating to St Quentin and Ollozy, covering 56 miles in 36 hours. Later they were to fight at the Marne and on the Aisne.

The brigade returned northwards and became a link between the British 11 and 111 Corps where it was to be heavily engaged in the region of Fromelles, south-west of Armentières, against units of the German XIII Corps.

At daybreak on 22 October Pte. Henry May was in a platoon under the command of Lt. D.A.H. Graham. This platoon was acting as a covering party in a ditch to hold the enemy in check while the main part of the Cameronians entrenched positions about 700 yards to the rear. This took place on the eastern side of the village of La Boutillerie. During this time the enemy, who were only 50 yards to the front of the platoon, attacked them in force which resulted in them falling back, but not before the trench-digging to the rear was completed. During the fighting L. Cpl. Lawton had been wounded, about a hundred yards to the right of May who quickly ran across the firing line through a hail of bullets. L. Cpl. James McCall and Pte. James Bell went with May to assist. Bell took off Lawton's equipment but he was shot dead as May and McCall tried to lift him to his feet. McCall too was knocked unconscious and May then flattened himself on the ground determined to fight to the last. At that moment he saw his platoon commander Lt. Graham fall to the ground with a bullet in his leg. May called to Bell to follow and ran over to their officer; the two men carried him step by step, zig-zagging as they stumbled on. When they had covered about 300 yards they reached a ditch where Bell was shot in the hand and foot but they managed eventually to reach safety. May was exhausted but struggled to drag Lt. Graham a little nearer safety when Cpl. Taylor came to his assistance. Lt. Graham who had lost a lot of blood by this time ordered the two men to return to their lines but they disobeyed him. Cpl. Taylor lifted Lt. Graham onto his shoulders but was then shot dead. May, by some supreme effort, then dragged the wounded officer to the British trenches and safety. Pte. May's heroism and utter disregard for the safety of his own life was in the true tradition of the holders of the Victoria Cross. On 2 November 1914, eleven days after May won his VC, he was wounded by shrapnel during the attacks on the town of Ypres. He was attended to at a base hospital before being invalided home. He was home with his family in Glasgow in time for Christmas. In mid-January 1915 he departed once more for France. His VC was gazetted four months later on 19 April 1915 and the King presented it to him at Buckingham Palace on 12 August.

Henry May was the son of Mr and Mrs William Henry May. He was born in Bridgeton, Glasgow on 29 July 1885. He went to school at Dalmarnock Public School in Glasgow and enlisted in the Army on 29 August 1902 at the age of seventeen.

After leaving the Army he became a reservist and was also a tenter with Forrest Frew & Company, muslin manufacturers close to Rutherglen Bridge, Bridgeton, Glasgow. As a reservist he joined the colours at the outbreak of war. After his VC was gazetted, he was told that he was entitled to return home for a short respite. He arrived at Glasgow Central station at 19.45 hours on Saturday 31 July 1915 and was met by a representative of the Lord Provost and by friends and former colleagues from Forrest Frew's mill. After leaving the train he was briefly carried shoulder high by the enthusiastic crowd. On 4 August, May was invited to a civil reception and in replying to a toast he said, 'I feel proud to be present. I only did what any other soldier would have done. Plenty of men have equalled what I did.' A week later he addressed a group of Clyde munition workers during a dinner break, telling them 'Stick to your work for the sake of the boys in the trenches.'

On 12 August, he travelled to London to receive his VC from the King. After the ceremony he was mobbed yet again by an eager crowd who was keen to shake him by the hand together with two other VC winners, Pte. Mariner and Cpl. Tombs. 'Good old May!' 'Good old Mariner!' 'Good old Tombs!' shouted the crowd. 'Come on, shake hands, old sports!' The three men were glad to make their escape.

May was discharged from the Army on 28 August 1915 when his regular engagement of thirteen years expired. He rejoined in 1918 and in March obtained a commission with the Motor Transport Corps. The next year he was demobilized with the rank of temporary Lieutenant. On 26 June 1920 he attended a garden party at Buckingham Palace but the official list gave his rank mistakenly as Pte. May.

May's former platoon commander Lt. D.A.H. Graham, whose life he saved, later became a Major General winning the DSO and the MC. He eventually became Colonel of the Regiment. May had been the first man from the Cameronians to win a VC for thirty-five years.

After the war he joined a hosiery firm the Glasgow Manufacturing Company in which he became a partner. He was taken ill at his home and died in the Glasgow Infirmary on 26 July 1942 just before his fifty-sixth birthday. He left a widow Christina, and four children.

His home address was No. 903 Cumbernauld Road, Riddrie, Glasgow, which still exists. His funeral took place at Riddrie Park Cemetery, Glasgow, and was the largest seen in the East End for a long time. It was attended by four holders of the VC: Messrs John McAulay, R. Downie, D.R. Lauder and W. Ritchie. The commanding officer of the Cameronians, Col. C.B. Vandaleur also attended. May's grave is listed as being in Lair No. 146 and although two of his children are listed on the tombstone, his own name is not mentioned.

May's medals are not publicly held.

W. KENNY

Near Ypres, Belgium, 23 October

The day after Pte. May won his Victoria Cross close to the village of La Boutillerie an Irishman, Drummer William Kenny, won his further to the north between Kruiseecke and Zandvoorde. He was a member of the 2nd Gordon Highlanders of the 20th Brigade of the 7th Division. The brigade line was to the south-east of the Menin road and the village of Gheluvelt, and from right to left were the 2nd Borders, 2nd Gordons and 2nd Scots Guards; on their left was the 22nd Brigade also of the 7th Division. The linking battalion between the two brigades was the 1st Grenadier Guards also of the 20th Brigade The position held by the Guards was a sort of salient and was to become a major objective for the enemy to capture.

The First Battle of Ypres began on 19 October. The German Army was desperate to bring about the fall of the town and was pressing in on it from all sides. In this area of the battlefield the Germans were employing many volunteer men in their ranks from the German middle classes, and their sheer numbers as well as their ardour was to be considerably underestimated by the British and French Armies. On 21 October the German attack by the XXVII Reserve Corps fell on the 21st and 22nd Brigades of the 7th Division rather than the 20th Brigade, with continuous assaults and shelling. The enemy certainly dug themselves in close to the positions of the 20th Brigade but never seemingly pressed an attack home.

On the south side of the Kruiseecke salient the 2nd Gordon Highlanders only had to deal with small or minor attacks. Occasionally they were subjected to shell fire and accurate sniping. It was against this background that Drummer Kenny, who was not much more than 5ft 3 in in height set about rescuing no fewer than five wounded men under very heavy fire on the 23rd. He was awarded the VC for his heroism and also for saving some machine guns and conveying urgent messages over fire-swept ground. The position of the 20th Brigade at the salient was given very close support by

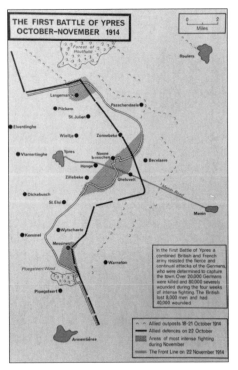

THE FIRST BATTLE OF YPRES
OCTOBER–NOVEMBER 1914

In the First Battle of Ypres a combined British and French army resisted the fierce and continual attacks of the Germans, who were determined to capture the town. Over 20,000 Germans were killed and 80,000 severely wounded during the four weeks of intense fighting. The British lost 8,000 men and had 40,000 wounded.

Allied outposts 18-21 October 1914
Allied defences on 22 October
Areas of most intense fighting during November
The Front Line on 22 November 1914

F Battery and 12th Battery who deterred the enemy from attacking at this point.

Kenny's VC was gazetted on 18 February 1915 and he was presented with the medal by the King at Glasgow Green on 18 May.

❖❖❖

William Kenny was born on 24 August 1880 in Drogheda, County Louth, although some accounts say he was born in Malta. In May 1915, a few days after being presented with his VC, he was given the Freedom of Drogheda. Later still he also received a watch at the Mansion House in the City of London.

He was discharged with the rank of Sergeant in 1919 and joined the Corps of Commissionaires, with whom he billeted. Several pictures exist of him in his uniform wearing his medals along with a full and pointed moustache, every inch an ex-military man. Kenny seems to have been the archetypal or stage Irishman. He became everybody's friend and a great favourite with his firm's customers, especially in Bond Street in the West End of London where he worked for some time – he was always chatting with people as they went in and out of the shops, hotels or car showrooms.

An article in the *Daily Express* described him well: 'He once filled Bond Street with his presence. Now he presides over the entrance to a house of motor-cars in Berkeley Square.' 'As Irish as ever they were bred,' he enlisted in the Gordon Highlanders, as a drummer in the nineties (and served in South Africa between 1899 and 1901). 'I'm a County Meath man . . . I'm a Drogheda man.'

In the same article Kenny tells of how he was once 'buried' as a result of a mix up with identity discs. His friend, Sgt. Bunn said that after Kenny had won his VC he had become too valuable a piece to be let near the front line again, but he slipped through once or twice – with some rum inside him. In the same article Kenny himself talks of being close to the Hindenburg Line in 1917.

He also served on the Somme in 1916 and there is a famous picture of him

Drummer W. Kenny marching at the front of his regimental drums and pipes

Brookwood Cemetery, Surrey

Drummer W. Kenny rescuing a wounded soldier at the First Battle of Ypres in October

proudly marching at the front of his regimental drums and pipes. Behind him can be seen the figure of Capt. (later Col.) Turnbull, Distinguished Service Order (DSO), riding a grey horse. The Gordons had recently been involved in the fighting at Ginchy and were probably on their way back to billets at Treux on 7 or 8 September 1916.

Kenny lived in the Corps Barracks in London until early 1936 when he was taken ill and died in Charing Cross Hospital on 10 January, shortly before the King died. Records show that he was buried and commemorated in Brookwood Cemetery, Woking, but he has no identifiable grave. His medals are not publicly held.

J. LEACH AND J. HOGAN
Near Festubert, France, 29 October

2nd Lt. Leach

Sgt. J. Hogan

By 23 October the British 11 Corps had crossed the Béthune-La Bassée Canal and had fought their way northwards. The 5th Division which included the 14th Brigade took up positions on the right, while the 3rd Division was to the north. The Corps was planning to reach the Lille-La Bassée road with the assistance of the French 10th Army. They were unaware that the Germans were in their turn planning to overwhelm the Allied positions.

The 2nd Manchesters of the 14th Brigade were instructed to establish a new position as rearguard to the 13th Brigade and to take up a line at La Quinque Rue, near Festubert, to the north of the La Bassée Canal and west of the industrial town of La Bassée itself. They were to spend the next few days improving their defensive positions and in maintaining them, despite heavy shelling and fighting with the inevitable casualties. During this time their sister battalion, the 1st Manchesters, came into the line to their left, the first time that the two units had met since 1882.

On the 27th the village of Neuve Chapelle to the north-east had been captured by the Germans but lost the next day. The Germans fought hard to retrieve the situation and tried to weaken the British position by shelling the junction of the 13th and 14th Brigades of the 5th Division, to the north-east of Festubert. On the 29th there was also very heavy fighting in the region of La Bassée.

It was in the subsequent fighting in the Festubert area that two deeds of great heroism occurred. On the 29th the 2nd Manchesters' trenches were heavily shelled from first light and then charged by the Germans, under the cover of a smoke screen. They attacked mainly at the centre and the right of the

2nd Lt. Leach and Sgt. Hogan recapturing a trench from the Germans

position, and captured one of A Company's forward trenches, but the remainder held their own. The Manchesters fought with great determination and courage, and two officers, 2nd Lt. C.L. Bentley and Lt. J.A.L. Reade, the acting adjutant, were killed in trying to stem the German thrust towards the supporting trench. As it was they were only stopped 10 yards from it. Two attempts were made to retake the forward trench but these failed. At 14.00 hours 2nd Lt. Leach accompanied by Sgt. J. Hogan and ten volunteers from A Company recaptured the forward trench and in so doing took six wounded and fourteen unwounded prisoners. The small party of brave attackers went forward along the communication trench, pushing the Germans back in front of them, and continued fighting from traverse to traverse. The casualties on the British side during the day included the two officers already mentioned and twenty other ranks. In addition nineteen men were wounded and eight men were missing. Capt. R.N. Hardcastle, DSO, was taken to hospital after his eye had been damaged by earth thrown up by a bullet.

On the 30th the Festubert area was again subjected to a forceful artillery attack but the British held their ground. The 2nd Manchesters were relieved at 02.00 hours by the Gurkhas, who had recently arrived in France with the Indian Corps. The 2nd Manchesters retired to Rue De L'Epinette and then withdrew to billets in La Couture. On the 31st they moved as divisional reserve to Le Touret.

Leach and Hogan had risked their lives in the action to regain their former positions; the 22-year-old subaltern and the more experienced non-commissioned-officer (NCO) must have made an excellent team. After the mawling that the 2nd Manchesters had received at Le Cateau and La Bassée, Leach had been given command of a company rather than a platoon.

Some time later 2nd Lt. Leach told the story to the Press in more detail. His advanced trench had room for about thirty-five men and was about 150 yards in front of the main trench which was 120 yards from the enemy. Leach was having his breakfast when he was warned that the Germans were attacking. He saw 250 men with fixed bayonets moving in on his position – they were running and making a sort of 'wailing noise'. Leach reported that they managed to shoot down about 150 of the enemy and the remaining 100 jumped into his advanced trench killing about 12 of his company. The Germans then pushed their way down the communication trench and into the main trench. Initially the enemy took over three out of four traverses, and eventually the fourth.

On learning that the 2nd Manchesters' positions were to be taken over by the Gurkhas later that day, Leach thought that it would be rather bad on his part to hand over his company trench to them. At 14.00 hours, therefore, he called for volunteers and Hogan and ten men agreed to join him. Leach, armed with his officer's pistol, had the idea of forcing the enemy back to their own trenches and shooting them as they retreated. In doing this he succeeded in releasing some of his own men who had been captured earlier in the day. They captured about fourteen men and twenty wounded along with an officer. 2nd Lt. Leach knew that his name had been mentioned in despatches, but the award of the VC came as a surprise to him. It was gazetted on 22 December 1914 together with Sgt. Hogan's. Leach was presented with his medal by the King at Buckingham Palace on 13 February 1915 and Hogan on 20 February.

James Leach was born in North Shields, Northumberland on 27 July 1892 and was the son of a colour-sergeant in the King's Own (Royal Lancaster) Regiment. The family moved to Manchester and lived at Cicero Street, off Ashley Lane, Blackley. Leach's first school was the Moston Lane Municipal School; his two brothers were also educated there. Leach acquired a good knowledge of the French language and left school in 1907 when his family moved to Leicester. His first job was that of an apprentice chemist before he joined the Army in the 1st Northamptonshire Regiment. He was at Aldershot when war was declared in August 1914, and on 1 October he was gazetted as Second Lieutenant with the 2nd Manchesters.

After his VC action he was made a full Lieutenant on 11 December 1914. On the day he was presented his VC in February the boys at his old school were given a half-day's holiday and welcomed Leach as a hero. He showed the pupils his medal and then went on a recruitment drive in the city. About a year later he was presented with an illuminated address by the people of Lancaster, his wife's home town. He was on half pay from 9 February 1918, and it is not clear from the records where he served between 1915 and 1918.

In 1938 he was named as a co-respondent in a divorce action and was ordered to pay £500 in costs. At that time the social stigma attached to a divorce was quite considerable and it caused much pain and ill-feeling among his family. He worked as a chartered secretary and became a councillor in Hammersmith. He attended at least three VC reunions before the VC Centenary Review of 1956 and also the 200th anniversary of the Manchester Regiment on 23 April 1958 when he was introduced to the Queen Mother. A few months later, on 15 August, aged sixty-six, he died at No. 4 The Lodge, Richmond Way, Shepherd's Bush, leaving a widow and six children. His funeral was held at St Matthew's church, West Kensington, and his cremation took place at Mortlake. His ashes were not scattered and his medals are not publicly held.

John Hogan was born at 134 Heyside, Royton, Oldham, Lancashire (the house no longer exists) on 8 April 1884. He was the son of Sarah Hogan whose name he took. She was employed as a cotton-speed tenter. After the South African war was over Hogan joined the 2nd Manchesters in 1903 and served in South Africa, India and the United Kingdom, for seven years. He left the Army as a reservist with the rank of Corporal. He returned home to Oldham where he became a postman in Heyside. He lodged with a Mr J. Naseby at 36, New Radcliffe Street for some time and also with relatives in Heyside. He was not a big man in stature and was known by his friends as a sociable, jolly and sensible young man. Early in August 1914 he became engaged to a woman who worked in a local hotel in Oldham. At the outbreak of war he rejoined the Army and his rank was made up to that of Sergeant. In the first five months of the war he sent back most of his pay along with many letters and war souvenirs to his fiancée.

He was an experienced soldier and survived the Battle of Mons and the subsequent retreat. After his VC action with 2nd Lt. Leach near Festubert on 29 October he was wounded on 14 December 1914, and was sent to hospital. He had been hit in the face by a piece of shrapnel shell and at one time was in danger of losing the sight of one eye. He was sent home and treated at the military hospital in High Street, Manchester, before recuperating at Macclesfield Infirmary. He was back in Oldham just in time for Christmas 1914 and was cheered by an enthusiastic crowd who carried him shoulder high.

On 2 January 1915 he married his fiancée, a widow from Miner Street named Mrs Margaret Taylor. The marriage ceremony took place at St Mary's Roman Catholic Church, Oldham. Hogan, who was still suffering from his head wounds, was on furlough until 11 January.

After the war Hogan was unemployed for long periods of time. A young man called Mike Lally met him after the war and in an interview with Frank Hearon in the 1980s told the following story:

> The next time I saw him [Hogan] was when I was walking down to my mother's from Piccadilly Station. I saw this man standing in the street with a tray of matches and a notice reading 'No Pension–Ex-serviceman'. I put two bob in his tray, then I looked and realized who it was. 'Excuse me, is your name Hogan?' I asked.
>
> 'Yes. Do you know me?'
>
> I said, 'I was in reserve to you and Mr Leach when you got your VC.'
>
> 'What's your name?'
>
> 'Well,' I said, 'Do you remember taking my bloody money before you got your VC? You had 100 francs off me on my twentieth birthday and spent it in the estaminet.'
>
> 'Lally,' he said. 'Bloody hell!'

Hogan had won the young soldier's recent pay in some sort of bet. A Press photograph exists of Hogan wearing his cloth cap and medals trying to sell

The sunken headstone of Sgt. J. Hogan

boxes of matches for a living, an occupation that he followed for three years. In 1936 the *Daily Express* heard of Hogan's financial difficulties and published an article which was seen by a music-hall star named Benny Ross. Ross gave Hogan a job as his valet and kitted him out in new clothes. This job, however, did not last very long and when the Second World War began in 1939 Hogan began work in a munitions factory. At the time he was living at No. 12 Alderson Street near the site of the Technical College in Oldham. His post-war life was tragic, but his fate was shared by many ex-servicemen who were unemployed.

Hogan died of cancer on 6 October 1943 at the Oldham & District hospital, Westwood Park Hospital, aged fifty-nine. It is not known what happened to his wife but her name is not listed among the mourners at his funeral on 12 October. The funeral took place at Chadderton Cemetery with a bearer party from the Pioneer Corps and a detachment of soldiers from his former regiment, the 2nd Battalion of the Manchester Regiment, under the command of Sgt. Stridgeon, DCM. The coffin was placed on a gun carriage with the Union Jack and a steel helmet. It was a Roman Catholic service and the 'Last Post' was played at the graveside. The mayor and the chief constable were among the mourners. Hogan's grave number is D9–63 and is difficult to find as his name is not listed on it. It has sunk down over the years and bears the following inscription: 'In Loving Memory of Robert Garlick Taylor. Died February 9th 1913 aged 39 Years. Also

Henry, son of the above, died October 21st 1914 aged 19 Years.' The grave plot was purchased by Mrs Margaret Taylor in 1913 before she married John Hogan. The grave also contains the remains of two Taylor children aged ten and three respectively. It seems likely that when Hogan married Mrs Taylor she was in her late forties while he would have been about thirty years old. In recent years the grave has sometimes become overgrown and neglected. However, at the time of writing there is a move afoot to erect a more appropriate memorial to Hogan's memory on the grave site. Enquiries are being made in order to try and contact any members of the Taylor family. It is proposed that Mr Norman Stoller, a local businessman, pays for the cost of a new stone and that the Manchester Regiment will supervise the lettering and the setting up of the new memorial.

The family address at the time of Hogan's funeral is given in the cemetery records at No. 55 Frank Hill Street. This was probably in Franklin Street but there is no trace of the house still existing.

After he died in hospital his family accused the hospital authorities of negligence and allowing his medals to be stolen. The truth of the matter was that Hogan had already sold them. He had not wished to tell his family about this. He had often pawned his medals until his pension came through. Hogan's family believed that the medals had been stolen and reported their suspicions to the local police. However, in the 1970s the medals turned up in a London dealer's catalogue with a reserve price of £10,000. The family, not unnaturally, asked for them back, thinking that they still legally belonged to them and they took out a court injunction to prevent the sale. However, Messrs Spink and Sons, the dealers, were able to produce documentation that proved Hogan had indeed sold the medals to a Mr Stanley Oldfield of Blackpool, a medal collector, in March 1942 for a price in the region of £60. In 1960 the medals were sold once more, for £15, and in the early 1970s for £785. Messrs Spinks sold them initially for about £6,000.

When the medals were offered for sale a second time by Spinks, Mr Norman Stoller, managing director of the Oldham-based Seton group, became interested in buying them back for the town. Mr Stoller negotiated a discount with the dealer and paid £7,250 with the local council contributing £2,500 towards the medals.

In October 1983, forty years after Hogan's death, *The Daily Telegraph* gave the following report of a parade in Oldham: 'The 5/8 King's Regiment marches with fixed bayonets, colours flying and bands playing through Oldham today (22 October), bearing a Victoria Cross won in 1914 by Sgt. John Hogan.'

One of those who attended the presentation was the now-elderly Mike Lally, Hogan's former colleague.

The medals were presented to the mayor by the Regimental Colonel Sir Geoffrey Errington and were then deposited alongside regimental colours and silver in the Oldham Civic Centre. Sadly, this parade in Sgt. Hogan's honour came rather too late for him. It does not appear from the regimental archives that his regiment took much interest in his plight.

Helen Hogan, John Hogan's daughter-in-law, told the local press about her reaction to the return of the medals:

> It's a lovely gesture and a happy ending to a very sad story. But I am a little upset that the medal won't be staying in our family, although I realize it is not a thing to be hidden away . . . I had virtually given up any hope of finding the medals. They are part of the history of Oldham and finding them after forty years means a great deal to my family.

Mrs Helen Hogan in a gesture of appreciation presented a clock to Norman Stoller in gratitude for all that he had done in her father-in-law's memory. Messrs Spinks made a special display case for the medals.

J.A.O. BROOKE

Near Gheluvelt, Belgium, 29 October

On 29 October 1914, six days after Drummer Kenny won his VC in the 2nd Gordon Highlanders, another man from the same battalion, Lt. J.A.O. Brooke won a second such medal for his regiment. Since the 23rd the fight for the possession of Ypres had continued and there was also heavy fighting around La Bassée and Arras. Despite considerable German pressure Gheluvelt, the gateway to Ypres, had not fallen. It will be recalled that the 2nd Gordons along with other battalions of the 20th Brigade (7th Div.) were occupying positions between Kruiseecke and Zandvoorde. The left of the brigade was on the Menin road about a thousand yards to the east of Gheluvelt.

It had been a quiet day on the divisional front on 27 October and the 20th Brigade moved back a couple of miles behind the firing line. Later there was a warning that the Germans might attack the Division on the 28th so the 20th Brigade was brought up again, with the 1st Grenadier Guards taking up positions immediately south of the Menin road with the 2nd Gordon Highlanders to their right. At about 15.30 hours a message came from General Headquarters to the Division to the effect that the German XXVIIth Reserve Corps had been ordered to capture the crossroads south of Gheluvelt. At 16.30 hours the 20th Brigade was ordered to send two battalions to the crossroads by 18.45 hours. Accordingly the 1st Grenadier Guards and the 2nd Gordon Highlanders were ordered up to a position stretching from the crossroads to the track running south-west from Gheluvelt. At night, the 2nd Scots Guards and the 2nd Border Regiment were to support them at Gheluvelt.

As there were no prepared trench positions and little cover the battalions were told that unless the enemy attacked very early the next day they were to withdraw. At daybreak on the 29th no such attack had materialized and subsequently the two supporting battalions withdrew to Veldhoek at about 06.45 hours. They had hardly been gone half-an-hour when the enemy opened a heavy bombardment on the Grenadier Guards and in the prevailing fog they swept down on the left flank in large numbers. The Grenadiers were gradually forced back westwards but the survivors, assisted by the 2nd Gordon

Lt. J.A.O. Brooke in action at Gheluvelt

Highlanders, made two counter-attacks, in order to regain the lost ground. The enemy numbers were, however, overwhelming and the Grenadiers had to retire to a ditch on the south side of the Menin road, east of Gheluvelt. There they were joined by the 2nd Borders from reserve. The Grenadiers remained in these positions for the rest of the day. At the end of the day they had lost 15 officers and 470 men out of the original 20 officers and 670 men.

The 2nd Gordon Highlanders on the right of the Grenadiers were attacked on their front and had just been able to hold to their trenches. Cyril Falls writes in the *Regimental History* that, 'At the worst moment, when a counter-attack had failed and the defence had seemed on the edge of disaster, the heroism of Lt. J.A.O. Brooke had done much to restore it. Brooke was killed, and received the posthumous award of the Victoria Cross.

The VC citation reads:

Brooke led two attacks on the German trenches under heavy rifle fire and machine-gun fire, regaining a lost trench at a very critical moment. By his marked coolness and promptitude on this occasion, Brooke prevented the enemy from breaking through our line at a time when a general counter-attack could not have been organized. Having regained the lost trench, he went back to bring up supports and in doing so was killed.

Brooke had been given a message by his Colonel who had noticed that the Germans were breaking through part of the line. He promptly rallied a group of cooks, orderlies, signalmen and servants for assistance with the attack; most of them were killed along with Lt. Brooke and their Captain. The battalion lost about 7 officers and 100 men during the day and some 240 dead Germans were counted in front of one platoon alone.

At about 16.00 hours the Scots Guards and the Queens (sent from 1st Brigade) advanced down the Menin road and retrieved the original line held by the Grenadiers in the morning. At nightfall the 20th Brigade was

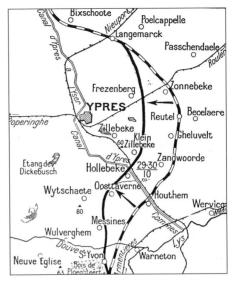

Ypres, 29 October

withdrawn to Veldhoek, while rain came down in torrents until midnight. The history of the 7th Division described the events in the following way:

> The stubborn resistance of the overmatched 20th Brigade had at least prevented the Germans south of the Menin road from keeping level with their progress north of the Menin Road (and some had nearly reached Gheluvelt). Two days later the village did actually fall to the Germans but was recovered by the Worcester regiment on a day of considerable crisis during the first battle of Ypres.

Lt. Brooke was buried in Zantvoorde British Cemetery VI, E, 2. His VC was gazetted on 18 February 1915 and presented to his father the following year.

James Anson Otho Brooke was the son of Capt. Harry Vesey Brooke, JP, DL, later 92nd Gordon Highlanders and his wife, Patricia Eyres. He was born on 3 February 1884 at Newhills, a few miles west of Aberdeen in Scotland. The family house was called Fairley. He was educated at Winton House, in Winchester, Wellington College and the Royal Military Academy, Sandhurst, where he was captain of the Shooting Eight. He was also an accomplished horseman and footballer and became Senior Colour-Sergeant of the Military College, and winner of the Sword of Honour.

On 11 October 1905 Brooke was commissioned into the Gordon Highlanders and joined the 1st Battalion at Cork in November. He was promoted to full Lieutenant on 5 August 1907, and then transferred to the 2nd Battalion in India. Here he was recognized as the smartest young officer in the regiment and the best of sportsmen (he killed many head of game). He took part in the Delhi Durbar in 1911 when he received the new battalion colours from the King and was awarded the Durbar Medal. In 1913 he left India and when the European War broke out he was serving in Egypt. He was promoted to Captain on 1 September 1914 although most accounts of his heroism describe him as being a Lieutenant. In October he reached Belgium, landing at Zeebrugge and took part in the severe fighting for several days. On 29 October he was the battalion assistant adjutant.

Brooke's VC was presented to his father, Capt. H.V. Brooke, at Buckingham Palace on 29 November 1916. Capt. Brooke had lost three sons in the First World War and one son-in-law. His health was badly affected by these tragedies. After the war, when the local war memorial was due to be unveiled by Capt. Brooke, his health was not up to it and the ceremony had to be performed by another local dignitary. Later this memorial was moved to a new position in front of the church at Kingswells. Although James Brooke is buried in Belgium his memory is also commemorated at the Springbank Cemetery, Aberdeen, in the family grave. The memorial bears the following inscription:

Erected by Captain Harry V. Brooke of Fairley late 92nd Gordon Highlanders in memory of his four sons.

Rupert born 12th September, 1896, died 27th September 1896.

Eldest son James Anson Otho Brooke, VC, Captain 2nd Gordon Highlanders. Born 3rd February 1884, killed in action at Gheluvelt 29th October 1914.

Henry Brian Brooke, Captain 2nd Gordon Highlanders. Born 9th December 1889, mortally wounded at Mametz, died 24 July 1916.

Patrick Harry Brooke, Sub-Lt. R.N. Born 21st May 1895. Died on active service from enteric fever, 25th May 1917.

Here lies the body of their father Capt. Sir Harry Vesey Brooke, KBE.
2nd son of Sir Arthur B. Brooke, Bart. of Colebrooke.
Born 23 September 1845, died 10th June 1921.
And his beloved wife Patricia Eyres Brooke.
Born 1859, died 1951.
GLORIA FINIS

Up to fairly recently a rough wooden cross which had marked the grave where James had been buried in Zantvoorde British Cemetery, Belgium, stood at the foot of the tombstone but this is now in the safe keeping of the Regimental Museum, along with his service revolver. The family gravestone is about 10 feet high and bears a Celtic Cross inscription within the family grave. There is a granite, waist-high stone on either side of the taller tombstone where other members of the family are commemorated.

The parish church at Kingswells also commemorates the names of the Brooke family.

Captain James Brooke also posthumously received the 1914 Star with clasp, the BWM, and the Victory Medal with MID Oakleaf. All his medals are in the collection of the Gordon Highlanders.

A. MARTIN-LEAKE

Near Zonnebeke, Belgium,
29 October to 8 November

Arthur Martin-Leake was awarded the very last Victoria Cross presented in the Boer War for his bravery and courage in February 1902. Nearly thirteen years later he won a second Victoria Cross in the third month of the First World War and was the first man to do so.

Leake had arrived in France from Calcutta where on 5 August news reached him of the declaration of war in Europe. He had immediately applied for permission to travel to France. He journeyed by a circuitous route and arrived in Paris via Marseilles on 30 August dressed in an ancient volunteer Indian uniform. After an adventurous journey, during which he only just missed being arrested in Malta, he was treated with some suspicion and was advised to go to the War Office in London and ask for instructions. Once there, he saw there were vacancies for Medical Officers in France and immediately applied for one of these posts, with the Fifth Field Ambulance attached to the 2nd Division (1 Corps). He was posted as a Lieutenant.

Leake first joined his unit when it was on the Aisne in September. This was before it was sent northwards to help cover the Channel Ports, to the north of the Belgian city of Ypres. The first battle for the possession of the town began in real earnest on 19 October and was to last for nearly five weeks. The Germans were determined to put pressure on the town from north-east, east and south-east and to 'pinch' out the position.

Similarly the Allies were going to use the town as a place to stand and fight for, although it was not particularly well-suited as a defensive position. During the rest of October the battles raged in great intensity and the 2nd Division was positioned on a line between Ypres and the village of Passchendaele to the north-east of Ypres. This was where the Allied Armies joined on the extreme left wing of the front line, always a point of weakness to be exploited by the enemy. The 1st, 7th and 4th Divisions together with the 1st Cavalry Division were to the right of the 2nd Division. The Germans opposite were units from the German Fourth Army.

At the end of October at Zonnebeke the British made an attack against the German trenches. This subsequently failed owing to the withering fire of the enemy machine guns and rifle fire. The British survivors, leaving a great number of dead and wounded, withdrew to their original lines. The enemy then appeared to expect a second attack and were nervous, firing off at any sign of movement in the Allied positions. It was during these circumstances, that Leake, at great risk to himself, crawled out to drag back as many of the wounded as he could. He was not concerned with the possible loss of his own life but more in saving the lives of his comrades.

On 26 November 1914 Maj. Gen. C.C. Monro, the Commander of 2nd Division wrote a letter recommending Leake for the VC as follows:

> This officer has shown such conspicuous gallantry that I recommend his case be favourably considered, and that he be granted a bar to the Victoria Cross that he already holds.
>
> At Zonnebeke, when he was with the Bearer Division of the 5th Field Ambulance, in a most exposed position, he went continually over the ground in between the English and German positions in search for wounded and though always fired at, and often having to crawl on hands and knees, he was able to get away large numbers of wounded men who would otherwise have been left to the inclemency of the weather and continual shelling of the enemy. These operations often took many hours to accomplish. There can be no doubt by his devotion many lives have been saved that would otherwise undoubtedly have been lost. His behaviour on three occasions when the dressing station was heavily shelled on the 5th November, 9th November and 12th November was such as to inspire confidence both with the wounded and the staff.
>
> In such a case it is not possible to quote any one specific act performed because his gallant conduct was continual, and the fact that he repeatedly successfully accomplished his dangerous mission makes his case, in my opinion, all the more worthy of reward.
>
> I also recommend Captain Loughman, RAMC, who accompanied Captain Leake should be awarded with a DSO.

Two days later Sir Douglas Haig also gave his recommendation for the award of the second VC. For this and similar actions in the days up to 8 November Leake was awarded a clasp to his Victoria Cross which was gazetted on 18 February 1915.

Since no man had won the medal twice before, there was some confusion as to how the award should be made. It was first listed as a clasp and later became known as a bar to his VC. There was even confusion as to the design of the new medal. Messrs Hancock, who had been making the Cross since its inception in 1856, sought instructions from the War Office and also submitted designs of their own which still exist in the PRO archive, ref. WO3/4992. In the end a clasp was fixed to Leake's original medal after it had been sent from India in the spring of 1915. The medal had been left in Calcutta when Leake left India for France. Leake's brother, Capt. W. Martin-Leake, sent it to the War Office from his home, 'Marshalls', in Hertfordshire on 31 March 1915.

The publicity surrounding Leake's second award aroused considerable interest in Britain and several other 'double VC claims' were put forward. Leake's was the first of what eventually were to be three such awards.

In March 1915 Leake was made Captain, and on 30 June he was awarded the British Medical Association's Gold Medal. He was presented with the bar to his VC by the King at Windsor Castle on 24 July 1915.

The Martin-Leake family had owned the house 'Marshalls', High Cross, near Ware in Hertfordshire, for about two hundred years and in the 1930s three brothers and one sister still lived there. This is the house where Lt. Col. Arthur Martin-Leake lived for the last fifteen years of his life. Arthur was the fifth of six sons and the seventh child of Stephen Martin-Leake and Isabel, née Plunkett. The couple had married in 1859. They also had two daughters. Stephen used the name of Martin Leake (without a hyphen) when he was a magistrate in the First World War. He himself was buried in Thorpe-Le-Soken, Essex, where many of his forebears lay. The family also owned Thorpe Hall.

Arthur was born at 'Marshalls' on 4 April 1874. He was educated at Westminster School, London, and University College Hospital, London, where he became Assistant Demonstrator in anatomy and physiology. He qualified as Member of the Royal College of Surgeons (MRCS), and Licentiate of the Royal College of Physicians (LRCP) in 1898, when he was appointed house-physician at the hospital. Leake later held a residential appointment at the West Herts Infirmary in Hemel Hempstead, in the capacity of House Surgeon and Assistant Secretary.

'Marshalls', High Cross, near Ware in Hertfordshire

Soon after the South African War broke out in October 1899 Leake joined the Hertfordshire Imperial Yeomanry as a trooper: his number was 5778. He had seen action during the South African War at Prinsloo's surrender and the relief of Hoar's laager. When his company returned to England, he remained in South Africa and became a civilian surgeon employed by the military. In 1900 he transferred to the Baden-Powell Police and later received the rank of Surgeon Captain with the South African Constabulary in May 1901. Ladysmith had been relieved, followed by Mafeking in May and yet the war still dragged on with the Boers employing guerilla tactics. The British, however, began to apply a slow method of attrition which brought the hostilities to an effective end in May 1902. Seventy-seven VCs had been awarded in the South African campaign and Leake won the seventy-eighth. The last to be awarded of the Boer War.

He won this first VC at Vlakfontein, in a district of Transvaal, south-east of Johannesburg, on 8 February 1902. A line of posts was to be moved forward in order to delay an advance by the Boers. At 03.30 hours a reconnoitring party found itself only 400 yards from the enemy and had to retreat to positions further back. The British opened a heavy attack on the Boers when suddenly a party of about forty Boers came within a hundred yards of them. The Boers advised the British to surrender but they refused to comply. During the height of the battle a number of the men were killed or wounded; Leake rescued Sgt. W.H. Waller, one of the injured, under heavy fire. The Boers were determined to prevent assistance being given to the wounded, but Leake lying flat on the ground bandaged Waller and dragged him under cover. The Boers continued to fire and Leake then went to the aid of a mortally wounded officer, Lt. D.O.P. Abrahams and in trying to make him comfortable he was himself shot three times in the left arm and right leg. But this did not stop him administering to the wounded until loss of blood made him too exhausted to carry on. All the men in the action were wounded and Leake refused to take water himself until he was sure that all others had been given some. He was invalided home with his wounds.

There was originally some disagreement about which medal Leake should be awarded. A board of officers met to discuss the merits of him receiving the VC or DSO and took evidence from several witnesses including Sgt. W.H. Waller who had been with Lt. Abrahams when he was shot in the leg. One officer said that Leake was 'only doing his duty' and therefore the most that he should receive was a DSO. The Commander in Chief in South Africa, Gen. Kitchener, also expressed this view and wrote the following letter to the Under Secretary of War from his Army Headquarters in Pretoria on 24 March 1902.

I have the honour to forward herewith a recommendation for the Victoria Cross in the case of Surgeon Captain Leake, South African Constabulary. I am of the opinion, though the Officer in question undoubtedly showed great devotion to duty, he at the same time was only carrying out his manifest duty, and I therefore consider that the bestowal of the DSO would be more appropriate than the VC, and I therefore recommend him for the former.

Field Marshal Roberts (who had been Commander in Chief, South Africa from December 1899 to December 1900) also submitted the case for the DSO to the War Office in a letter dated 23 April. Sir R. Buller (the former Commander in Chief, South Africa) thought it a clear case for the VC. In 1881, twenty-one years before, the regulations for the VC had been slightly amended so that the award could be conferred in cases of marked gallantry in the performance of duty.

Trooper Grindley gave evidence saying, 'The Boers who were there expressed great regret that they had shot Captain Leake and stated that he had rushed forward; he had previously dressed Sgt. Waller under heavy fire, and had gone to Lt. Abrahams to attend him.'

Finally, the case was made out for both points of view and submitted to King Edward VII on 4 May 1902 to make up his mind on the issue. He came down on the side of the Victoria Cross which was duly gazetted eleven days later and presented to Leake on 2 June. Leake had used the period of convalescence for further medical study and as a result was admitted as Fellow of the Royal College of Surgeons (FRCS) in June 1903. A few months later he left for India and took up the position of administrative medical officer of the Bengal-Nagpur Railway. In the railway's well-equipped hospital Leake was able to practise and improve his surgical skills. He was also the medical officer to the two battalions of volunteers who staffed the railway. Apart from leaves of absence Leake retained his post for thirty-four years.

In 1912 when Montenegro declared war on Turkey Leake was in England and was able to apply for a position with the British Red Cross which had been formed for service with the Montenegrin Army. He was presented with the Order of Montenegrin Red Cross by Nicholas, King of Montenegro.

In November 1915 Leake was promoted to Major and sent to the Balkans with the 'Adriatic Mission' which arrived too late to be of much use and had to flee with the Serbian forces to Corfu and Italy before returning to England on 6 March 1916. He returned to the Western Front on 20 March to 30th Casualty Clearing Station. A year later he was made up to Lieutenant Colonel and given command of No. 46 Field Ambulance and a casualty clearing station between March 1917 and June 1918.

Only three men have won the Victoria Cross twice and Leake was the first. Capt. Noel Chavasse, another doctor was the second, and the third was Charles H. Upham, a New Zealander, in the Second World War. Coincidentally, Leake had treated Noel Chavasse at Brandhoek during the early part of the Battle of Passchendaele in August 1917. Leake took charge of 42nd Casualty Clearing Station, having left the 46th, from June to September 1918.

After the war Leake returned to his job as medical officer with the Bengal-Nagpur Railway in Calcutta and became a keen big game hunter, sending skins home to Hertfordshire. In 1930 he married a widow, Winifred Frances, who sadly died two years later of a tropical disease. There were no children of the marriage.

In 1937 Leake resigned from his job with the Indian Railway and returned to England after a shooting trip in East Africa. He took up residence at 'Marshalls' once more, with various members of his family.

In the Second World War Leake commanded a mobile Air Raid Precaution (ARP) unit at Puckeridge near his home which won many prizes for efficiency. In his retirement he occupied himself by managing the Hertfordshire estate and gardens at 'Marshalls'. He also wrote and illustrated a book on hunting in India. He was president of the local branch of the British Legion for over twenty years; his brother, William, had previously been an officer on the committee. After Leake died of cancer at home on 22 June 1953 there were many obituaries published about his remarkable career and achievements but it was left to a friend, Dr Aubrey Barker, to write a particularly touching appreciation:

The family were typical of the best Victorian traditions and they were all imbued with a strong love of their country. He had many hobbies: a keen motorist, he even rode a motor-bicycle a year before his death, and rather resented the insurance company requiring a medical certificate. At one time he held a pilot's licence and flew his own plane. He spent much of his later years in the garden and was proud of his vegetables. One of the memories I have is of Arthur in the kitchen, wearing a surgical coat, cooking herrings, with his cheeks all floured and a cigarette in his mouth. He was not interested in himself; his friends and neighbours came easily first. He was a great man, a simple man, and a character to admire and love.

At Leake's funeral which took place at High Cross church, Ware, the Director-General of the Army Medical Services attended, along with representatives of the various organizations that Leake had been associated with. His body was cremated and his ashes placed in the family grave. Seven members of his family are buried in the same grave and the eighth, who died in a ballooning accident, is buried in Dorset. In his will Leake left £110,320 (duty paid £54,421) and directed that his medals should be presented to the Royal Army Medical Corps. On 26 June 1955 this was carried out by his cousin, Dr H. Martin-Leake at a special service.

On 13 June 1986, thirty-three years after his death, a plaque commemorating Leake was unveiled in the parish church of St Mary's, High Cross. Those who attended the service of dedication included the Bishop of St Albans and the Surgeon General of the RAMC along with two classes from the local High School. Leake's medals were on display at the service.

In 1989 the neglected appearance of the Leake family grave caused concern locally. Subsequently the grave was cleaned and tidied up and a surrounding paving laid down at the expense of the RAMC.

KHUDADAD KHAN

Hollebeke, Belgium, 31 October

While the First Battle of Ypres was being fought, the Indian Divisions were involved in fighting to the south, at La Bassée and at Messines. On 31 October and 23/24 November two Indians won their country's first Victoria Crosses which were gazetted on 7 December. Conditions for the Indians could not have been much worse with continuous wet, low temperatures and soggy ground. However, they distinguished themselves despite these.

Sepoy Khudadad Khan of the 129th Duke of Connaught's Own Baluchis Regiment won the award on 31 October at Hollebeke. The Baluchis were part of the Ferozepore Brigade of The Lahore Division. Other units in this brigade were the 1st Connaught Rangers, 9th Bhopal Infantry, and 57th Wilde's Rifles, Frontier Force.

The Indians had arrived in the line on 23 October and the Ferozepore Brigade was initially supported by the Cavalry Corps and two of its sister units. Some of them had been brought up by bus. During the Battle of Messines and early in the morning of the 23rd the Baluchis relieved the 3rd Cavalry Brigade. The positions were close to the Ypres–Comines railway and parallel to the Comines Canal, close to the village of Hollebeke to the north-east of Messines. Several ineffectual German attacks took place and the enemy made very little progress as the British positions were very strong in this sector. On the 26th the 2nd Cavalry Division attacked from the Hollebeke Château on the north of the railway line, down the canal in a south-easterly direction towards the village of Houthem. The 4th Hussars were in the lead with the Baluchis in support who were, at one time, in front of the Hussars. However the new trench lines were inferior to their former ones which had been worked on for several days.

While the Battle of Gheluvelt was being fought at the end of October the British line to the south-west was becoming too thinly spread in the line between Ploegsteert Wood and the Douve stream to Armentières. The troops holding it came from three cavalry divisions supported by two Indian

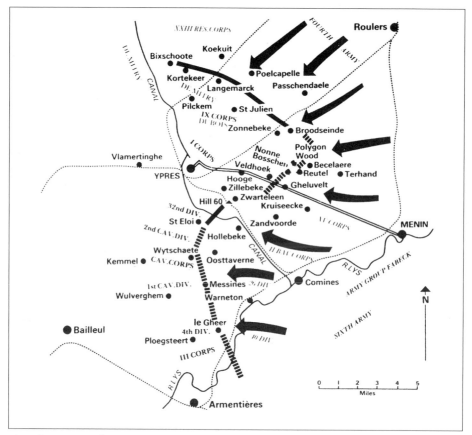

The Salient, 31 October

battalions, the 57th Rifles and the Baluchis. They were comparatively short of ammunition and did not have a great deal of artillery support. The cavalry was forced to fall back from Hollebeke and the enemy closed round the château. In the Ferozepore Brigade one of the companies of the 57th Rifles lost 80 out of 140 men before escaping and most of one company of the Baluchis was also cut off.

In the attack on the line from Wytschaete to the Comines Canal on 31 October the 2nd Cavalry Division with about 3,250 troops was outnumbered by the enemy by about five to one. Some 600 of these 3,250 men were contributed by the Baluchis.

In a report by Col. W.M. Southey, the Commanding Officer of the 129th Baluchi Regiment he wrote as follows: 'We formed up about 3 a.m. and advanced on the left of the farm. We killed about three and wounded three and the remainder who had not bolted, surrendered, fourteen in number.' Each battalion had two Maxim guns and with the team of one gun from the Baluchis were three men who continued to work until their gun was blown to bits by a shell. They only retired when ordered to do so by Capt. R.F. Dill who was their commander. He was himself wounded in the head and had to be carried back to the rear. He received the Distinguished Service Order (DSO) for his work on that day.

The men who worked the remaining gun, causing considerable havoc among the ranks of the enemy, were Havildar Ghulam Mahomed, Sepoy Lal Sher, Sepoy Said Ahmad, Sepoy Kassib and Sepoy Afsar Khan. Sadly, they were all killed. Khudadad Khan, who was wounded, continued to work the gun after the five men had been knocked out. All the men manning the second gun received posthumous awards. The wounded Khudadad managed to rejoin his company but not before rendering his gun useless.

Some 164 men of the Baluchis were killed or wounded and 64 missing, mostly killed. They also lost six British officers, three killed and three wounded; three Indian officers were also killed and two wounded. Gen. Sir O'Moore Creagh, VC, was their Colonel.

Khudadad's VC was gazetted on 7 December 1914 but he was too unwell to be decorated. At the time he was recovering at the Indian Convalescent Hospital in New Milton, Hampshire. He finally received his medal from the King at Buckingham Palace on 26 January 1915.

Khudadad Khan (4050) was a Punjabi Mussulman and was born in Dabb village, Chakwal in the Jhelum district of the Punjab, on 26 October 1888. In August 1914 his regiment, which bore many battle honours and was one of the few Indian regiments composed entirely of Mohammedans, was mobilized. When it received orders it was stationed at Ferozepore in the Punjab, apart from 200 men who were on guard duty at Simla. The Baluchis, with the 57th Rifles, was one of the first two Indian units to come into action in the First World War.

In 1956 Khudadad attended the VC Centenary celebrations in London where he was photographed standing proudly among his colleagues. He died in Pakistan on 8 March 1971 at the age of eighty-two. His medals are not publicly held.

S.J. BENT

Near Gheer, Belgium, 1/2 November

No. 8581 Drummer Bent arrived in France with his battalion, the 1st East Lancashires, eighteen days after the First World War began. The battalion was part of the 11th Brigade of the 4th Division and it took part as a reserve unit at Mons and in the fighting at Le Cateau on 26 August. Later it was involved in the retreat towards Paris and the retreat of the German Army at the Marne, and subsequently in the Battle of the Aisne.

At the end of September, the French Army took over the Aisne front completely and the British units left by train for Flanders. Their next fighting engagement was the First Battle of Ypres which lasted from 19 October to 22 November. It was during this battle that Drummer Bent won his Victoria Cross.

On the eastern edge of Ploegsteert Wood was the small village of Le Gheer, in which there was a convent. On 21 October the village was captured by the Germans and they took up positions to the west of it facing Ploegsteert. The 11th Brigade re-took the village and the position was furiously fought for during the next few days, with ammunition running short. It was during this period that Bent brought ammunition up to the trenches to this advanced position. The trenches gave very little cover or protection to the men using them as they were merely scraped out of the ground. Bent, in carrying out this work, was in constant danger of being hit by bullets or shellfire.

On the 27th the village was the centre of renewed attacks by the enemy on the seven mile line between Messines and Armentières. The brigade was heavily shelled but managed to repel the German infantry attack. The night of 1/2 November was a crisis time for the East Lancashires and at one point word was passed down the line to withdraw.

Drummer Bent was interviewed for *The Suffolk Chronicle and Mercury* dated 18 December 1914 and said of the incident:

We were as usual taking our hourly turns alternately watching for the enemy, and I had snuggled down into my hole. We had no officer in our trench and

Drummer S.J. Bent rescuing Pte. McNulty

my platoon leader had gone to visit a post, when someone passed the word down the line the battalion was to retire. This was being done when I woke up. I started to follow them, but remembered a French trumpet which I had found, and carried with me for some long time. I did not want to lose it and went back for it, chancing a bullet. When I got into the trench I saw someone just coming round the corner. Thinking it was a German, I waited for him till he crawled up to me, and then poked my rifle into him and asked him who he was. It was Sgt. Waller, who told me that it was a wrong order. I at once jumped out of the trench and ordered the men back. Whilst doing this an officer came up, and after I had told him what had happened he told me to get the men back, whilst he went after some others. We all got back to the trench safely and waited. In the early morning the Germans evidently thought we had left the trenches, for after a bombardment they attacked. The Germans came on, doing a sort of goose step. Our officers kept our fire back, and in the meantime Lt. Dyer brought up a machine gun. When the Germans were about 400 yards off, the order was given to fire, and the Germans went down in hundreds, very few getting safely back to their own trenches.

On the following morning, after we had had breakfast, Private McNulty went out of the trench, and on returning was hit in the pit of the stomach. He fell, and the Germans were trying to hit him again; you could see the earth flying up all around him. I said, 'Why doesn't someone go and help him?' and got the reply, 'Why not go yourself?' I went, and to make it difficult for the Germans to hit me I zig-zagged to him. They did not snipe at me whilst I was advancing, but as soon as I got hold of McNulty's shoulder something seemed to take my feet from under me, and I slipped under McNulty. This took place close to the walls of a ruined convent, and just as I fell several bullets struck the wall, sending a piece of plaster against my left eye. I thought I was wounded, and started to rub the blood away, as I thought, but fortunately the skin was only grazed. I felt it was time to get out of it, and knowing it was impossible to stand up, I hooked my feet under McNulty's arms, and using my elbows I managed to drag myself and him back to the trenches about twenty-five yards away. When I got him there safely I went for a doctor and stretcher bearers. As far as I know he is still alive, at any rate it was the last time I heard of him. On November 10th I got a bullet through the flesh of my right leg, and had to be taken to hospital.

The opponents of the 11th Brigade had been the German 40th and 26th Divisions from their Sixth Army.

Bent was first sent to Oxfordshire and then to the 15th Northern General Hospital at Leicester. He then returned home to Suffolk. When interviewed he was still limping very badly and only walked with the aid of a walking stick. His Victoria Cross was gazetted on 9 December 1914. Bent received his medal from the King at Buckingham Palace on 13 January a few weeks later.

Spencer John Bent was born at Spikes Farm, off the Bury Road, Stowmarket, or so he wrote in a letter to Canon Lummis. However, most accounts state that he was born in the Pickeral Inn, Station Yard, Stowmarket, Suffolk on 18 March 1891. He was the son of Spencer Bent and Gertrude Baker. His father was killed in the Boer War, when serving with the Royal Horse Artillery. Spencer junior was, therefore, brought up from the age of seven by his uncle and aunt, Mr and Mrs William Baker. They lived at Verandah Cottage, Witnesham, near Ipswich. Bent decided to enlist at the very young age of fourteen, in July 1905. He signed on in Ipswich as a Drummer with the 1st East Lancashire Regiment.

As a young man in the Army he seems to have enjoyed boxing and football. He quickly obtained the nickname of 'Joe' during the early part of his Army service. He was stationed with the East Lancashires in a camp at The Curragh, Ireland from 1905 to 1908, followed by four years' service in Woking, until 1912. He then moved with his unit to Colchester, where he heard of the outbreak of the First World War declared on 4 August 1914. Ten days later he journeyed to France. By this time he had served in the Army for nine years.

After Bent had won his Victoria Cross at the beginning of November 1914 he was sent home to recover from his wounds. The *Daily Sketch* of 11 December 1914 published a front-page photograph of him greeting a former farmer-friend at Witnesham. In Ipswich a week later, he was presented with a cheque for £50 in a special casket, a reward sponsored by a local businessman, a Mr T. Curtis. It was presented by the mayor of Ipswich, Mr J.D. Cobbold in recognition of the first Ipswich winner of the VC in the war. It was clearly thought that Witnesham was near enough Ipswich to qualify.

In January 1915 Bent was promoted to the rank of Corporal. On 16 January the *Bury Free Press* reported:

Nearly all the recipients of honours drove to and from the Palace in closed motors and taxi-cabs, and of the little group of Victoria Cross heroes, only one left the Palace on foot. This was Drummer Bent, a sturdy lad, who was warmly congratulated by several relatives who awaited him outside the gates. Bent is a modest man. He had divested himself of his decoration and passed through a crowd of people unnoticed as a Victoria Cross hero. It was not until a group of photographers had persuaded him again to pin the Cross to his breast for the purpose of a picture that his identity as a hero of character was revealed.

Bent spent several months helping with recruiting while he was still convalescing and was promoted to Sergeant. In 1916 he returned to the Western Front with the 1st East Lancashires but was invalided home in November after the Battle of the Somme. In the spring of 1917 he was back in the Le Gheer region where he had won his VC in 1914. In June 1917 he took part in the Messines Ridge battle with the 7th Battalion and at the same time was promoted to the rank of Company Sergeant Major. In February 1918 Bent returned once more to the 1st Battalion and later in the year at the end of October he commanded a successful patrol in the Mons area, and was subsequently awarded the Military Medal on 3 November 1918, for 'bravery in the field.'

Bent left France in December and decided to stay in the Army. Initially he served in the United Kingdom and in March 1920 he was appointed to the role of recruiting officer in Blackburn, Lancashire. He stayed in the town in lodgings with his wife. Later he served with his regiment in the West Indies. During this time he attended the funeral of Sgt. W.J. Gordon VC of the 1st West India Regiment, and had the honour of carrying his VC medals. Bent was also part of the Guard of Honour for the Unknown Warrior at Westminster Abbey in November 1920.

In 1923 Bent received the Long Service and Good Conduct Medal. He was finally discharged from the Army while stationed in Malta in July 1925. He had served for twenty years. In 1927 he was present at Mons for an Armistice Service – he was after all one of the 'Old Contemptibles'. After leaving the Army he became a janitor at the Paragon School, New Kent Road, London. In the Second World War Bent again served with his regiment. On 1 July 1950 he was present when new colours were presented to the 1st East Lancashires in Chester. In 1956 he attended the Centenary of the Victoria Cross in Hyde Park, London. During that same year he retired from his job at the Paragon School and became a commissionaire.

The Bents had three children: Spencer Powell, born on 18 June 1920, Beryl Helena Bent, born in Jamaica on 13 November 1922, and Pauline Patricia Bent born on 5 September 1929. In later years Bent fell out with his son who at one time stood as a candidate for the Communist Party. In August 1968, when Bent was employed as a commissionaire with Courage, the brewers, he was invited to open a public house in Lordswood Lane, Chatham, Kent, named The Victoria

Sgt. Maj. Bent 'hoisting the ale garland' at The Victoria Cross, Chatham, 20 August 1968

Cross. The mayor of Chatham was at the ceremony along with the directors of the brewery. The service of hoisting the traditional ale garland, which signified that the beer was in good condition, was duly carried out by Bent himself. The inn sign was of a Victoria Cross, and a raised terrazzo in the shape of the medal was built for use as outdoor seating. Inside the public house the VC motive was continued in the saloon bar with a photo-mural and the walls were decorated in the VC colours. In addition a three and a half foot fibre-glass model of the award in bronze was also on display. Prints illustrating VC deeds were hung on the walls.

In his later years Bent seems to have become a rather belligerent man and was suspicious of historians researching his life history, often seemingly being on the defensive. An Army Major wrote a letter to Canon Lummis in 1949 in which he said the following of Bent: 'He was not a clever man and probably would have had to relinquish his rank of CSM, had he not retired on pension. You will remember that many who were extremely brave in war did not possess great intelligence.'

An author, a Mrs Margaret Pratt, who was researching for a book on the lives of men who won the VC had a confrontation with Bent in June 1968. She wrote a distraught letter to Canon Lummis about Bent's rudeness and his lack of cooperation in assisting her with information for her project. She had been an army welfare officer and had handled thousands of soldiers but 'Bent was the very first British soldier ever to best me.'

Throughout his life Bent attended many functions and reunions, both in connection with his former regiment and the Victoria Cross and George Cross Association. He worked with Courage, the brewers, for thirteen years and finally retired in 1976 when he was eighty-five. In the same year he and Alice attended what was to be their last Somme Sunday Service together, on the sixtieth anniversary of the battle. Bent laid a wreath to his former colleagues' memory. The following year on the occasion of the couple's Diamond Wedding, they were given a special dinner by the East Lancashire Regimental Association.

Bent died later that year in London on 3 May at the age of eighty-six. His funeral was held at West Norwood Crematorium two days later. Six weeks later on 15 June a service of thanksgiving for Bent's life took place at the Chapel of the Royal Hospital, Chelsea.

Bent's widow, Alice, lived on for another five years and died on 7 December 1984 aged ninety. Bent's medals were displayed at the Imperial War Museum in 1978 and remained there until purchased by a former member of the East Lancashire Regiment for £11,000 on 27 June 1985 at Sotheby's.

J.F. VALLENTIN

Zillebeke, Belgium, 7 November

When war was declared the 1st South Staffordshire Regiment travelled from the Cape of Good Hope in South Africa to join up with the 22nd Brigade of the 7th Division. On 22 October 1914 the regiment joined the battalion in the fighting in the first Battle of Ypres which had begun three days earlier. It was continuously involved in heavy fighting during the next fortnight as the Germans were determined to capture the town of Ypres. The 22nd Brigade was involved in attacks near Zandvoorde, south-west of Gheluvelt, on the Menin road and two days later they lost a large number of men in the fighting near the Gheluvelt crossroads. On the 25th the South Staffordshires were put at the disposal of the 20th Brigade and lost 13 officers and 440 other ranks. On the 26th they were back with the 22nd Brigade and suffered yet again, this time at Kruiseecke, to the south-east of the Gheluvelt crossroads, which the enemy captured. On the 30th the 22nd Brigade was fighting at Zandvoorde again and it was during this time that Captain Vallentin was wounded and sent to hospital in Ypres.

Although the BEF had been heavily outnumbered in the battle for Ypres, which was to continue until 22 November, the town had not fallen. The human cost to both sides was considerable but the enemy having more men in the field probably lost more. The South Staffordshires lost 80 per cent of their men including all their senior officers.

While in hospital Vallentin, who had distinguished himself in the fighting around the village of Gheluvelt, heard that his regiment was going to be involved in the fighting again. He therefore requested permission to rejoin and take command as he was the most senior officer remaining.

The following account is based on the 22nd Brigade *War Diary* (WO95/1660):

In the afternoon of 6 November the Germans had attacked part of the 4th Guards Brigade of the 2nd Division and occupied their trenches. It was decided that the 22nd Brigade should make an attack on these trenches in order to recover them. The 1st South Staffs were joined by the 2nd R.

Warwicks and the 2nd Queen's also of the same Brigade. The German units were from the 30th and 39th Divs. and the French Army was to the 22nd Brigade's right. Starting off at 04.00 a.m., 2 miles to the east of Zillebeke Vallentin personally led his men to the point of deployment from which the counter-attack was launched. The British had 1,100 men with 14 officers in the attack which was entirely successful. The Queen's supported on the right by the 1st South Staffs with the R. Warwicks in reserve, drove the Germans from the previously British forward trenches and pushed on a further 100 yards. Three machine guns were captured and the enemy suffered considerable losses. The main lines of enemy trenches lay about 150 yards inside a wood, part of which consisted of very thick undergrowth and presented great difficulty to the advance. The Germans brought forward a considerable quantity of infantry and delivered a counter-attack which forced back the British to the edge of the wood, where the German trenches made during the night were ... The position was held all day, but it was decided to withdraw to the trenches which had been dug on a line about 600 yards in rear as the present positions formed a salient with the left flank exposed. The French troops not having come up on the right as expected and agreed upon.

Vallentin, who had personally led his men against the Germans was soon wounded again. Pressing on with the charge he was caught by a burst of

Capt. J. Vallentin recapturing the vital trench

machine-gun fire. Nevertheless, the vital trench had been recaptured, owing in full measure to the Captain's extreme courage, for which he was rewarded with a posthumous Victoria Cross. He was also mentioned in despatches in January 1915. His VC was gazetted on 18 February and presented to his mother.

John Franks Vallentin was the son of Mr and Mrs Grimble Vallentin. He was born in Lambeth on 14 May 1882. He was also the grandson of Col. Finnis, the first victim of the Indian Mutiny. His uncle, Maj. Vallentin, was killed in the Boer War.

Vallentin's home was in Hythe in Kent. He was educated at Wellington College and at the age of seventeen joined the 6th (Militia) Battalion Rifle Brigade and became a Lieutenant in July 1900. The unit was stationed at The Curragh in Ireland for a year after the beginning of the Boer War. Vallentin transferred to the 3rd (Militia) Battalion Royal Sussex Regiment and served with it for three years in South Africa between 1899 and 1902. He took part in the operations in the Orange River Colony and also in Transvaal. He subsequently received the Queen's Medal and five clasps.

In July 1903 he received a regular commission in the Royal Garrison Regiment. He transferred to the South Staffordshire Regiment as Second Lieutenant in June 1905. He was promoted to Lieutenant in September 1907 and to Captain in June 1909.

Vallentin's posthumous Victoria Cross was presented to his mother, Mrs Grimble Vallentin, at Buckingham Palace on 16 November 1916. Mrs Vallentin erected a memorial plaque to the memory of her son in St Leonard's parish church, Hythe.

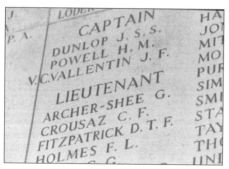

There is also a memorial to him in the garrison church, Whittington Barracks, Lichfield.

Vallentin's body was never found and his name is included in the panels of the Missing on the Menin Gate – on panels 35 and 37. In 1924 his mother presented a set of silver to the regiment in memory of her son. His VC is in the possession of Wellington College.

W.L. BRODIE

Near Becelelaere, Belgium, 11 November

The 2nd Highland Light Infantry was part of the 5th Brigade of the 2nd Division, along with the 6th Brigade, and the 4th (Guards) Brigade. They arrived in France in August 1914 and took a brief part in the fighting at Mons and then helped to repair damaged roads at Etreux a few days later. They also fought in the Battles of the Marne and Aisne, before going northwards to the Ypres Salient. They were, like so many British regiments, to become heavily involved in the desperate fight to prevent Ypres from falling into German hands.

On 23 October the 2nd Division having defeated a German attack, was relieved in its trenches in front of Poelcappelle, to the east of Langemarck. It re-assembled a mile to the east of Ypres, on the Menin road at the infamous Hellfire Corner. The Division was used again as part of a 1st Corps attack. The 2nd HLI was in a defensive brigade position close to Polygon Wood, due north of Gheluvelt. There was no possibility of being able to improve their trench positions, as they were under constant shellfire and were also interrupted by occasional infantry attacks. It was equally dangerous for both sides. The Germans were members of the 54th Reserve Division, of their Fourth Army, and they adopted the same tactics as the British, namely to sap towards the other's positions. In places the lines were extremely close to one another. Raiding parties armed with grenades and bayonets could appear at any time.

On 7 November, according to the Battalion *War Diary* (WO95/1347), signed by Lt. Col. A. Wolfe Murray: 'The 2nd HLI were on the extreme left of the 2nd Division's positions, close to Polygon Wood. To their right was the British 3rd Division and beyond them were units of the French Army. Together these units formed a crescent shape which half encircled the beleagured town.'

B Company trenches under the command of Capt. Buist, were little more than 15 yards from the German positions. The company expected an attack at any time and hid behind the parados. They did not have long to wait and at 04.30 hours they were suddenly attacked by a party of about three hundred Germans.

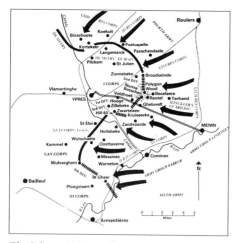

The Salient, 11 November

The Highlanders jumped down on their attackers and inflicted great carnage, in a hand to hand fight, where the bayonet was the predominate weapon. In the morning light it was discovered that about eighty Germans had been killed, mostly by the bayonet, but some by Lt. W.L. Brodie's two Maxim machine guns. About fifty-four Germans were taken prisoner.

It had been the German plan to capture the guns and turn them against the Highlanders. However, despite the guns being momentarily captured, Lt. Brodie personally bayoneted four men and shot five others. The losses of the HLI amounted to one officer, sixteen other ranks and twenty-eight wounded or missing. It was this incident, for which Brodie gained the Victoria Cross, an incident that he was to describe in a letter home 'as a bit of a scrape'.

Brodie's Victoria Cross was gazetted on the 12 December. The citation records the date of the VC as 11 November whereas Regimental records state it was 7 November. Brodie was the second man from Edinburgh to win the VC in the First World War – Pte. George Wilson being the first. He received his medal from the King at Windsor Castle on 17 July 1915.

Walter Lorrain Brodie was the son of Mr and Mrs John Brodie. He was born at Belgrave Crescent, Edinburgh on 28 July 1885. His father was a chartered accountant. Walter Brodie was educated at Edinburgh Academy and from there went to the Royal Military College at Sandhurst. He obtained a commission when he was eighteen years old with the Highland Light Infantry in March 1904. He joined the 2nd Battalion in Jersey and was stationed subsequently at the Castle in Edinburgh and at Fort George. He passed through various courses successfully and became an expert on the use of machine guns. He was promoted to Lieutenant on 30 June 1908. In the period from 1909 to 1913 his regiment was stationed in Ireland. In 1913, the year before the First World War broke out, his battalion moved to Aldershot and in August 1914 Brodie left for France as battalion Machine-Gun Officer. A few days later, on 10 September he was made up to Captain.

In January 1917 Brodie was awarded the Military Cross. At the end of that year he took command of the 2/10th Liverpool Scottish and was made a Brevet

Major the following January. In April 1918 he was back with his former battalion as Commanding Officer – something he had always wished for.

In the Battle of Albert, which began on 21 August 1918, the 3rd Division advanced on Gomiecourt with the 5th Brigade in reserve. If the 3rd Division was successful the plan was for the 5th Brigade to attack the line Behagnies–Sapignies while the Highlanders were to take Behagnies, with the assistance of 'whippet tanks'. They crossed the Achiet-le-Grand railway and wheeled round the edge of Gomiecourt under heavy fire. The leading units established themselves 500 yards to the north-west of Behagnies but Brodie was killed along with 160 other casualties. They had found Behagnies a harder position to take than had been thought. Brodie was killed eleven weeks before the end of the war; he was shot by a bullet and died instantaneously.

A brother officer wrote the following about his former colleague:

From the first he entered the regimental spirit with enthusiasm, and his love for and pride in the regiment were unbounded. . . . He was keen on all sports . . . [and when in Ireland] he took to hunting very eagerly. [In the war] . . . His machine gunners soon proved themselves worthy of the labour he had expended on them . . . he had much hard fighting as Company Commander

with his old battalion in 1915, especially in the neighbourhood of Richebourg, Givenchy and Festubert. Later he was attached for intelligence duties to the Staff, first of Sir Hubert Gough, and afterwards of Sir Henry Rawlinson, and later became Brigade Major of 63rd Infantry Brigade in May 1916. Brodie had taken an active part in the 1916 Somme battle and Arras battles and other engagements in 1917. He was a professional soldier in the very best sense and he was delighted when he was given command of his battalion.

Brodie was buried in Bienvillers Military Cemetery, Row F, Grave 15. His medals are not publicly held.

J.H.S. DIMMER

Klein Zillebeke, Belgium, 12 November

The 2nd King's Royal Rifle Corps was sent to France in August 1914 with the BEF and served with the 2nd Brigade of the 1st Division of 1 Corps. The other two brigades in the division were the 1st (Guards) Brigade, and the 3rd Brigade

The main part of the Battle of the Aisne was fought in mid-September. In the small hours of 14 September, in pouring rain and mist the KRRC was part of the divisional attack launched from the village of Vendresse with the high ground above the small hamlet of Troyon as its target. Once this ground was secured, it would then allow the rest of the Division to proceed. At about 04.45 hours, the leading company of the battalion, accompanied by the 9th Lancers, reached the top of the hill and came up against a German piquet. Reinforcements were called up as the Germans seemed to be present in considerable numbers. The right flank was protected by the 1st Northamptons of the same brigade as the riflemen and leading companies of the 2nd Royal Sussex moved westwards to try and take the enemy in the flank. There was fierce fighting between the hamlet of Troyon and the sugar factory to the north.

Three days later, a White Flag incident occurred there – these were common in the early stages of the war. The usual pattern was that one section of the enemy decided to surrender flinging up its hands and displaying at least one white flag. On this particular occasion most of the officers of the 1st Northamptonshire Regiment (2nd Brig. 1st Div.) had been killed. Capt. Savage of B Company, however, left his front trench along with Lt. Dimmer as it was rumoured that the enemy was showing the White Flag and laying down their arms. Savage climbed out of his trench and lay down his revolver and sword and marched the few yards to the German positions. Dimmer was close behind him. Savage and a German officer saluted one another and were seen to converse for about five minutes. The two British officers then began to walk back to their trenches when Dimmer turned to look back at the enemy and saw them levelling their rifles. He shouted to Savage to get down but it was too late and Savage's body was riddled with bullets and he died immediately. Many Northamptons became casualties during this incident until a machine gun from the 1st Queens retaliated.

There was another similar incident shortly afterwards near the Troyon sugar factory. The Germans seemed to be waiting for the British to come up in order to receive their surrender but they then fired indiscriminately at their own troops and foe alike. The enemy tried 'surrendering' again three days later but this time a machine gun was trained on their positions.

The Battle of Aisne was virtually over by the end of September when the French took over the rest of the line. This allowed the British to travel north to take part in the operations to save the town of Ypres from falling into German hands. The 2nd KRRC was at first heavily involved in operations around Kortekeer, near the town of Langemarck, to the north-east of Ypres.

During the last few days of October the battalion was engaged in the fighting at Gheluvelt, a village which was the gateway to Ypres, a short distance down the Menin road. Later the unit was in action to the south-east of Ypres. On 12 November the enemy shelled the French troops out of the village of Zwarteleen, to the north-east of Klein Zillebeke, and two miles to the south-east of Ypres. The enemy, from the 39th and 30th Divisions, began to attack in large numbers.

At Klein Zillebeke the Germans were faced by units of the 3rd Division; to the north were the 1st and 2nd Divisions and to the south-west the French Army. The 2nd KRRC was in the part of the line which bordered on the French positions and Lt. J. Dimmer was in charge of four machine guns set up in a rough emplacement. Early on, a German shell killed three of his men and also wounded him in the shoulder with two shrapnel bullets. Despite these wounds and other injuries Dimmer staggered to one of the machine guns and managed to fire off over nine hundred rounds before falling to the ground unconscious. His action had saved the day and the line from being broken. It gained him the last Victoria Cross to be awarded for bravery in the First Battle of Ypres. When he came round he insisted on reporting to Earl Cavan, Commander of the 4th Guards Brigade, to whom the 2nd KRRC had been attached before collapsing.

He was sent to Bellevue Hospital, Wimereux, near Boulogne where he read of the news of his VC award in a newspaper, a week after it had been won. He was, apparently, a little surprised at the news according to his brother officers in hospital. He wrote to his mother telling her that his condition was much improved. He also told his mother about the incident as follows:

At about one o'clock we were suddenly attacked by the Prussian Guards. They shelled us unmercifully, and poured in a perfect hail of bullets at a range of about 100 yards. I got my guns going, but they smashed one up almost immediately, and then turned all their attention on the gun I was with, and succeeded in smashing that, too, but before they completed the job I had been twice grounded,

Lt. J.H.S. Dimmer in charge of four machine guns at Klein Zillebeke

and was finally knocked out with the gun. My face is spattered with pieces of my gun and pieces of shell, and I have a bullet in my face and four small holes in my right shoulder. It made rather a nasty mess of me at first, but now that I am washed and my wounds dressed I look quite all right.

Dimmer's VC was gazetted on 19 November, a week after the deed. He went to Buckingham Palace on 13 January 1915 where he received the Military Cross with his Victoria Cross. The MC was awarded for devotion to duty during the period 29 to 31 October and on many other occasions.

Dimmer was attached for a time to the 6th Battalion at Sheerness and was involved in duties such as inspecting the Southern Battalion of the Volunteer National Guards at Southend. He also addressed the boys of Harrow School OTC in February 1915, a visit that was filmed. He was then sent to join the 3rd Battalion in Salonika as Brigade Machine-Gun Officer to the 10th Division. He suffered from malaria but refused to return home. He joined the local Flying Corps and gained his Observer's Certificate. He then became ill again and was sent home to England to recover his health. In February 1917 he re-joined the 2nd KRRC but contracted blood poisoning and once more had to enter hospital. He was then made Commander of the 2/4th Royal Berkshire Regiment and took part in the Battle of Cambrai in November 1917.

Dimmer was eventually killed during the beginning of the March Retreat on 21 March 1918 at Marteville, north-west of St Quentin. He was shot when leading his battalion on horseback. His horse survived and was taken over by a brother officer. He was buried at Vadencourt British Cemetery in France, grave number 46, row B, plot 11.

A brother officer wrote of Dimmer on his death: 'The Colonel was like a father to us, we all had implicit faith in him, and loved him dearly. He was full of energy with a natural ability for military work . . .'

John Henry Stephen Dimmer was one of four sons of John Dimmer, a railway worker. He was born at 37 Gloster Street in South Lambeth on 9 October 1883 and spent his boyhood in

Lt. Dimmer on his horse

Wimbledon living at No. 55a Griffiths Road, now a block of flats. He attended the local elementary school in Melrose Road, Merton, Surrey. At the age of thirteen, with the help of a scholarship, he went to Rutlish Science School, also in Merton. Many years later a future British Prime Minister, John Major, was also to attend Rutlish School.

When Dimmer left school at the age of fifteen he worked briefly in an engineer's office but had a hankering for military life. He subsequently started up the Boys' Brigade at the local Presbyterian Christchurch at Copse Hill. In 1900–1 he joined the 1st Cadet Battalion of the KRRC (Militia) and was made a Sergeant when still only seventeen years old. In 1902 he joined a regular battalion of the KRRC and won prizes for drill and shooting and for other military work. He was made a Lance-Corporal. In the autumn of that year he joined the 4th Battalion in South Africa where he served until June 1904. He became a Corporal following reconnaissance work in the Orange River Colony. Later he was promoted to Lance-Sergeant for scouting and signalling in the Mounted Infantry serving at one time on Salisbury Plain in Wiltshire. He was commended by Gen. Sir Ian Hamilton for military sketching and for some time he served as an instructor to non-commissioned officers (NCOs).

In 1906, at his own expense, he visited Belgium and Germany to study their military systems. The following year he carried out some intelligence work and was thanked by the Army Council for this. He attended the School of Signalling and passed at the top of his course subsequently becoming a sergeant instructor. His duties and responsibilities at this time seemed to be those more associated with the rank of a commissioned officer. At the end of 1906 he attended an officer's examination and passed with high marks. In March 1907 he obtained a first-class Army School certificate but it was not until January 1908 that he was finally recommended for a commission by Lord Methuen. This delay may have been caused by his background. The KRRC was second only to the Guards in terms of class consciousness.

During the next few years Dimmer did 'special work' in Africa, serving with black troops. He came home on leave in May 1914 and was called up over the August Bank Holiday, on the outbreak of the First World War.

Dimmer, like many other VC holders, became a temporary national celebrity. In January 1918 he had married the daughter of a carpet millionaire, a Miss Mary Bailey Parker. After her husband's death, she was remarried to an Irish Peer, Lord Garvagh, at St Matthew's church, Bayswater, London on New Year's Day 1919, just three months later.

After the war the local council at Wimbledon discussed erecting a suitable memorial to Dimmer's memory. His mother, however, was invited to lay one of the wreaths at the unveiling of the Wimbledon war memorial.

Dimmer's VC is in the possession of the Green Jackets Museum at Winchester, Hampshire. At one time his family owned his ceremonial sword presented to him by the King. He was mentioned twice in despatches.

Dimmer had been offered the freedom of the borough of Wimbledon in April 1915 but declined the offer in the following letter written the following month and published in the *Suffolk and Essex Free Press*: 'Whilst appreciating the great honour, I beg to decline the same. Too much publicity has been given my name already, and has caused me a great deal of worry and annoyance. To accept the freedom would only bring further publicity, and such is not in accordance with the traditions of the service.' This shy hero was, however, commemorated

on the KRRC memorial at Winchester Cathedral and in the Civic Offices of the London Borough of Morden in an office block called Crown House.

J.F.P. BUTLER

Cameroons, West Africa,
17 November and 27 December

In August 1914 Germany's African Colonies consisted of German East Africa, German South-West Africa, the Cameroons and Togoland. It was the aim of the British and French Armies to drive the enemy out of these territories.

Captain J.F.P. Butler of the King's Royal Rifle Corps was attached to Pioneer Company, Gold Coast Regiment, West African Forces, and on 17 November 1914 he won the Victoria Cross for conspicuous bravery in the Cameroons. He was with a party of thirteen men in thick bush when they attacked about a hundred of the enemy, including some Europeans. They defeated them and captured their machine gun and a great deal of ammunition as well. Nearly six weeks later, on 27 December, Capt. Butler was on patrol with a small group when he swam the River Ekam which was in enemy hands. He was alone and in the face of brisk fire he carried out his reconnaissance on the far bank and then swam back to safety.

The following March he was made a Captain before later returning to England. His VC was gazetted on the 23 August 1915 and he went to Buckingham Palace the next day in order to receive his medal from the King.

Capt. Butler was once more involved in fighting in the Cameroons in December 1915. He fought with the Gold Coast Regiment when they got behind the German lines and captured a village, together with a machine gun and the papers of the local German commander, and then established their base there. Two weeks later Dschang Mangas, between Wum Biagas and Jaunde, on the fringe of the Jaunde district, was taken by them. By this time most of the forestry region was behind them. Before them was a cultivated area which would be much easier to cope with. By 30 December they were entirely clear of the bush and a small party marched into Jaunde on New Year's Day 1916.

On 6 July 1916 the Gold Coast Regiment left the West African capital of Accra and sailed to East Africa, landing at Kilindini on the 26th. They reached

The Cameroons, 17 November

the firing line on 8 August; the enemy was then pushed back across the Central Railway. In German East Africa the first firm contact with the enemy occurred on 4 September near the main highway to the east of the Matombo mission station. This was south of the railway in the Uluguru Mountains which the Germans were preparing to strongly defend. The Allied positions were overlooked by the Kikirunga Hill which is about 3,000 feet high and covered with trees and undergrowth. It was a landmark which had to be captured. The action lasted two and a half days and ended with the capture of the hill. But the day was marred by the loss of Capt. Butler. The full details of the incident are recorded in the history of the Gold Coast Regiment by Sir Hugh Clifford:

At 7 a.m., on the 4th September the Regiment moved out of camp, and about two hours later the enemy opened fire with a couple of howitzers upon the road a little ahead of the marching troops. No casualties were inflicted but the Regiment was halted, moved off the road and took up a sheltered position on the right side of it, in a gut between two hills.

Captain Butler was then sent forward with a Pioneer Company to reconnoitre the enemy positions and the small party climbed towards the head of the pass that led to the Uluguru Mountains, that had Kikirunga as its culminating point. The Pioneer Company reached a point where they could

River Ekam, 27 December

overlook the enemy positions but they must have been spotted as a German machine gun opened up from the right and another gun about 100 feet higher also opened up on the small party.

It was not until about 5 o'clock in the afternoon that the Pioneer Company became seriously threatened and it was when Butler had gone forward to check his picket on the bend of the road that he and several of his party were wounded by a sudden burst of machine gun. They had been lying down, close to the road and the machine gunners were either aware of them, or just fired off a round or two at random. Twelve men were wounded during the afternoon but the party managed to stand firm. Later B Company under a Captain Shaw, were sent up to reinforce the Pioneers, and to make the ground won, good. They settled down for the night after attending to the wounded.

Butler had been wounded in the shoulder but more seriously a bullet had penetrated one of his lungs and according to Maj. G.H. Parker, MC, RA, Butler lay dying by his side all through the night. The regimental history says the following of Butler:

> . . . a young officer, possessed at once with a charming and forceful personality, of an absolutely fearless disposition, and of more than ordinary ability, he has won for himself a conspicuous place in the Gold Coast Regiment, and had earned the devotion and affection of the men in a very special degree. His death, in this first action in which the Regiment had been engaged since its arrival in East Africa, was felt to be a specially malignant stroke of ill-fortune and he was mourned as a personal loss by his comrades of all ranks.

Unofficially Butler died of his wounds on 5 September 1916 near Matombo. He was later buried in the Morogoro Cemetery, Tanganyika, Plot 111, Row C,

Grave 43. He was mentioned in despatches three times. At the end of the war the Allies were to confiscate all German-held territories in Africa.

John Fitzhardinge Paul Butler was the son of Lt. Col. F.J.P. Butler of Wyck Hall, Gloucestershire and his wife the Hon. Elspeth Fitzhardinge, daughter of the 2nd Lord Gifford. He was born at Berkeley, Gloucestershire on 20 December 1888. He was a nephew of Maj. Lord Gifford, VC, the third baron who had won the VC in the Ashanti War.

John Butler was educated at Mr Kempthorne's House at Wellington and from there he went on to the RMA at Sandhurst. While there he won the Military History Prize. In February 1907, when he was eighteen years of

Morogoro Cemetery, Tanganyika

age, he was given a commission in the KRRC. In August 1909 he was promoted to Lieutenant and served in India until 1913. On 1 October 1913 he was seconded to the Gold Coast Regiment in West Africa where he was to win his VC.

After the war he was commemorated on the war memorial in Cirencester and by a large candleholder at St Lawrence's church, Bourton-on-the-Water, also in Gloucestershire. His medals are with the Royal Green Jackets in Winchester, Hampshire.

T.E. RENDLE

Near Wulverghem, Belgium, 20 November

The 1st Duke of Cornwall's Light Infantry arrived in France in mid-August 1914 and took part in the Battle of Mons on 23 August, where they were in positions near Pommereul station.

In the early evening the battalion had its first casualty. Rendle commandeered a car to take the injured man to hospital. Soon afterwards Gen. De Lisle of the 1st Cavalry Division intercepted them and sent Rendle back to his unit and took charge of the injured man himself.

The battalion went on to serve at Le Cateau, in the Battle of the Aisne and the First Battle of Ypres. This last battle formally ended on 22 November when trench warfare set in for the rest of the war. Three days later the 1st DCLI of the 14th Brigade of 5th Division, were in positions between Lindenhoek, to the east of Mont Kemmel, and Wulverghem, to the south-west of Ypres. They had taken over the line from troops of the French XVI Corps who had left the positions in a very poor state with an inadequate trench system. These positions faced the Messines Ridge which was in enemy hands. In places the trenches were little more than ditches and there was no proper system of communication trenches. The battalion did its best to improve the defences. The lines to the right were only 50 yards apart and to the left they were 150 yards apart.

On 20 November the enemy snipers were busy and at 09.00 hours a heavy bombardment suddenly opened up. The first few shells from the enemy fell on their own positions but they then found their range and hit the left centre of A Company's positions, when a shell landed on the parapet. About fifteen men were buried and several wounded or killed. Capt. Leale, the Company Commander, was one of those buried and about 40 yards of trench were destroyed together with a support trench occupied by C Company.

Later in the day it was thought that the artillery fire was being directed from an aircraft. When the shelling was at its height, 2nd Lt. R.M. Colebrooke was sitting in the bottom of a trench when he was hit. He was in need of urgent medical attention. Bandsman Rendle came to the rescue as bandsmen operated as stretcher bearers in times of war. Rendle had to be extremely careful in crawling to rescue the officer as the enemy snipers had the position very well covered. He applied temporary first aid to the officer and then scratched a path through the fallen earth, and carrying him on his back, he slowly crawled his way to safety. This gallant action was to earn him the Victoria Cross. During the day, the battalion lost twelve men killed and sixteen wounded and one missing. The shelling occurred at the end of a period of snow and rain, and the enemy guns were doing less damage because many shells were sinking harmlessly deep into the soft earth.

Rendle was eventually invalided home as his sight had been badly affected by high explosives. He was promoted to Lance-Corporal and was first sent to recuperate at No. 1 Temporary Hospital in Exeter. His family stayed in the town in order to be near him. His VC was gazetted on 11 January 1915.

Rendle was invited along with Drummers Bent and Kenny to a reception at the Mansion House, London, in March 1915 but he was still recuperating from his wounds and was unable to attend. He did manage to attend a civic welcome at Launceston in Cornwall and he went to Buckingham Palace on 12 July 1915. Being a modest man Rendle did not particularly welcome the publicity that went with winning the VC and he, together with some other award winning soldiers, turned up at the Palace in taxis which were ordered to drive into the inner courtyard in order to avoid the crowds.

Rendle left the hospital in Exeter for Bristol, his home town, and on arriving at Temple Meads railway station he was not recognized as he stepped off the express from Plymouth. A local newspaper even went as far as reporting Rendle's homecoming in his own city as 'furtive'.

Thomas Edward Rendle was the son of James and Charlotte Rendle. He was born at No. 4 Mead Street, Bedminster, Bristol, on 14 December 1884. His father was a painter and decorator and his mother, who gave birth to three sons and four daughters, died on 4 October 1898. All three boys were to serve in the First World War.

Rendle was educated at St Luke's School, New Cut, Bedminster and then went to Kingswood Reformatory. After leaving school he wanted to join the Gloucestershire Regiment but there were no suitable vacancies. In due course, he joined the Army at Bristol on 5 September 1902 at the age of seventeen. His number was 7079. He then joined the DCLI at Bodmin on 8 September. On 3 January 1903 he was sent with a draft to join the 1st DCLI at Stellenbosch, Cape Colony. The battalion moved from there to Middleburg and in July 1904 they went to Wynberg, Cape Colony, where they remained until 12 March 1906.

They then left for England, arriving at Plymouth on 5 April 1906 and travelled to Crowshill.

Shortly before Rendle left South Africa he married Lillian Crowe, the daughter of a bandsman, on 7 February 1906. They had two children, a daughter Ruby, born on 23 May 1907, and a son Edward, born on 10 October 1909. During his service in the Army Rendle had always been a bandsman.

He served in various parts of the British Isles and in March 1914 he went with his battalion to Newry in Northern Ireland. Four months later at the end of July they returned to The Curragh in Ireland before leaving for France on 13 August 1914. After he won his VC on 20 November 1914 Rendle took some time to recover in hospital. His was the only VC to be awarded to a member of the DCLI in the First World War. When he was decorated by the King he was also awarded the Order of St George, 4th Class (Russia).

In the meantime he was promoted to the rank of Corporal and Sergeant on 24 March 1915. When he was well enough he was employed in a recruiting campaign and also visited his old school at St Luke's, Bedminster, much to the delight of the teachers and children. During the rest of the war Rendle was employed as a musketry instructor.

In 1919 he returned to Northern Ireland and the following year he went back to South Africa, having been invalided from the Army on 12 November 1920. He was for many years a part-time bandmaster with the Duke of Edinburgh's Own Rifles, Cape of Good Hope. He also worked at the Standard Bank as caretaker and stationery controller in their branch at Strand Street. In 1927 a South African Veterans' organization was founded under the name of The Memorable Order of Tin Hats, or 'Moths' for short. Their headquarters was in Durban and their motto was 'Mutual Help, Sound Memory, and True Comradeship'. Rendle had the name of 'Provincial Old Bill' within the organization. He used to attend its various meetings.

Between the two world wars he carried out a great deal of work on behalf of the local ex-service organizations and was a 'fine and popular character'. He used also to arrange an annual dinner to commemorate the Battle of Mons on 23 August in Cape Town. In 1939, Cape Town celebrated the twenty-fifth anniversary of Rendle's historic deed.

In the late 1930s while Rendle was in South Africa a man called Joseph Rendle began to impersonate him in England and Scotland. He wore a VC which he had purchased for fifteen shillings and he styled himself Corporal and attended various functions. He was eventually caught and fined.

In the Imperial War Museum file on Rendle, there is a note about a conversation Rendle had with the then Prince of Wales. He was asked why he had not attended the last VC dinner. Rendle replied that he could not afford the fare. The Prince then said, 'No, I suppose you couldn't. Anyway we had a jolly good evening.'

Rendle died at the Groote Shuur Hospital, Cape Town, on 1 June 1946 after a short illness. The streets of Cape Town were crowded for his funeral on 3 June. The arrangements were made by his regiment, the Duke of Edinburgh's Own Rifles, and he was buried at Maitland Number 1 Cemetery, Cape District. His medals are in the DCLI Regimental Collection at Bodmin, Cornwall.

DARWAN SING NEGI

Festubert, France, 23/24 November

Naik Darwan Sing Negi of the 1/39th Garhwal Rifles was the second Indian to win the Victoria Cross in the First World War, the first being Sepoy Khudadad Khan, who had gained the medal on 31 October in Belgium (see earlier chapter). Darwan Sing, whose rank was the equivalent of a Corporal, did, however, receive his medal before Khan who was still in hospital.

When war broke out in Europe orders were received for mobilization on 9 August 1914. The battalion was detailed with the 2nd to the 20th Brigade of the 7th Division. Later it became known as the Garhwal Brigade, of the Meerut Division, Indian Expeditionary Force. The other units in the brigade were the 2nd Leicestershires and the 2/3rd Gurkha Rifles. The 1st Garhwalis left their headquarters at Lansdown, a hill station, on 20 August and after a delay at a railway terminus they departed from Karachi on 3 September. They did not sail until the 21st and disembarked at Marseilles on 14 October. They were issued with equipment and arrived at Orleans on the 21st, eventually reaching Lillers six days later. They then proceeded to march to the Rue de l'Epinette where arrangements were made for them to take over trenches occupied by units from British 11 Corps.

It has been said that the Indian Army could not have arrived at a better time as the BEF was suffering badly and fast becoming exhausted from continuous fighting against a larger army. The German attack against Lille had ended and the enemy was now attacking along the line from La Bassée to Messines.

The Indian Corps arrived on the Western Front at the end of October 1914. They took over a line that ran for about eight miles from north of Givenchy to the south, east of Richebourg l'Avoue to the back of Neuve Chapelle and then beyond Capigny to Fauquissart before turning in an easterly direction to Rouges Bancs, north of Fromelles. The Indian units were ill used by the British High Command and were fed piecemeal into the fighting and attached to British formations. They were often broken down into half battalions.

Conditions in the area were deplorable, the whole region was little more than a sea of mud, with fetid pools and ditches. Communication trenches were little more than streams. The environment could not have been more alien than this for these men from the Indian sub-continent. The brigade order from right to left was Bareilly, Garhwal, Dehra Dun, all of the Meerut Division, then four British battalions on attachment from 11 Corps and lastly the Jullundur Brigade of the Lahore Division. The 1/39th Garhwalis relieved the 1st East Surreys in the period 29/30 October and were involved in the Battle of La Bassée until 2 November. During the next three weeks they were in and out of the trenches on this part of the Front.

At Festubert on the morning of 23 November part of the section of trenches occupied by the Ferozepore Brigade had been lost. In spite of numerous attempts to recapture the lost positions the Germans were still in occupation of a 300 yard portion of them at dusk. Allied troops were on both of the two flanks and in effect were sharing the same trench as the enemy. The 1/39th Garhwalis under its commander, Lt. Col. E.R.R. Swiney, was instructed to recapture this portion and to restore the broken line at 19.30 hours. There was confusion over the line that the Germans were occupying and Swiney was not at all keen to make a frontal attack on the positions. He therefore obtained permission to change the plan of attack and gave orders to advance through the trenches occupied by the 57th Rifles and to attack the enemy from the British left flank. This attack began at 03.00 hours.

Several traverses were captured with the use of bomb and bayonet and about thirty prisoners were also captured. When the supply of bombs ran out the Garhwalis were ordered to charge. After very hard fighting in which the bayonet predominated as the main weapon the lost portion of trenches was recaptured at about 06.00 hours on the 24th. The BEF was able to join hands once more. This was achieved by men jumping on the parapet at each traverse while the party in the trench charged round the traverse and quickly took the position. At the time it was considered a novel fighting approach for trench warfare was still in its infancy.

The regimental history writes about the role of Darwan Sing Negi in this action as follows:

This non-commissioned officer, from the beginning to the end, was either the first, or among the first, to push around each successive traverse, facing a hail of bombs and grenades. Although twice wounded in the head and once in the arm, he refused to give in, and continued fighting without even reporting that he was wounded. When the struggle was over and the company fell in, his company commander saw that he was streaming with blood from head to foot . . .

Darwan Sing Negi fighting in the trenches at Festubert 23/24 November

The attack was well planned by Lt. Col. Swiney and skilfully carried out by the Indian and British troops. The battalion losses were comparatively small and the achievement was considerable. The 1st Garhwalis continued to occupy the positions until the night of the 25th when they were relieved by the 2nd Garhwalis, of the same brigade. The trenches were by this time in a terrible condition and the putrefying bodies of both Germans and Indians had to be removed, under the fire of the enemy who was only a short distance away.

Darwan Sing Negi's well-deserved Victoria Cross was gazetted on 7 December 1914 but presented to him two days earlier by the King at General Headquarters in St Omer when he was visiting his Armies. Darwan Sing Negi was escorted to St Omer from Locon by car. St Omer was within sight and sound of operations. The presentation ceremony took place in front of Indian troops. It was the first time that a VC had been awarded to a native Indian and the event was received with great enthusiasm in India. At the pre-war Durbar at Delhi King George V had made a promise that native Indian troops would be eligible for the award.

On 23 November, the day that Darwan Sing Negi had won his award, he was commissioned as Jemadar. He returned to India for recruiting purposes in January 1915. After the fighting at Festubert the Garhwalis were again in action, this time at Neuve Chapelle, in March 1915, when they charged a line of trenches where the wire was still uncut. Most of the British and Indian officers involved in the attack were killed but the men managed to bayonet the German garrison and remained all day with no officer in command.

Darwan Sing Negi was the son of Kalam Sing Negi, a landowner and cultivator. He was born in the village of Kabartir, Karakot, Garhwal, north of the Pindar river in India, in November 1881. He was brought up in the Hindu faith and during boyhood he used to help look after his father's herds of goats and sheep in the glacier valleys. He was often alone for weeks at a time and became hardy to extremes of weather. He was educated at the Regimental School and at the age of eighteen he married Chandpur Garhwal, the daughter of another cultivator and landowner.

On 4 March 1902 Darwan Sing Negi enlisted as a Rifleman in the 1st Battalion, Garhwal Rifles. They recruited mainly from the Himalayan foothills that lay within the British territory called Garhwal, to the west of Nepal. The men were often short of stature but became active and sturdy mountaineers. The Garhwalis had a kinship with the more famous Gurkhas and wore the same slouch hats and used similar equipment. The regiment was first raised in Almora in 1887 as the 2nd Battalion of the 3rd Gurkha Regiment and became the 39th

Neuve Chapelle Indian Memorial, France

Bengal Infantry in 1890. In 1892 they added the title of The Garhwal Rifles. A second battalion was raised in 1901.

In August 1915, almost nine months after his VC and promotion to Jemadar, Darwan Sing Negi was made a Subadar.

Five years later on 1 February 1920 Darwan Sing Negi retired from the Army with a pension and returned to his home. On 11 November 1923 he attended the unveiling of the Royal Garhwal Rifles War Memorial at Lansdowne, the Regimental Headquarters. The unveiling was carried out by Lord Rawlinson to whom Darwan Sing Negi was introduced. The memorial, which was designed in England, showed a Garhwal Rifleman in the act of fixing a bayonet, and was set on a marble plinth.

Another better-known memorial exists at Neuve Chapelle in France, which is dedicated to the 5,000 missing Indians from the First World War. It was erected in an area that had become particularly associated with the Indian Army Corps.

Darwan Sing Negi died on 24 June 1950 at the age of sixty-eight. His regiment acquired his medals.

F.A. DE PASS

Near Festubert, France, 24 November

The Indian Corps did not take part in the First Battle of Ypres but was based in the region of La Bassée-Armentières. The town of Estaires was the centre of the Indian Corps positions which stretched from Armentières in the north to Givenchy in the south-west. The Ferozepore Brigade of the Lahore Division, however, did take part in the Battle of Messines, in early November when the Indian Corps was sent to the north-west of Givenchy.

It was on 23 November 1914 that a detachment of the 34th Poona Horse of the Secunderabad Cavalry Brigade of the 2nd Indian Cavalry Division, under the command of Capt. Roly Grimshaw, took over part of the trenches of the Ferozepore Brigade of the Lahore Division. They arrived in the line at 04.00 hours on the 24th only to find that the Germans had driven a sap right up to the parapet which had been destroyed. This made a gap of 8 feet wide and exposed the Allied trench to enemy fire from the sap, which was about 2½ feet broad and about 6 feet deep. A party under Lt. F.A. de Pass guarded the breach, at his own request, and the position was inspected by Grimshaw as soon as it was daylight. Grimshaw asked for a volunteer to reconnoitre along the line of the sap to the German lines. Sowar Khan volunteered and crawled out, and on his return reported that the Germans had erected a sandbag traverse about 10 yards from their trench, at the first bend in the sap. Khan discovered that the traverse was loopholed when a German guarding it fired at him but missed.

At 08.00 hours the Germans began to throw bombs from their side of the traverse; they continued doing so throughout the day causing several casualties. At the same time the following morning, de Pass asked Grimshaw to allow him to put an end to the continuous bombing. Grimshaw was not very keen on the idea as it would risk the lives of others should de Pass and his party need rescuing. However, he relented, and de Pass, with two Indians, Sowars Fateh Khan and Firman Shah, entered the sap and crawled along it until they reached the German traverse. With great coolness de Pass then proceeded to place a

Lt. de Pass bombing the enemy after entering one of their saps

charge of gun cotton at the loophole. He subsequently fired it and completely destroyed the traverse. The Germans quickly retaliated with a bomb which landed just behind de Pass but fortunately failed to explode. The detachment was not troubled anymore that day by the enemy bombers.

Later, when de Pass was visiting the neighbouring positions occupied by the 7th Dragoon Guards, who were also members of the Secunderabad Brigade, he spotted a wounded sepoy from the 58th Rifles (Bareilly Brigade) lying outside the Indian trench. Several bodies were showing signs of life.

Accompanied by Pte. Cook of the 7th Dragoons, he went out in broad daylight to bring the Indian back to safety. He was exposed to enemy fire for about 200 yards. Capt. Grimshaw was not pleased about this action and was to write in his diary: 'A British Officer is worth more than a wounded Sepoy, I know these things cannot be measured in that way . . . '

During the cover of darkness the enemy had managed to repair their traverse and de Pass again volunteered to repeat his exploits of the night before. Grimshaw felt this would lead to de Pass' certain death and permission was refused.

On the 25th the Germans returned and began to bomb with increasing violence. Lt. de Pass made an attempt to repair the sap head and to supervise the mending of the parapet which had again been badly damaged. He spotted a sniper at work behind the traverse and tried to shoot him but the sniper was too fast and blew half of de Pass's head away with a bullet at close range.

A grieving Grimshaw reported the incident in his diary when he was exhausted and was trying to snatch some sleep:

> I was dozing off when an orderly hurriedly came up with the news that de Pass was very badly wounded. Alderson (a brother officer) and myself both jumped up and the former ran along the trench to try and help. I picked up my flask and followed. I just caught Alderson up and could see de Pass lying on the ground with half his head gone when I felt a blinding crash and fell forward on Alderson who had also fallen. [They had both been stunned by the explosion.]

Grimshaw was far from well and scribbled a note to de Pass in case he became conscious explaining why he had not come sooner. But de Pass was certainly dead and a message from Headquarters said that the Germans were massing in their trenches for an attack. Grimshaw observed some time later that de Pass's defence works had once more been destroyed by the enemy, allowing them to snipe at will at the Indian unit's positions along with those of the 7th Dragoon Guards.

Thus ended the short life of a very brave soldier. In the book *The Indian Corps in France*, J.W.B. Merewether describes de Pass as 'the very perfect type of British officer. He united to singular personal beauty, a charm of manner and a degree of valour which made him the idol of his men . . . '

Although Grimshaw does not exactly say it in his diary, he appears to have been a little annoyed that de Pass took matters into his own hands. It was as if he was determined to make a mark in the shortest possible time. He was surely successful and was awarded the Victoria Cross for his action. Sowars Abdullah and Fateh Khan and Firman Shah, who had supported their officer so well, received the Indian Distinguished Service Medal and Pte. Cook was awarded the Distinguished Conduct Medal (DCM).

In his report, dated 27 November, Grimshaw wrote: 'I consider that Lieutenant de Pass's conduct throughout was most intrepid, and that this action was a magnificent example to the men of the Detachment.' Another officer, Lt. Elphinstone of the same regiment, in writing to de Pass's parents said of him: 'He was quite the most gallant fellow it had ever been my good fortune to meet.'

A few days later, Grimshaw who was far from recovered, had to inspect de Pass's body at a local mortuary at Béthune where it had been taken by the 7th Dragoon Guards. He was required to search the young man's pockets for his personal effects and described the scene in the following way: 'I felt an unpleasant pang when I stood beside poor Bumpty's body. That lifeless clay was all that was left of his brilliant accomplishments. It was only with an effort I

could bring myself to search his pockets. It was soon over and, giving his hand one last press, I left the room feeling very wretched . . . ' On the 28th Grimshaw had to write to de Pass's father and his fiancée, 'a very sad business'.

On 7 December Lt. de Pass was buried at Béthune Town Cemetery at 16.00 hours. Grimshaw wrote: 'We held over the burial to get a reply from de Pass's people as to their wishes as to the disposal of their son. Just as he was lowered into the grave our guns thundered out their wicked-sounding salvos . . . ' The grave number is 1, A, 24.

When Grimshaw was next on leave he visited de Pass's family. The Lieutenant's posthumous VC was announced in the *London Gazette* on

18 February 1915. He was the first Jew to win the award in the First World War. Grimshaw described the award as satisfactory. Sadly, de Pass's father was not fit enough to receive his dead son's medal and it was, therefore, posted to him.

Frank Alexander de Pass came from a Jewish family and was the son of Sir Eliot Arthur and Beatrice de Pass. He was born at No. 2 Lancaster Gate Terrace, London W8 on 26 April 1887.

He went to school at the Abbey School in Beckenham, Kent, and then moved on to Rugby School in 1901. From there he went to the Royal Military Academy at Woolwich and in 1904 was third on the list of successful candidates. In January 1906, at the age of eighteen, he was commissioned in the RFA and three years later on 20 March 1909 he was promoted to full Lieutenant. His battery was then stationed in India and de Pass applied for a commission in the 34th Prince Albert Victor's Own Poona Horse, Indian Army, and was successful. He was a natural linguist and quickly learnt the necessary standard of Hindustani which was necessary when dealing with native Indian troops. He also studied Persian and was an accomplished rider, both on the flat and across country. He played a great deal of polo and was also a fine shot. In November 1913 he was appointed Orderly Officer, with the local rank of Captain, to Sir Percy Lake, Chief of General Staff in India.

After the war broke out in August 1914, de Pass rejoined his regiment in September and travelled with it to France. It was part of the Secunderabad Cavalry Brigade and belonged to the 2nd Indian Cavalry Division. The regiment arrived in France on 12 October 1914 docking at Marseilles, and became the first Indian cavalry regiment to serve in the war. They first saw action at Neuve Chapelle on 2 November, where they assisted in repelling a German attack. The Battle of Ypres was still being fought and the enemy withdrew from most of the left bank of the Yser in order to concentrate on the capture of Ypres.

During the next three weeks the 34th Poona Horse continued to serve dismounted, and was mainly involved in providing working parties in the day while acting as a mobile reserve by night. Many units from the Indian Army Corps were badly used. They were totally unused to the wintry weather and the shell-torn and flooded landscape. Their brigades were broken up into separate battalions and even on occasions into companies. This was very disheartening practice for the native Indian troops who had come to expect a fairer deal from the British High Command. Later in November they were involved in the fighting near Festubert where de Pass won his VC.

H.P. RITCHIE
Dar-es-Salaam, East Africa, 28 November

At the beginning of the First World War in August 1914 the Germans held various parts of the African Continent. These included the Cameroons, German South-West Africa and German East Africa. The British attacks so far in East Africa had been unsatisfactory and an ill-judged action at Tanga in November ended with a reverse. Land operations as a result of these reversals were suspended and responsibility for them was transferred from the control of the India Office to the War Office.

Gen. Wapshare took over command of the operation against the Germans in East Africa in December 1914 a few days after an audacious raid by Commander Ritchie. He was to confine himself to mainly defensive operations. One Victoria Cross had already been earned in Africa, by Capt. J.F.P. Butler of the Gold Coast Regiment and Commander Ritchie was to gain the second in a very dramatic action at Dar-es-Salaam on 28 November 1914.

Dar-es-Salaam was in the hands of the Germans. A powerful wireless telegraph station was situated in the port which was capable of communication with the Cameroons and German West Africa. The Allies thought that a floating dock which had been sunk in the harbour no longer closed off the exit and that subsequently the ships inside the harbour would be able to move out and in their turn block the British Allied harbours at Killindini and Mombassa. The port, therefore, constituted a source of danger to the British, and it was decided to destroy all craft that might be used to operate in support of the *Konigsberg*, a German raiding cruiser, which was barricaded down the coast in the reaches of the Rufiji.

Soon after hostilities began Ritchie, who was second in command of the battleship HMS *Goliath*, was employed on the East African coast giving support to those cruisers which were trying to keep the *Konigsberg* bottled up. The plan was for *Goliath*, along with the cruiser *Fox*, to sail as far as the harbour at Dar-es-Salaam. Ritchie was to then sail in the *Duplex*, a former German cable-laying ship which had been converted to an armed auxiliary vessel, and to destroy as many enemy boats as he could find. But Ritchie realized that the *Duplex* would be too large to enter the harbour and decided to arm another and much smaller steam boat, and to man it with a Maxim gun. He also protected the sides of the boat with such material as he could find. He set sail accompanied by two small support boats, and entered the harbour unchallenged.

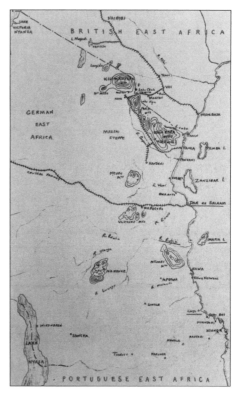

In the harbour white flags were flying on the flagstaff as a token of truce. Although the enemy was clearly watching they allowed Ritchie to continue. He then proceeded to create havoc and to sink or damage every craft which was afloat in the harbour. Ritchie expected a trap and after thoroughly searching the main creek, which flowed into the harbour, he took over two steel lighters and leashed them to each side of his small boat. The enemy could wait no longer and began to fire from all directions. Field

Dar-es-Salaam, 28 November

guns were used, as well as machine guns and rifle fire. *Goliath* and the *Fox* opened fire and the Governor's house was burnt to the ground and many other buildings destroyed. Many of the crew were severely wounded and Ritchie himself was wounded at the outset. Petty Officer Clark and A.B. Seaman were both so badly injured they could not carry on with their duties at the wheel. Ritchie was wounded eight times before becoming unconscious at about the same time as his boat sailed back through the harbour mouth. PO Clark who had his wounds bound up, now took over the steering and pointed the craft out to the open sea.

Ritchie subsequently spent six weeks in the Zanzibar Hospital and regained his fitness. He was awarded the VC for his audacious raid while PO Clark was awarded the Conspicuous Gallantry Medal and Upton won the Distinguished Service Medal.

Ritchie's VC was gazetted on 10 April 1915 shortly before he returned to naval duties. He did not receive it from the King until 25 November 1916. He was the first naval officer to win the VC in the First World War.

On 13 May 1915 the battleship *Goliath* (12,950 tons) under Capt. T.L. Shelford was torpedoed by the Turkish destroyer *Muavenet-Millieh*, commanded by a German officer, off the Eski Hissarlik Point, just inside the Dardanelles Straits. Some 570 men were lost including the Captain and Upton out of a complement of 750.

The Germans, however, lost all their African possessions after the war.

Henry Peel Ritchie was born at No. 1 Melville Gardens, Edinburgh on 29 January 1876, the eldest son of Dr and Mrs R. Peel Ritchie MD. He attended the George Watson's Boy's College, Edinburgh, 1883–6, when he left to continue his studies at Blair Lodge, and joined the Navy as a cadet in HMS *Britannia* on 15 January 1890, when he was almost fourteen. He qualified as a Gunnery Officer and was made a full Lieutenant on 30 June 1898. In the following year he was acting Junior Staff Officer at the Sheerness Gunnery School. In 1900 he became Army and Navy lightweight boxing champion, and runner up in 1901.

Ritchie was married to Christiana Lilian Jardine, only daughter of James Aikman, a wine merchant, on 31 March 1902 at St Cuthbert's church in Edinburgh. They had two daughters.

In 1911 he was made a Commander and retired from the Navy in 1917. He was made a Captain on the retired list on 29 January 1924.

The Ritchies lived at Craigroyston House, Davidson's Mains, Edinburgh. This is now part of the Scottish Gas Offices. In 1957 his wife died and the following year on 9 December 1958 he himself died at the age of eighty-two. He was cremated at Warriston.

N.D. HOLBROOK

HM Submarine B-11, Dardanelles, 13 December

In August 1914 Lt. N.D. Holbrook was twenty-six years old and after being trained to be a submarine officer he found himself based at Malta in command of the British submarine B-11. The 'B' Class to which the submarine belonged was built in 1905/6 by Vickers, and was of a fairly primitive design – the boat performed poorly on the surface and was not at all easy to manage when submerged. Its overall length was 143 feet with a displacement when on the surface of 285 tons. In all it was about a third of the size of the submarines used in the Second World War. It possessed a single petrol engine which only gave it a surface speed of 12 knots. In addition a storage battery fed an electric motor which could only produce 6½ knots when the boat was submerged.

When the submarine dived for long periods the speed of the craft was considerably reduced. It is difficult to stress just how primitive these early submarines were in their design; there was no sort of consideration given to the comfort of the crew, and there was no room for extra crew space. These factors underline the considerable bravery and forbearance of the crews who manned them. It took a special sort of temperament for a man to work in these conditions.

Originally the submarines had been designed for coastal defence. After a long sea journey of 2,000 miles to Malta in the Mediterranean, Holbrook was ordered to take the craft a further 1,000 miles to the Dardanelles Straits between Asia Minor and the Gallipoli Peninsula. The Allied powers from early in December 1914, kept up a dawn to dusk patrol at the entrance to the Dardanelles. Here they were able to look down the Straits and observe the many ships and smaller craft belonging to the Turkish Navy, which were often manned by German crews. Turkey had come down on the side of the Central Powers against the Allies soon after the outbreak of war.

Lt. Commander Pownall was in command of the mixed fleet of French and British shipping outside the Straits at this time and decided to send a submarine to attack a Turkish battleship in Dardan Bay to the north of Chanak. The battleship was being used as headquarters for the German Naval Staff and was virtually 'bottled up' in the Straits. Holbrook's submarine, the B-11, manned by his First Lieutenant, Lt. Winn, in the Control Room, and a crew of fifteen ratings, was detailed for the job, mainly because the boat possessed a new and reliable battery. Holbrook's task was not an easy one and it would have to be carried out with the boat submerged for as long as possible and often only a few feet off the bottom of the channel.

The danger of the proposed voyage encouraged each of the crew to write a final letter to their families and friends in case they did not return. The difficulties of navigation alone made the trip a hazardous one and the current in the Sea of Marmara could run as fast as 5 knots while the submerged B-11 could only travel at 6 knots. Any return journey, however, would be a speedy one with the current then assisting the passage.

The enemy searchlights which were in position on both sides of the Straits were usually switched off at dawn, one by one. It was also known that there would be a minefield to negotiate and Holbrook had special shields placed on his submarine to fend off mines and other obstructions.

At 03.00 hours on 13 December the B-11 cast off from its supply ship the *Hindu Kush* on its way to attack the battleship at Chanak. The strong searchlights continuously swept the waters to the south of Kephez Point and Lt. Holbrook decided to wait for nearly an hour, knowing that the lights would go out at dawn, when it was still fairly dark. Soon, however, the submarine was experiencing an unexplained vibration and on breaking surface Holbrook saw that one of his shields on the port side had been damaged. He decided to jettison it and to continue without it. It took two men half an hour to complete the job, adding considerably to the tension on board.

After rounding the point at Sedduel Bahr Holbrook then proceeded to treat the narrow Straits as a wide river with a strong current and to navigate accordingly. As daylight grew he hugged the European shore, where there was still a strong current. Holbrook had intended to sail the first 7 miles at 50 feet below the surface until he had reached the first minefield at Kephez but having come from fresh water, when it submerged B-11 found itself in very much muddier salt water. This affected her trim and forced her upwards nearer the surface. The submarine continued at this level for two and a half hours, surfacing every three-quarters of an hour in order to check its position in the Straits.

At 08.30 hours Holbrook identified the mouth of the Saundere river on the port side close to the five lines of mines across the Straits which formed the Kephez minefield. Now the B-11 had to descend 80 feet and slowly move forward 'blind' for the next hour. At 09.40 Holbrook surfaced again to check his position and found himself further on than he had expected. Already he could see a Turkish battleship a mile away, but it was too early to fire a torpedo. B-11 moved across the mouth of the bay close to Kephez Point, dived again, came up less than a mile away from the Turkish battleship, identified as the *Messoudieh*, in the Sea of Marmara.

Holbrook gave the order to fire, targeting the ship's bow, and the subsequent explosion violently shook the small boat. Immediately the submarine surfaced and the guns from the battleship began to fire almost at once. Holbrook could see the ship beginning to settle by the stern and very soon her guns ceased firing. He dived again and made for the waters in mid-channel because the current had carried the B-11 too far inshore. A torpedo boat and other vessels appeared and Holbrook kept to 50 feet below the surface. During the return journey the craft often touched bottom and once more had to go under the five lines of mines. After about eight or nine hours submerged, the B-11 made it back to safety and her supply ship outside the Dardanelles entrance.

Holbrook had grown a beard during the Dardanelles campaign and there is a picture in the archives at the IWM of him in front of his crew wearing a large cardboard Iron Cross which had been presented to him by his fellow officers. The B-11 became the first ever submarine to sink a battleship. Nine days later Holbrook's name was gazetted for the Victoria Cross which he well deserved. Each one of his crew received the Distinguished Service Medal (DSM), and his First Officer the Distinguished Service Order (DSO). Holbrook received his medal from the King at Buckingham Palace on 5 October 1915.

In addition to their medals the Prize Court awarded Holbrook and his crew £3,500 for destroying what amounted to almost one-third of the Turkish Navy's strength. The prize was calculated as £5 per man in the Turkish crew. The sinking was written up as a major triumph by the British Press and a Canon H.D. Rawnsley even responded to the event by publishing a special commemorative poem on the theme of the action.

After August 1915 Holbrook was mainly involved in patrolling duties, and served in F-3, V-4 and E-41. At one point he was wounded by fire from a ship which was displaying the white flag. Later in the war he was involved in mine-laying duties and was mentioned in despatches in July 1917. He retired from the Royal Navy in 1920.

Norman Douglas Holbrook was one of six sons and four daughters of Lt. Col. A.R. Holbrook, DL, JP, and Amelia Mary, daughter of Alexander Parks. He was born in Southsea on 9 July 1888. He went to a private school first but later attended Portsmouth Grammar School. He became a cadet in HMS *Britannia* in 1903 and a Midshipman on 9 January 1905. He was gazetted as Sub-Lieutenant three years later. On 30 September 1909 he was made a full Lieutenant and was subsequently trained in submarine work. He joined *Bonaventure*, the submarine depot ship, in the Home Fleet on 4 April 1911 and two and a half years later was appointed to *Egmont* in Malta in command of B-11 on 30 December 1913.

His father, Col. Holbrook, was a newspaper proprietor and at the outbreak of the war he was appointed by the War Office to be in charge of the Supplies and Transports, Salisbury Plain Division. At one point in the war all six sons were serving and they became known as 'the fighting Holbrooks'. He was to receive a knighthood for his services, becoming Col. Sir Arthur Richard Holbrook.

Norman Holbrook was to be the first member of the Royal Navy to be gazetted with the Victoria Cross in the First World War and he was the first submariner to win the award. By the end of the Second World War, there were to be another thirteen. In August 1918 Holbrook left the submarine service and went to Russia as Lieutenant Commander in the Russian cruiser *Askold*.

After the war he married a widow, Viva Dixon, at Holy Trinity, Kensington Gore in London on 21 June 1919. They had one son who was killed in action in the Second World War in 1945.

Stedham Mill, Midhurst, West Sussex

In September 1919 at Portsmouth, the Lower Deck invited Earl Beatty and forty-two other Admirals to a special dinner to mark the end of the war. During the evening all the toasts were made by members of the Lower Deck; Holbrook was one of the responders.

When he left the Royal Navy in 1920 he was promoted to Commander on the retired list published on 9 July 1928. He was then forty years old and took up farming in Midhurst, West Sussex, where he kept a pedigree herd of Guernsey cattle. At home in Midhurst he also cultivated a very fine garden and continued to fish with great enjoyment, a pastime that he had followed all his life. He was recalled for service by the Admiralty in the Second World War.

Viva Holbrook died in 1952 and in the following year Holbrook married an Austrian, Gundula Feldner, daughter of Dr A. Feldner of Innsbruck.

In 1915 the local council of the Australian town of Germanton, wanting to change its name to something less associated with Germany, drew up a list of alternative names for consideration. Martin was the favoured choice for a while but suddenly the newspapers were full of Lt. Holbrook's daring exploits in the Dardanelles and the town council decided to choose Holbrook for its new name. Holbrook himself was delighted and honoured to have a town named after him and this remote place, in far away Australia, made much more fuss of him and his heroic deeds than did his home town of Southsea.

The Holbrooks first visited the Australian town on 9 March 1956, when the people turned out in force to meet them. A special reception was held in the local park and a luncheon was provided at the Returned Servicemen's Club. The Holbrooks visited the town again in 1969 and as a couple for the last time in February 1975, not long before Norman Holbrook died. During this final visit they inspected a replica of the B-11 submarine which had been placed in Holbrook Memorial Park.

On each visit they were treated as honoured guests. Holbrook's widow returned alone once or twice more and not only presented the town with many of her husband's papers but also with his Victoria Cross and other war medals, including the French Legion of

Honour, on 11 May 1982. Mrs Holbrook said that it had always been her husband's wish that the town should own the medals, and he had wanted them presented as an acknowledgement of all Holbrook had done to commemorate his name. The medals were handed over at a ceremony in front of a large crowd of local residents. Three duplicate sets of the medals were made for display purposes. These were exhibited at the Woolpack Inn Museum, the Returned Servicemen's Club, and in the council's own offices. A statue of Holbrook was also erected and unveiled in the town.

Holbrook died six days short of his eightieth birthday on 3 July 1976 at his home at Stedham Mill, Midhurst. He is buried in the local cemetery and in his will he left £81,445 (£81,708 gross).

In 1993 Mrs Holbrook was still living in Midhurst and the family firm of Holbrooks Printers was still operating in the Portsmouth/Southsea area.

H.H. ROBSON

Near Kemmel, France, 14 December

The 2nd Royal Scots were sent to France in August 1914 as part of the 8th Brigade of the 3rd Division. They fought in the Battle of Mons where they inflicted heavy losses on the enemy in the afternoon of 23 August, while suffering only light casualties themselves. They also took part in the Battle of Le Cateau three days later. In September they fought on the Aisne and then went north with the rest of the BEF to take up positions in the Ypres Salient. When the First Battle of Ypres began in October the battalion took part in the heavy fighting at La Bassée, to the south-west of the industrial city of Lille.

Pte. Robson won his Victoria Cross in the attack against Petit Bois to the north of Kemmel, on 14 December 1914. The British trenches were just in front of Irish Farm. A heavy bombardment by British and French batteries began at 07.00 hours. At 08.00 hours the 8th Brigade with the 1st Gordons on the right and the 2nd Royal Scots on the left, attacked the German trenches situated on the high ground south of Petit Bois and also Petit Bois itself. On the left, the Royal Scots were partly successful in capturing two lines of enemy trenches but elsewhere the attack failed. In the afternoon the 2nd Suffolks moved up from reserve to relieve the 2nd Royal Scots. During the fighting considerable gallantry took place and the battalion history records 'men facing death over and over again in noble efforts to succour wounded comrades . . . '. Robson particularly distinguished himself by crawling through mud during heavy fire and rescuing a wounded non-commissioned officer (NCO). In an attempt to save another man Robson was hit by a bullet as he left the trench. He continued to crawl forwards, however, until a second bullet incapacitated him. Later in the day he was rescued. The remains of the 2nd Royal Scots marched back in companies to Kemmel where they stayed in reserve during the night. The wounded Robson was sent back to hospital in England and was taken to Cambridge, where he recuperated from bullet wounds. His battalion remained in the Kemmel area for the rest of the year.

Robson's name was gazetted for a Victoria Cross on 18 February 1915. On 12 July he went to Buckingham Palace to collect it.

Henry Howey Robson, always known as Harry, was the son of Mr and Mrs Edward Robson. He was born at No. 40 Hampden Street, South Shields, Durham, on 27 May 1894. At one time the family lived in Garrick Street. Robson was educated at the Mortimer Road Council School. His father worked at St Hilda's Colliery in South Shields. Later the family resided at Shotton Bridge, a district in Shotton Colliery, a mining village to the west of the City of Durham. The bridge was over the colliery mineral line.

Robson joined the 2nd Royal Scots (Lothian Regiment), in Edinburgh in 1912, when he was not yet eighteen. He chose a life in the army rather than one in the coal mines, where he had already worked for a short time.

At the outbreak of war in 1914, Robson was stationed in Plymouth waiting to be drafted to India. Instead, his regiment was called up to join the BEF in France. After recovering from his war wounds in a Cambridge hospital he returned to South Shields in mid-July 1915. In the same month he was presented with his medal. He was the first man from South Shields to be awarded it.

On his return to South Shields, Robson was given a very warm welcome and cheered as he arrived at the station. He was limping and could only walk with the aid of a stick. He was met by the mayor and other local dignitaries. He was only able to use his left hand for shaking hands as the right one had been injured. He was ushered into an open carriage which was preceded by a band from the Durham Light Infantry. The carriage was driven through the streets to the Municipal Buildings. Robson received a formal address of welcome from the mayor and replied with a brief speech of thanks. He also used the occasion to promote recruitment saying that 'We want more men, and still more men.' The National Anthem was then played and three cheers were called for. In October he was given the Freedom of the Borough.

On 24 May 1916 Robson was invited to return to his old school at Mortimer Road and later a presentation took place in the spacious yard of Stanhope Road School where the Mortimer Road pupils were billeted. The school children were present in large numbers and the general public was also assembled. The school was celebrating Empire Day and wished to honour one of its most famous scholars. Robson was presented with a gold watch which had been subscribed for by pupils of Mortimer Road.

Empire Day was celebrated all over the country and parades took place in schools throughout the British Isles. These generally took the same form with pupils parading in their playgrounds singing patriotic songs and saluting the Union Jack. At Mortimer Road during his address the mayor, Alderman Taylor, told the audience that observing Empire Day was 'The emblem of everything that went to make a good citizen and a good nation.'

Robson eventually went back to the front, but only for a brief period. The regimental history mentions him in the following extract about the Battle of the Ancre:

> The 2nd Royal Scots had better fortune on the night of 3 November. A small group of volunteers, including Private Robson, VC, under command of 2nd Lt. Callender, reached the enemy's first line and drove back a hostile listening-post. The party then proceeded to the next line which was found to be strongly manned. Callender and his men, having taken careful stock of the Boche position, then commenced to withdraw, and though the foe kept up a heavy rifle fire and threw numerous grenades, they arrived back at our lines without a casualty.

Ten days later Robson was seriously wonded at Serre. He took no further active part in the war after this incident.

After the war Robson worked in the local shipyards and then with the Corporation Highways Department. He then went to sea and became a steward on board oil tankers on the run between England and South America for two and a half years. It was after this job that he decided to sell his medals for £90 to help pay for his passage to Canada where he proposed to make a new life. There is a certain amount of confusion about the medals at this period and he may have acquired a duplicate set.

His first job was that of a streetcar conductor, and in 1934, he got a job as a civil servant working in the Parliament buildings in Ontario. He was Sergeant-at-Arms to the Ontario Legislature for six years and then became an information clerk. This job meant that he was meeting the public all the time which he did with relish, and besporting his medals he acted as guide to the thousands of people visiting the buildings. He must have dealt with about 100,000 visitors a year. Showing a party around the buildings took him about 45 minutes and many visitors were especially curious about Robson's display of medals. In 1930 Robson came over to Britain from Canada for the Prince of Wales' banquet in London for holders of the Victoria Cross. In his own words 'the trip was splendidly arranged' and he was able to stay very briefly in North and South Shields. Robson wrote to Mr George McVay, the mayor's secretary to thank him for his kindness during his brief visit. Mr McVay became a sort of keeper of the local archives and local historian and noted down many of the events which occurred in South Shields and district. In 1939 Robson was presented to the King and Queen at Queens Park, Ontario during their Canadian visit on the eve of the Second World War. In 1953 he returned to England for Queen Elizabeth II's coronation with a number of VCs from Canada. Once more he paid a brief visit to South Shields where he was given a civic reception. He also visited Mortimer Road School. In Edinburgh he visited the Royal Scots' Monument before returning to London.

His wife, who came from Edinburgh, was not with him on the trip as she was frightened of flying. Asked if he would like to settle in South Shields again he replied, 'I guess my heart and soul are still right here in South Shields.'

A year later he retired from his job in the Parliament buildings, and devoted his energies to the welfare of ex-servicemen and women. In 1956 he paid what was to be his last visit to England when he attended the Centenary celebrations of the Victoria Cross. He also visited South Shields for what was to be the last time.

In recent years Hampden Street, the street in South Shields where Robson was born, has almost been demolished and the land used for a new tax office and car park. Shotton Colliery has long gone and Mortimer School has also been demolished but it has been replaced by a new school.

Robson died of cancer on 4 March 1964 at the age of sixty-nine in Sunnybrook Hospital in Toronto after a long illness. He was buried in the military section of the York Memorial Cemetery in Toronto. At his death he left a widow, five children and fourteen grandchildren.

There seems to be some confusion about the ownership of Robson's medals. After he had sold them he spent thirty-five years tracing their whereabouts. In 1951 they were bought by a Dunfermline solicitor, who lent them to Robson to wear for the 1956 Review. It was understood that they would then be returned but Robson seems to have refused to do this and made out that he had purchased them. Maybe in time he did buy them as his family presented them to the Royal Scots after his death. The handing-over ceremony took place in Toronto where one of Robson's daughters, Mrs Bruce Gaskin, gave them to an ex-officer of the regiment who passed them on to their headquarters in Edinburgh.

W.A. MCCRAE BRUCE

Near Givenchy, 19 December

On 19 December Lt. W.A. McCrae Bruce 59th Scinde Rifles (Frontier Force) won the Victoria Cross for the Indian Army in the fighting near the town of Givenchy west of La Bassée. He was in charge of a small party during a night attack on an enemy trench. The Germans had made signs of surrender and had held up their rifles, but as soon as Bruce's party put their heads over the parapet they were shot at. During the fighting Bruce was wounded in the neck but remained at his post walking up and down the trench giving words of encouragement to his men. The Germans fired all day and also used bombs as they continuously counter-attacked the Indian Corps' positions. Eventually Bruce was killed, but by his heroic example the little group, by now under the command of Havildar (Sgt.) Dost Mahomed, kept the Germans at bay. An ever-growing pile of German corpses in front of their trench was evidence of their determination. They held out until dusk when the trench was finally taken by the desperate Germans who had brought up a trench mortar. This forced Dost Mahomed to order his men to retire. They refused to obey, however, stating that they had been ordered by Lt. Bruce Sahib to hold on to the end. Finally only two survivors crawled out.

It was not until 4 September 1919, ten months after the war had ended, that Bruce's VC was gazetted. The reason for this delay is that the deed was not known about until repatriated troops told the full story of his bravery and surviving fellow officers made their recommendations. Bruce's father, Col. Bruce, was not well enough to go to Buckingham Palace for the presentation of the posthumous medal. Instead it was given to William Bruce's mother by the Lieutenant-Governor of Jersey, Maj. Gen. Sir Alexander Wilson KCB, at a private ceremony. Bruce's other medals were the 1914 Star with clasp, BWM and VM.

William Arthur McCrae Bruce was the only son of Col. and Mrs Andrew M. Bruce whose family home was at La Fontaine, Pontao, Channel Islands. William was, however, born in Edinburgh, on 15 June 1890. He was educated between the ages of fourteen and eighteen at Victoria College, Jersey and was a member of the cricket eleven in 1907 and 1908. He left the college in 1908 and entered the Royal Military College at Sandhurst in the same year. The following year he was commissioned and attached to the Northumberland Fusiliers. In 1910 he was transferred to the 59th Scinde Rifles (Frontier Force) in India.

When war began in August 1914 Bruce was home on leave and he left immediately to rejoin his regiment in India but was ordered to meet up with them in Cairo. He joined his regiment with three officers (who were all to be killed in the war). The battalion had embarked in Karachi on 29 August 1914, in HMT *Takada* which disembarked *en route* at Port Tewfik before proceeding to Cairo where they stayed for two days. They then re-embarked at Alexandria, once more on HMT *Takada* and finally arrived in France at Marseilles on 26 September.

The 59th Scinde Rifles were part of the Jullundur Brigade, one of three Indian Brigades of the Lahore Division which formed part of the Indian Corps. It was involved in the La Bassée fighting at the end of October, and later at Givenchy in December.

Bruce has no known grave; his name is listed on the Neuve Chapelle Indian Memorial, north-west of La Bassée, in France. A memorial to the officers of the 59th Scinde Rifles is dedicated in the garrison church at Kohat Church, on the

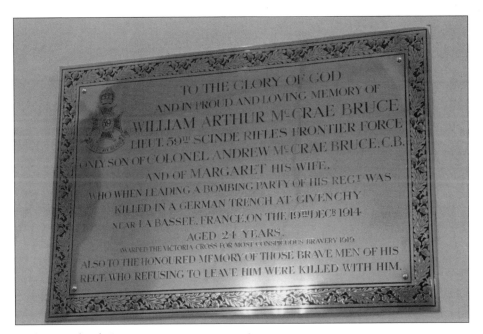

St Clement's church, Jersey

north-west frontier of India, which is now in Pakistan. In the chancel of St Clement's church, Jersey, there is a brass plaque to Bruce's memory along with that of his wife Margaret. It is also dedicated to the memory of the brave men of his regiment, who refusing to leave him, were killed alongside him. Bruce's name was also commemorated when Victoria College, his former school, named a house after him in 1919.

In November 1992 Bruce's VC came onto the market at Christies. A group of old boys decided to try and buy it and present it to the college. The sum required for the purchase was £20,000 which was raised and at a special service the medal was duly handed over by Mr Dixie Landick, an ex-pupil of the college. On receiving the medal, the Headmaster said, '. . . its acquisition was a tribute to the strength of support among Old Victorians and to their enduring pride in the college.' It was decided that the medal would be displayed at the Jersey Museum and on special occasions at the college. At the presentation ceremony the head boy, Neil Hussey, carried the medal on a cushion to a display table for the boys and other members of the congregation to have an opportunity to look at it.

P. NEAME

Near Neuve Chapelle, 19 December

Lt. Philip Neame arrived in France as a subaltern with the 15th Field Company (Royal Engineers), 8th Division, which began its war service in France in October 1914. The Division occupied positions between Neuve Chapelle and Armentières, in a dreary, waterlogged and desolate landscape.

On 27 November, Neame with a small party of Royal Engineers under the protection of 2nd Lt. L.M.J. Kerr and nine men of the 2nd West Yorks (23 Brig., 8th Div.) went across to the German lines near Neuve Chapelle and blew up a farm building called Moated Grange, which was being used by German snipers. The explosion was successful. For the next three weeks the Division carried out a series of attacks on the enemy positions. On the 18/19 December the 2nd Devons (23rd Brig., 8th Div.) accompanied by a section of the 15th Field Company, RE, under a Subaltern attacked the enemy positions at the Moated Grange. The sappers had first to cut the barbed wire in front of the enemy trenches and then attempt to link the German trench system to the British one by digging new trenches in No Man's Land.

During the night the West Yorks relieved the Devons and began to consolidate the British position but at dawn the enemy began to counter-attack using bombs. Subsequently Neame was sent for and told by the Commanding Officer of the 2nd West Yorks to consolidate the position. So with a party of Royal Engineers he went up to the captured enemy trenches close to the Moated Farm. Nearing the front line Neame heard fighting and bombing, which in effect was caused by hand-grenades. Leaving a sergeant in charge of his party of thirty-six sappers, Neame crawled forwards along a ditch in order to find out what was going on. He was informed by the forward infantry commander that the Germans were indeed throwing bombs but that his own bombers had all been wounded so he was unable to retaliate.

Neame sought out one of the wounded bombers and discovered that he had been unable to throw the bombs owing to a lack of fuses. Furthermore, he had not

199

known how to light a safety fuse without a proper fusee. Neame knew that the bombs could in fact be used without a fuse. This could be done by holding a match head on the end of the fuse on the bomb and striking a match-box across it.

The position was meanwhile hectic and the trench was overcrowded and movement restricted. Neame gave orders to gather up all the bombs available so that he could then try and throw them accurately at the two German positions which were giving trouble. He concentrated on the position directly to the front and had to stand up on the fire-step and expose himself before throwing each bomb. Each time he did this a German machine gunner would fire at him but always a moment too late. It appeared by the sound of German screams and a lessening of the enemy bombing that Neame's one-man attack was paying dividends. Eventually the enemy bombing petered out and finally stopped altogether. During the time of his action Neame had been protected by three members of the 2nd West Yorks and he held on to this advanced position with his three infantrymen until he received orders to move back.

Despite Neame's heroism there had been heavy casualties especially of men wounded or killed before he arrived on the scene. He then met up with his original party of sappers. At one point he tried to help a wounded man along a road ditch which became impossible and consequently he risked taking him along a road in full view of the enemy who did not fire. He then handed over the injured man to stretcher bearers. Next Neame reported at Battalion Headquarters where the Colonels of the Devons and West Yorks were based. He told them that he had completed his task which included preparing the captured German trenches for defence. The Colonel of the West Yorks then told him to take a party up to repair the British front line defences, as they were worried that the Germans might begin a counter-attack at any time.

When Neame returned, Col. Travers of the 2nd Devons told him that he would make sure that Brig. R.J. Pinney would hear about his oustanding work during the day. Two days later the Corps Chief Engineer visited the position and he told Neame that he would make sure that the Corps Commander was informed. Six days later, on Christmas Day, the Divisional Commander Maj. Gen. F.J. Davies came to the Engineers' billets to wish them a Happy Christmas and told Neame that he had recommended him for the Victoria Cross.

In later life when Neame was interviewed by David Lance of the Imperial War Museum he was asked, 'Did you find that having the VC was a significant help to you in your later career in any way at all?' Neame replied that he supposed it had helped a little, especially when it came to promotion on the Staff.

Neame was made Captain in February 1915 and took part in the Battle of Neuve Chapelle in March. On 30 March he became Adjutant, Royal Engineers, 8th Division. In May he fought in the Battle of Fromelles and Festubert. His VC was gazetted along with about ten others on 18 February 1915. On Saturday

17 July 1915 he returned home to Faversham, in Kent, to a hero's welcome together with a civic reception. His train arrived at about mid-day and he was greeted at the station and taken, together with his parents, in an open horse-drawn carriage. A band preceded the carriage and a mounted escort was provided by a contingent from the Royal East Kent Mounted Rifles. The carriage was greeted by a cheering crowd and drove down Preston Street and then into the Market Place. The square and the windows of the local shops and houses were full of spectators and in front of the Guildhall, a dais had been erected to take the local dignitaries. Here the mayor, town clerk and Lord Harris in uniform were awaiting the hero's arrival. Lord Harris described the incident 'as a bomb-throwing match with the enemy'.

A Territorial Guard of Honour made up from men who were billeted in the Faversham area, was arranged around the dais. Neame was addressed by several 'local worthies' and despite drizzling rain the crowd continued to roar its approval of their hero. In his reply Neame made kind remarks about the Territorials and the New Army raised by Lord Kitchener. He talked of the war effort in general and made a local reference to the nearby explosive works as doing a valuable job. At the end of the speeches, the National Anthem was sung and three further cheers were called for Neame. He and his parents were then taken by car to the mayor's house at Gatefield House in Preston Street, where they were entertained for lunch.

Neame had not yet received his medal and was wearing the VC ribbon only. At the local cinema, the Empire Picture Hall in Tanners Street, a well-known local singer, Bert Holmes, included in his recital a song called 'The Victoria Cross' as a reflection of the moment.

Two days later Neame travelled by train from Paddington to Windsor, with a group of other servicemen, to an investiture at Windsor Castle. The King asked Neame about the fight and afterwards the servicemen were entertained to lunch by some of the King's equerries.

Philip Neame came from yeoman stock, descending from a family that had lived in East Kent for several hundred years. He was the son of Frederick Neame, JP, of Luton House, Selling, and his wife Kathleen. He was born on 12 December 1888 in the historic house of Macknade near Faversham, which had been re-built in the eighteenth century. He was the youngest son of six children – five boys, four of whom were to serve in the First World War, and one girl. In 1908 when the agricultural and hop industries both slumped Frederick Neame moved his family to Colkins, a small house on one of the family farms. The local industry revived shortly afterwards and he therefore moved his family back to Luton House, which was later demolished.

Philip was educated at St Michael's School, Westgate, and at Cheltenham College. He then went to the Royal Military Academy at Woolwich, passing out seventh in his year. The Boer War had influenced the young man when deciding to follow a career in the Army. He was commissioned into the Royal Engineers as Second Lieutenant at the age of nineteen on 29 July 1908. He was made a full Lieutenant on 18 August 1910, and served with 56 Field Company at Bulford Camp on Salisbury Plain in Wiltshire.

In October 1913 he was sent on his first foreign tour to Gibraltar where he was stationed when the war began in August 1914. He was very keen to get to France and he sailed with 15th Field Company in a convoy of ships bringing troops from India and the Middle East for service in France and Flanders. They were to be part of the 8th Division and reached France in November just missing the last great assault of the Germans in the First Battle of Ypres. They went into the line close to Ploegsteert. Neame was made Captain in February 1915 (seniority 30 October 1914) and was Adjutant, Royal Engineers, 8th Division, from 30 March to 10 October 1915. On 11 October he became GSO3, 8th Div. In January 1916 he was awarded the DSO for work carried out with the 8th Division since his VC in December 1914. On 13 February 1916 he became Brigade Major with the 168th Infantry Brigade (56th (London) Div.), in time to witness the attack on Gommecourt on the Somme on 1 July 1916. He took part later in the battles at Ginchy, Combles and Les Boeufs. On 29 November he was promoted to GSO2, and joined the staff at 15th Corps Headquarters.

On 1 January 1917 he became Brevet Major and took part in the advance to the Hindenburg Line in the spring of that year. He later participated in the coastal operations around Nieuport which was part of the Third Battle of Ypres. In December Maj. Neame joined the staff of 1st Army Headquarters and was with them at the time of the German breakthrough on the Lys. In June he became GSO1, 30th Div., and was promoted Lieutenant Colonel. He took part, with his division, in the final operations of the war in Flanders, during September to November. Armistice Day found Neame 25 miles from Brussels.

In June 1919 Neame was made Brevet Lieutenant Colonel and then full Colonel in 1926. He was awarded the Belgian and French Croix de Guerre and the French Legion of Honour, in addition to his VC and DSO for services in the First World War. When the war was over Neame served as an instructor at the Staff College and then moved to India. He became part of the Army revolver team and in 1925 was member of the Olympic Games team which won a Gold and Bronze medal. He joined the King's Own Bengal Sappers and Miners and in 1930 became the GSO1, Waziristan District.

He spent his leave in exploration, big game hunting and in climbing expeditions. In 1933 he fought with a tiger which badly mauled him. He was taken to Lansdown Hospital where he was tended by a nurse named Miss

H. Alberta Drew. The couple subsequently became engaged in December and married in Bombay in April 1934. Neame became Commandant of the Royal Military Academy 1938–9, and was now an expert on Tibet and the North West Frontier. He was a keen polo player and point-to-point rider.

Neame was Deputy Chief of the General Staff and was involved in the BEF in France in 1939/40. He then had various appointments in the Middle East including Major-General commanding the 4th Indian Division in the Western Desert of Egypt. Next he was Lieutenant-General, General Officer Commanding Palestine and Trans-Jordan. Finally he was GOC and Military Governor of the former Italian Colony, Cyrenaica, in 1941. In the Western Desert he was in command of the British, Australian and Indian Forces against Rommel's first attack on Cyrenaica. He was later taken prisoner, along with Gen. Sir Richard O'Connor in rather unfortunate circumstances, by a group of armed German motor-cyclists. The British senior officers were captured just off the main Derna road in April 1941, and flown to detention in Italy. The two Generals along with two staff officers had left for their new headquarters further eastwards, but chose not to follow the main Derna road as there was demolition work in progress on it. Instead they took an alternative route and came across a stationary British convoy at about midnight. The two cars were attempting to thread a way through the convoy when a German patrol of motor-cyclists and sidecars which had travelled from the direction of Mechili suddenly appeared taking the staff by surprise. It was to be a typical desert incident, the like of which was to occur many times with the opposing armies so close to each other. According to a British Army witness, a German with a tommy-gun approached the staff cars and ordered the Generals to get out. A British soldier nearby challenged him and was promptly shot, another British soldier fired back. In the confusion the two Generals disappeared. Meanwhile, the staff cars carrying the two Generals' aides-de-camp got through to headquarters by using the main Derna road with no trouble at all.

Neame and his fellow prisoners were handed over to the Italian authorities and spent six months in Sulmona on Sicily before being sent to the Castello di Vincigliata near Florence. As a prisoner of war, Neame assisted other officers to escape before attempting to do so himself. One of his fellow prisoners was Carton de Wiart who won the VC on the Somme in 1916. During this period of confinement Neame wrote his autobiography and he subsequently hid it from his captors; miraculously it was found and returned to him after the war. In September 1943 he left the Castello di Vincigliata, with a group of Allied officers and other ranks having negotiated their departure with his Italian jailers. This was during the period that Italy changed sides in the war which resulted in reprisals from both the advancing Germans and Italians still loyal to the Fascist cause.

In his autobiography Neame writes of four very adventurous months, during which he and his colleagues continuously risked being captured. He finally reached home with O'Connor and Air Marshal O.T. Boyd, on Boxing Day 1943, having been a prisoner of war for two years.

After the Second World War Neame retired in 1947. He was Lieutenant-Governor of Guernsey between 1945 and 1953, and in addition he was also Colonel Commandant of the Royal Engineers during this time. He served as President of the Institution of the Royal Engineers from 1954 to 1957. He was a member of the Council of the National Rifle Association. In 1939 he had been made a Commander of the British Empire (CBE) and a Knight of the British Empire (KBE) in 1946. Neame's name was mentioned in despatches no fewer than five times.

The Neames had three sons and one daughter. He found time to publish two books, *German Strategy in the Great War* in 1923, and his autobiography *Playing with Strife* in 1946.

In the 1930s he had bought the house Woodlands in Selling to which he gave its original name of Brookes Court. In 1955 he became Deputy Lieutenant of Kent. In April 1967 he was involved in a serious car crash in his MG 1100. He crashed into another car killing his brother, A. Bruce Neame, and injuring his sister-in-law.

On 28 April 1978 Sir Philip Neame died at his home at Selling. His funeral was held at Selling church, St Mary the Virgin. It was attended by a large and distinguished congregation. During the service two trumpeters from the Royal Engineers at Chatham played the 'Last Post'.

Sir Philip's career in the British Army had been extremely successful. He was the last man from the Royal Engineers to win the VC in 1914, and the only 1914 VC to have his autobiography published. His medals are not held in the public domain.

J. MACKENZIE

Rouges Bancs, France, 19 December

The 7th Division was continuously involved in the First Battle of Ypres which officially lasted from 19 October to 22 November. On 18/19 December it found itself at Rouges Bancs to the north-west of Neuve-Chapelle. The 20th Brigade consisted of 1st Battalion the Grenadier Guards, 2nd Battalion Scots Guards and 2nd Battalions of The Border Regiment and The Gordon Highlanders.

An attack carried by the 2nd Borders to establish a lodgement, failed, according to the divisional history 'mainly to the impossibility of hearing the signal for the start of the assault'. They had moved forward when they heard shouts and saw movements to their right where the Guards had begun, but their attack was a mixed success. The Germans had received adequate warning and had manned their trenches accordingly. As a result when the Borders did advance they faced murderous fire at point blank range suffering heavy losses. Capt. Askew, the Company Commander, was able to reach the enemy trenches but was killed when still brandishing his revolver. A German counter-attack drove the rest of the attackers back to their start lines. A second attack, under Maj. Warren, was later organized but it was soon realized that it was hopeless to continue. The failure of the attack by the Borders led to the collapse of the supporting attack of the Scots Guards. It was during this fighting that Pte. James Mackenzie of the 2nd Scots Guards gained the Victoria Cross. It was gazetted on 18 February 1915. The citation read as follows:

> For conspicuous bravery at Rouges Bancs on 19 December 1914, in rescuing a severely wounded man from in front of the German trenches under very heavy fire, and after a stretcher-bearer party had been compelled to abandon the attempt. Private Mackenzie was subsequently killed on that day while in the performance of a similar act of gallant conduct.

A comrade of Mackenzie wrote of the incident as follows:

He was returning to the trenches along with me and another stretcher-bearer when it occurred. We had only two or three cases that morning, so the last one was taken by us three. After we took the wounded soldier to hospital we returned to see if there were any more. There was a very dangerous place to pass. I went first, followed by another, then James came behind, which caused his death. He was shot in the heart by a sniper, and only lived five minutes.

Two days later, also at Rouges Bancs, two more VCs were won by Pte. A. Acton and Pte. J. Smith both of The Border Regiment.

Mackenzie's body was subsequently lost and his name is listed on the Ploegsteert Memorial to the Missing (Panel One).

James Mackenzie was the son of Alexander Mackenzie, a mason by trade, and Marion Mackenzie. He was born on 2 April 1884 (not 1889 as listed in the reference books), at his grandmother's house at West Glen, New Abbey, Kirkcudbrightshire where his mother had gone for the birth of her child. The Mackenzie family moved from West Glen around twelve years later to Terregles Street, Maxwelltown.

Mackenzie was educated at Laurieknowe Public School (formerly Maxwelltown School). The school was originally built in 1872. By coincidence

another boy, named James Tait, who was to win the Victoria Cross also attended the school. He won the medal on 18 August 1918, as a Lieutenant in the Canadian 78th Infantry Battalion

On leaving school Mackenzie had several jobs; firstly he worked on farms at Locharbank Bankend and for his grandparents at Barncleuch Shawhead before being employed by McGowans Joiners of Terregles Street in Maxwelltown. He left them to enlist in the Army in Dumfries on 16 February 1912. The Scots Guards were having a recruiting drive when he applied and he understated his age to ensure being accepted. He said he was twenty-three but in reality he was twenty-seven. He gave his occupation as groom. His army number was 8185 and for two years he was based at the

Guards Depot, Caterham, in Surrey. On 5 October 1914 the Scots Guards received orders to go to France where they arrived in mid-October.

Mackenzie died only shortly after winning his Victoria Cross. His name is commemorated not only in Belgium but also on the family gravestone at Troqueer parish church. In addition his name appears on the Maxwelltown Memorial in New Abbey Road, Dumfries, and he is commemorated on a plaque on the east porch of Troqueer parish church where his age is given as twenty-seven when he was in fact over thirty years old. Mackenzie's former school proudly displays a photograph of him in full uniform, and includes his name on the School Roll of Honour.

Mackenzie's medals were presented to the Scots Guards by his mother. These included the 1914 Star, War Medal, Victory Medal and the Victoria Cross itself. It was the first VC to be won by a member of the Scots Guards since the Crimean War.

Maxwelltown Memorial, Dumfries

Mackenzie's family home was occupied until the late 1950s but has since become derelict.

A. ACTON AND J. SMITH
Rouges Bancs, France, 21 December

Pte. A. Acton

Pte. J. Smith

The First Battle of Ypres officially ended in stalemate during the third week of November 1914. Both sides were exhausted. This was followed by a period of very bad weather and the establishing of a trench system along the whole of the front which marked the beginning of static warfare. Fighting, however, did flare up in the period from 18 to 22 December in and around Givenchy.

The unsigned *War Diary* of the 2nd Border Regiment states that 10694 Pte. A. Acton and 6423 Pte. J. Smith gained their VCs on 19 December at Rouges Bancs, 3½ miles from Neuve Chapelle, when saving the lives of the wounded. All other accounts, however, give the date as 21 December, two days later. The two Privates had allegedly rescued two wounded men who had been lying out in No Man's Land for more than forty-eight hours.

The 2nd Borders *War Diary* WO95/1655 is quite detailed about this action. Maj. Warren, who was Battalion Commander, received orders from 20th Brigade on the 18th for B and D Companies to attack at 18.30 hours after two companies of the Scots Guards had attacked. Warren and Capt. H.A. Askew also of the 2nd Borders arrived at the trenches at 15.00 hours when Warren decided to change the orders and to employ A and C Companies instead of B and D. It is not clear why. The left of the position was to be the road running south-east of La Cordonnière Farm and the right was the position of the Scots Guards, whose own left was the Sailly–Fromelles road. This meant that the whole of C Company had to be moved to the right with A Company also adjusting its position.

B and D Companies were to get behind each man of A and C Companies and assist them out of their trenches. The companies were not in position until after dark and as a result nobody really knew the correct front of the attack.

The 300 men advanced at 18.15 hours and crossed the 150 yards to the enemy positions being fired on all the time, which resulted in many casualties. The attacking force was also hit by shells from British artillery which caused it to retreat to a safer position about 50 yards back. The position became completely untenable and the Borders then went back 100 yards to their original start positions. Maj. Warren followed up with a smaller party but with no better results. He was hindered by a lack of wire cutters and sent back for some. When he returned for a second attack he went to see the 7th Division Commander, Maj. Gen. Capper, who was at La Cordonnière Farm. He was away from his position for an hour and a half and when he got back he found that Capt. Jenkins had brought the companies back to the trenches. No further attacks had been ordered and operations ceased. The collecting of the dead and wounded was therefore carried out. During the attacks Capt. H.A. Askew had been killed on top of the enemy trenches, and other rank casualties from the attacks of 18/19 December totalled 123. Two men received the DCM for bringing in Capt. C. Lamb of the 2nd Borders. The Captain had recently received his DSO from the King on 1 December for gallantry in action at Kruiseik in October. Tragically he died of his wounds eleven days later.

Ptes. A. Acton and J. Smith, Rouges Bancs, 19 December

Le Touret Memorial, France

Pte. Acton and Pte. Smith both volunteered to save two wounded men in broad daylight. The men had both suffered severe thigh injuries and they carried them on their backs to the British trenches. This involved going through a hail of machine-gun bullets, and the whole operation took an hour to complete. Sadly, the two wounded men subsequently died. The awards of the Victoria Cross were compiled on the 21 December according to the *War Diary*. On Christmas Day an armistice was agreed with the enemy and this was to last until 16.00 hours. The dead were buried close to the trenches. The next day there was no firing either and men walked along the tops of the communication trenches which were in a very poor state.

The fighting in the northern section of the Western Front subsequently died down in 1914. Acton and Smith were to be the last men to win the Victoria Cross in that year. Acton's VC was gazetted on 18 February 1915. He was killed three months later during the Battle of Festubert on 16 May. His name is commemorated on a panel on the Le Touret Memorial in France. James Alexander Smith of the 3rd Borders, attached to the 2nd Battalion, received the same citation as Acton. His medal was also gazetted on 18 February 1915. He received his VC from the King at Buckingham Palace on 22 April 1915.

Abraham Acton was the son of Mr and Mrs Robert Acton. He was born at Whitehaven, Cumberland, on 17 December 1892 and went to school at Crosthwaite Memorial School. He later joined the 5th Battalion (TF) of the Border Regiment before enlisting in the 2nd Borders (10684) in January 1914. He served in the First World War from 25 November until his death nearly six months later.

A letter from Acton to the proprietors on the merits of Zam-Buk was published in the *Bury Free Press* on 10 April 1915. It read: 'You can't place too much faith in Zam-Buk. It had been very useful to me on many occasions. I have used Zam-Buk for my feet especially to keep frost-bite out, and to cure sprains; also for quickly and cleanly healing cuts from barbed wire and other things. Zam-Buck is indeed a grand thing to carry in my haversack.'

This letter was published five weeks before his death. It was to provide a perfect example of how the winning of a Victoria Cross could be exploited commercially. After his death Acton's medals were donated by his family to the town of Whitehaven. They are now in the Whitehaven Museum. His name is listed on St James's church war memorial in the town.

James Alexander Smith, whose real name was Glenn, was born in Workington on 5 January 1881. He enlisted under his mother's maiden name in about 1901/2 and it is thought he served with the 2nd Battalion in Burma between 1902 and 1905 and in South Africa between 1905 and 1907. He probably took his discharge after seven years with the colours and in 1914 was a reservist.

He was married twice, his first wife dying in 1928 and his second in 1966. He had no children. Between the wars he was a labourer and served in the Home Guard in the Second World War.

He was given a place of honour in the 1953 coronation. In 1968 he was invited to attend a biennial dinner in London along with 200 other medal holders from all over the world. Sadly, he died a few weeks before at No. 73 Thorntree Avenue, Brambles Farm, Middlesborough, on 21 May 1968. He was cremated at Acklam Crematorium and his ashes were scattered in the May section of the Garden of Remembrance. His funeral service took place at St Thomas's church, Brambles Farm, and was attended by four holders of the Victoria Cross: Stanley Hollis, Edward Cooper, Tom Dresser and William McNally. The 'Last Post' was played by a member of the British Legion and a large detachment of Legion members was present together with the mayor of Teesside.

Smith's VC was bequeathed to The Border Regiment OCA and presented to the regiment at a ceremony on 5 September 1968 at Carlisle Castle.

SOURCES

The sources used in the preparation of this book include the following:

The Lummis VC files at the National Army Museum, London
The Victoria Cross files at the Imperial War Museum, London
The Public Record Office, Kew, Surrey
The Royal Artillery Institution, Woolwich
Regimental Museums and Archives
The London Gazette 1914–20 (HMSO)

M.J. Dease
David Rowlands
Major French, MBE

S.F. Godley
Daily Express, 23 August 1953
This England, spring 1980

T. Wright
The Royal Engineers Journal: Demolition at Mons, 1914, March and June, 1932
The Sapper

C.A. Jarvis
The Royal Engineers Journal: Demolition at Mons, March and June, 1932
The Sapper 1915
John M. Cameron
St Andrews Citizen, 27 November 1948
The Fraserburgh Herald, 9 September 1917

C.E. Garforth
This England, spring 1980
Beeston Gazette and Echo, 5 July 1973

F.O. Grenfell
The Ypres Times, May 1924
Daily Mail, 11 October 1926
The Sphere, 28 August 1915
The Oak Tree, autumn 1964
Nick Forder at the Derby Museum and Art Gallery
9/12 Lancers Records at the National Army Museum
This England, spring 1980

E.W. Alexander
Lindsay, S., *Merseyside Heroes* (unpub. ms)
Ramsden, Lt. Col. J.V. Adj. 27th Brig. RFA. *Report on Alexander* dated 30 September
    1914

G.H. Wyatt
The Other Side of the Hill – Landrecies. The Army Quarterly No. XII
Pearce, LSGT L., *A Short History of the Regiment's Victoria Cross Holders*. Coldstream
    Guards, 1988
Benows Worcester Journal, 20 November 1915
Doncaster Gazette, 26 November 1915 and 30 November 1964
Hereford and Worcester County Libraries

C.A.L. Yate
The Bugle (1906 and 1922)
Wellingborough Journal and Shrewsbury News, 28 November 1914
Leisure Services Department, Shropshire County Council
The Torgau History of the Retreat from Mons in August 1914 (CAB 45/129 PRO)

F.W. Holmes
Daily Mirror, 25 January 1915
The Bugle, 1922
Daily Mail
The Green Howards' Gazette, May 1970?
Tit-Bits, 13 March 1915 to 3 April 1915

D. Reynolds
Michelle Young

J.H.C. Drain
Libraries Department, London Borough of Barking and Dagenham
Diary of the 37 Battery and its experiences in the war, J.H.C. Drain
Barking and Dagenham Post, 6 August 1975

F. Luke
Carroll, F.G., *For Valour*. Hampshire Magazine, September 1972
Hampshire Chronicle, 28 November 1914
South Side News (Glasgow), 19 November 1976

E.K. Bradbury
XI Hussars Journal, October 1915 and March 1921
Pitman, T.T., *The Attack on the First Cavalry Brigade at Néry, September 1st 1914*.
    Cavalry Journal, 1936
Gunner Darbyshire, *The Immortal Story of 'L' Battery (I Was There, 29 September 1914)*
Gillman, H.C.R., *'L' Battery, R.H.A., at Néry, 1st September 1914*. Journal of the R.A.
    (Vol. LXXXI) 1954
The Epic Fight at Néry – Immortal Stand of 'L' Battery
The Legionary, October 1935

The Observer, 25 October 1914
The Daily Telegraph, 21 October 1914

G.T. Dorrell
Those Néry Guns – Soldiers. January, 1964
Surrey Advertiser, 3 July 1970 and 14 January 1971

D. Nelson
Account of the Practical Annihilation of 'L' Battery, R.H.A., at Néry, Oise on 1st September 1914

W. Fuller
Private Diaries of Sir Henry Rider Haggard, edited by D.S. Higgins, Cassell, 1980
West Glamorgan County Library
Andrew Vollans

W.H. Johnston
The Sapper

G. Wilson
How I Won the V.C. by Pte. Wilson, Imperial War Museum

R. Tollerton
The 79th News, 1915 and 1931
I.H. Macdonald and John Cameron

E.G. Horlock
Hampshire Telegraph
Battery Sergeant Major E.G. Horlock VC, RFA (*The Gunner*, 1969)
The Gunner, December, 1974

H.S. Ranken
War Diary of the 1st KRRC (first draft)
Kilmarnock Standard, 5 December 1964
Diary of Lt. H. Robinson RAMC (WO95/1358 PRO)

F.W. Dobson
Pearce, L. SGT. L., *A Short History of the Regiment's Victoria Cross Holders*, Coldstream Guards, 1988
Evening Chronicle, Newcastle, 28 September 1989
2nd Btn. Coldstream Guards War Diary (WO95/1342 PRO)

H. May
Daily Sketch, 2 August 1915
Glasgow Evening News, 6 March 1940
Glasgow Evening Standard, 2 August 1941
VCs of the Regiment, Cameronians – March, 1956

W. Kenny
Daily Express
Daily Mirror, 14 January 1915
The Times, 10 January 1936
Steve Wall

J. Leach
Great Deeds of the Great War, 9 January 1915
The Sunday Times, 17 August 1968
2nd Manchesters War Diary (WO95/1564 PRO)

J. Hogan
Daily Mail, 21 February 1915
McInnes, *The Medal Box*
The People, 9 February 1969
Evening Chronicle (Oldham). Various issues between 1914 and 1983
Oldham Chronicle, April and May 1993
Tom Brophy and John Lester

J.A.O. Brooke
2nd Btn. Gordon Highlanders War Diary, October 1914 (WO 95/1656 PRO)
Norman Adams

A. Martin-Leake
The Daily Telegraph, 1915
Paper collected by H.C. Benson (86/67/1 IWM)
The Times, 24 June 1953
British Medical Journal, 4 July 1953
Military Historical Society Bulletin. Vol. V, No. 20. May 1955
The Hertfordshire Mercury, 16 May and 20 June 1986
Ann Clayton

Khudadad Khan
The Daily Telegraph, 15 December 1914
Daily Mirror, 26 January 1915
The Times, 27 January 1915

S.J. Bent
Daily Sketch, 11 December 1914
Suffolk Chronicle and Mercury, 18 December 1914
Bury Free Press, 16 January 1915
Daily Mirror, March 1915
Courage (Eastern) Ltd

J.F. Vallentin
22nd Infantry Brigade War Diary (WO95/1660)
The Stafford Knot, April 1969

W.L. Brodie
2nd Btn. Highland Light Infantry War Diary (WO95/1347 PRO)

J.H.S. Dimmer
Wimbledon and District Gazette, 2 May 1908
The Daily Telegraph, 20 November 1914
Daily Mail, 21 November 1914 and 1 January 1919
Suffolk and Essex Free Press, 12 May 1915
Wimbledon Series, 8 November 1984
David Harrison, *Jack Dimmer, VC, MC*

J.F.P. Butler
Sir Charles Lucas, *The Empire at War*. Vol. IV

T.E. Rendle
Lloyd's Weekly News (Bristol)
Daily Sketch, March 1915 and 13 July 1915
Daily Mail, January and March 1915
Daily Chronicle, 13 January 1915

Darwan Sing Negi
East Anglian Daily Times, 7 December 1914

F.A. de Pass
The War Budget, 6 March 1915

H.P. Ritchie
The Times, 24 May 1918 and 12 December 1958

N.D. Holbrook
The Times, 15 December 1914 and 5 July 1976
The Daily Telegraph, 15 December 1914, 5 July 1976 and 24 September 1976
Daily Sketch, 6 February 1915
Border Mercury Mail, May 1982 (Australia)
The News, 7 April 1987

H.H. Robson
North Mail, 24 May 1916
The Northern Echo
The Gazette (South Shields) Issues between February 1915 and December 1989
Jack Cavanagh

W.A. McCrae Bruce
Malcolm Beal and Douglas Ford from Jersey

P. Neame
East Anglian Daily Times, 12 April 1941
Kent Messenger, 12 February 1954
Gazette and Times (Kent), 11 May 1978

This England
Faversham Library
Interview with David Lance (IWM)

J. Mackenzie
John M. Cameron

A. Acton
Bury Free Press, 10 April 1915
2nd Btn. The Border Regiment Diary, December 1914 (WO95/1655)

J. Smith
Evening Gazette (Teesside), 22 May 1968
Northern Echo, 23 May and 25 May 1968

BIBLIOGRAPHY

The following list is a selection of the published sources used in this book. It does not include regimental, brigade or divisional histories which are too numerous to list.

Ascoli, D., *The Mons Star: The British Expeditionary Force 1914*. Harrap, 1981

Bancroft, J.W., *Devotion to Duty: Tribute to a Region's VCs*. 1990

Becke, A.F., *The Royal Regiment of Artillery at Le Cateau, Wednesday 26th August, 1914*. Woolwich: R.A., H.Q., 1919

Bloem, W., *The advance from Mons, 1914*. Davies, 1930

Brice, B. (comp), *The Battle Book of Ypres*. Murray, 1927

The Bond of Sacrifice. The Naval & Military Press re-issue, 1993

Bridges, Sir T., *Alarms and excursions: reminiscences of a soldier*. Longmans, 1938

Buchan, J., *Francis and Riversdale Grenfell: A Memoir*. Nelson, 1920

Chance, R., *Draw Swords*

Chronology of the War 1914–15. Constable, 1918

Coleman, F., *From Mons to Ypres with French: A Personal Narrative*. Sampson Low, 1916

Craster, J.M. (ed.), 'Fifteen Rounds a Minute', *The Grenadiers at War, 1914 August to December 1914*. Macmillan, 1976

Creagh, O'Moore and Humphris, E.M., *The V.C. and D.S.O.*, 3 vols. Standard Art Company, 1924

Crook, M.J., *The Evolution of the Victoria Cross*. Midas Books, 1975

Deeds that Thrilled the Empire. Hutchinson

Doyle, A. Conan, *The British Campaign in France and Flanders 1914*. Hodder & Stoughton, 1916

Edmonds, J.E. (ed.), *Military Operations France and Belgium 1914–1918*. Macmillan/HMSO, 1922–1949

Farndale, General Sir Martin, *History of the Royal Regiment of Artillery: Western Front 1914–18*. R.A.I., 1986

Gleichen, A.E.W., *The Doings of the Fifteenth Infantry Brigade August 1914 to March 1915*. Blackwood, 1917

Grimshaw, R., *Indian Cavalry Officer 1914–15*. Costello, 1986

Hamilton, E., *The First Seven Divisions*. Hurst and Blackett, 1916

Home, A., *The Diary of a World War I Cavalry Officer*. Costello, 1985

Jameson, W.S., *Submariners V.C.* Davies, 1962

Kirby, H.L., *Drummer Spencer John Bent, V.C.* T.H.C.L. Books, 1986

Kirby, H.L. & Walsh, R.R., *The Seven V.C.s of Stonyhurst College*. T.H.C.L. Books, 1987

McCrery, N., *For Conspicuous Gallantry – A Brief History of the Recipients of the Victoria Cross from Nottinghamshire and Derbyshire*. J.H. Hall, 1990

Lucy, J., *There's a Devil in the Drum*. Faber, 1938

Macdonald, L., *1914*. Michael Joseph, 1987

Martin, A.A., *A Surgeon in Khaki*. Arnold, 1915

The Medical Victoria Crosses. RAMC

Maurice, F.B., *Forty Days in 1914*. Constable, 1919

Memorials of Rugbeians Who Fell in the Great War, Volume 1, 1914. Rugby School, 1916

Ypres and the Battles of Ypres. Illustrated Michelin Guides to the Battlefields 1914–1918

Neame, P., *Playing With Strife: The Autobiography of a Soldier*. Harrap, 1947

Osburn, A.C., *Unwilling Passenger*. Faber, 1932

Pillinger, D. & Staunton, A., *Victoria Cross Locator*. Highland Press, Australia, 1991

Richardson, S. (ed.), *The Recollection of Three Manchesters in the Great War*. Richardson, 1985

The Register of the Victoria Cross. This England Books, 1988

The Royal Artillery War Commemoration Book. G. Bell, 1920

Smyth, J., *The Story of the Victoria Cross*. Muller, 1963

Spears, E.L., *Liaison 1914*. Heinemann, 1931

Swinton, E.D., *Twenty Years After: the Battlefields of 1914–18, Then and Now*, 3 vols. Newnes, 1936–38

Terraine, John, *Mons: The Retreat to Victory*. Batsford, 1960; (ed), *General Jack's Diary 1914–18*. Eyre & Spottiswoode, 1964

Uys, I., *For Valour, the History of Southern Africa's Victoria Cross Heroes*. South Africa, 1973

Williams, W. Alister, *The VCs of Wales and the Welsh Regiments*. 1984

INDEX